ST ANTONY'S/MACMILLAN SERII

General editors: Archie Brown (1978–85) ⟨
 both Fellows of St Antony's College, Oxford

To my mother and father

Contents

List of Maps

Foreword

The air-raids on Libya in April 1986 raised in an acute form the question of the use of the United States Air Force bases in the United Kingdom. The bases were first established in the Second World War but little information has been published about their continuation after the war and the agreements between the two governments which have regulated not only conditions of their use but also the more detailed administrative and legal arrangements. The same is true of the later Polaris submarine bases.

Simon Duke's book has developed from his doctoral thesis at Oxford which drew largely on sources in the USA to provide a far more comprehensive account of these matters than has hitherto existed. Its appearance now is most timely.

MARGARET GOWING

Acknowledgements

My thanks are due to many people, both in Britain and in the United States, who have given generously of their time and knowledge. Although space does not permit mention of all who have in one way or another helped me, a few deserve special mention. Professor Adam Roberts of Balliol and St Antony's Colleges, Oxford, in spite of his many other commitments, read through all stages of the study and made many suggestions. Mention must also be made of Professor Margaret Gowing, who discussed some of the ideas in the early period covered by the thesis and whose own works have proved to be an inspiration.

Without help in various archives the researcher's job would be difficult and much valuable material would pass by. In Britain my task was made simpler and pleasant through the help of Humphrey Wynn at the Ministry of Defence, and Barry Nickle, who was Historian at the Third Air Force headquarters, RAF Mildenhall. He also gave me a valuable insight into base life for the United States servicemen in the United Kingdom. Debbie Christie and Gerry Northam of the BBC also unselfishly discussed and shared their own findings on the bases' arrangements. Duncan Campbell also proved to be a lively and stimulating 'sounding-board' for many of the ideas contained in an earlier version of the study. I must also thank the Library Staffs at the Codrington Library, Oxford; the Public Record Office, Kew; and Chatham House press-cuttings library.

In the United States special mention must be made of the staff in the Modern Military Archive section of the National Archives, Washington, DC. Their help was unfailingly courteous and efficient. Bill Heimdahl and Master Sergeant Roger Jernigan at Bolling Air Force Base, Washington, DC, were also of great assistance in spite of administrative upheaval. Much of the material pertaining to naval matters was supplied by Dr Allard and his staff at the US Navy Yard, Washington, DC, to whom my thanks are also due. Of immense value were the staffs of the Congressional Research Service and the Manuscripts Division, Library of Congress, as well as those at the Harry S. Truman Library, Independence, Missouri, and the Dwight D. Eisenhower Library, Abilene, Kansas. There were also many who gave generously of their time to answer my questions on both sides of the Atlantic.

A special word of gratitude is due to Martha Bremser, who has given generously of her time to read through and suggest improvements to various drafts of the study.

Even though I have had invaluable help from many sources, any errors and inadequacies of the book remain entirely my own.

Oxford SIMON DUKE

List of Abbreviations

ADM	Atomic Demolition Munitions
AFSWP	Armed Forces Special Weapons Project
ANF	Atlantic Nuclear Force
AUTODIN	Automatic Digital Network
AUTOVON	Automatic Voice Network
BDSW	British Defence Staff Washington
CEATO	Central Treaty Organisation
CIGS	Chief of the Imperial General Staff
CINCEASTLANT	Commander in Chief Eastern Atlantic
CNO	Chief of Naval Operations
COMNAVEU	Commander in Chief, (US) Naval Forces Europe
CSCE	Conference on Security and Cooperation in Europe
GCHQ	Government Communications Headquarters
HAS	Hardened Aircraft Shelter
HB	Heavy Bomber
HLG	High Level Group
ICBM	Intercontinental Ballistic Missile
IEPG	Independent European Programme Group
IISS	International Institute for Strategic Studies
IND	Independent Nuclear Deterrent
INF	Intermediate Nuclear Forces
IRBM	Intermediate Range Ballistic Missile
JCS	Joint Chiefs of Staff
JPS	Joint Planning Staff
JSPC	Joint Staff Plans Committee
JSPG	Joint Strategic Planning Group
JSSC	Joint Strategic Survey Committee
JWPC	Joint War Plans Committee
LORAN	Long Range Aid to Navigation (LORAN-C used for submarine navigation and communication)
LRTNF	Long Range Theatre Nuclear Force
MATS	Military Air Transport Service
MBFR	Mutual Balanced Force Reductions
MCP	Military Construction Programme

MIRV	Multiple Independently Targetable Re-entry Vehicle
MLF	Multi Lateral Force
MRBM	Medium Range Ballistic Missile
MRCA	Multi-Role Combat Aircraft
NADGE	NATO Air Defence Ground Environment
NPG	Nuclear Planning Group
NSA	National Security Agency (HQ: Fort Meade, Maryland)
NSC	National Security Council
POL	Petroleum-Oil-Lubricants
POMCUS	Pre-positioned Military Core Unit Stocks
SAC	Strategic Air Command
SCP	Special Construction Programme
SEALS	Special Forces (US) Unit Europe
SEATO	South East Asia Treaty Organization
SIGNIT	Signals Intelligence
SILVERPLATE B-29	especially modified for an atomic role
SMART (weapons)	so called for their ability to home in on targets, otherwise known as PGMs (Precision Guided Missiles)
SOFA	Status of Forces Agreement
SOSUS	Sound Surveillance System
SSBN	Strategic nuclear-powered Ballistic Missile Submarine
TACAMO	'Take-charge-and-move-out' aircraft (S-130 Hercules): part of Minimum Essential Emergency Communications System
TDY	Temporary Duty
TFW	Tactical Fighter Wing
TNF	Theatre Nuclear Forces
USAAF	United States Army Air Force (became USAF)
USAFE	United States Air Force Europe
USN	United States Navy
VHB	Very Heavy Bomber
WIMEX	Worldwide Military Command and Control System

Postscript

In the early evening of 14 April 1986 a strike group took off from RAF Lakenheath and RAF Upper Heyford simultaneously. The F-111Fs from the 48th Tactical Fighter Wing at Lakenheath and the EF-111As of the 42nd Electronic Combat Squadron at Upper Heyford were part of the strike force destined for Libya. The fighters operating from these bases were to rendezvous with tanker aircraft (KC-10 and KC-135s) operating out of RAF Fairford and RAF Mildenhall, *en route* to their targets around Tripoli and Benghazi.

The role of the American forces operating out of Britain, it was claimed, was crucial to the military success of the operation aimed at suspected terrorist training and bivouac sites in Libya. In the debates following the raid Mrs Thatcher said that President Reagan had asked for British assistance and support under the 'consultative arrangements which have continued under successive governments for over thirty years'.[1] The precision of the Ford Aerospace 'Pave Tack' laser designator–ranger system, used by the F-111Fs operating out of Lakenheath, was at the centre of Reagan's guarantee that only clearly defined targets having a relation to terrorist activities would be hit. Since there were no other F-111s based anywhere in Europe that could be used for the attack, Britain was therefore approached and, on 12 April, Mrs Thatcher gave Reagan's special envoy, General Vernon Walters, her permission for the American use of the bases.

In the aftermath of the raid, which put the British government under considerable pressure from all quarters, the case for British involvement in the raid seemed less clear. The main reason for British involvement, it emerged, was probably not so much military as political. It was seen as vital that the United States had the support of at least one European ally in the raid, although the fact that it was Britain who gave support made it look more like the strings of the old special relationship were being pulled, rather than a wider European consensus being achieved. Indeed, in the light of subsequent European criticism of the raid Britain has stood out. In Bonn, Chancellor Helmut Kohl said, 'Force is not a very encouraging way of dealing with things',[2] and in spite of tacit government support, there were massive demonstrations. The Italian Prime Minister, Bettino Craxi, said Europeans were disappointed that the sanctions agreed to by the EEC were considered inadequate by the US administration, whose action was interpreted by some as a deliberate overriding of European opinion. The Danish Prime Minister, Poul Schlueter, and the Dutch Foreign Minister, Hans van den Broek, also issued statements deploring the US action which had also sabotaged EEC efforts to solve the problems of terrorism by meeting with officials of Arab countries.

Within Britain, the debate over the future of the bases yielded unclear results. During the debate on the Libyan raid that took place on 15–16 April the 'agreements' assumed a central position. Mr David Steel said:

> The Attlee–Truman accord is very much out of date. It was never published, and it should now be revised, published and approved. If damage is not to be caused to the NATO Alliance, there must be no doubts as to the conditions under which the American bases in this country are used.[3]

Mr James Callaghan also spoke of the 'terms of the Attlee–Truman agreement'[4] while Dr David Owen, closer to the truth, spoke of the terms of the agreements of 'Attlee with Truman, Churchill with Truman *and* those of successive Prime Ministers'.[5] Dissatisfaction and confusion over the exact terms of the agreement was rife on the opposition benches. On the Conservative benches the picture was different. Mr Edward Heath reaffirmed his understanding that 'a right of veto exists'[6] (the example of his veto over the American use of British bases in the middle of the Yom Kippur War was mentioned,[7] but the later involvement of US forces in the war when all US forces were put on alert without prior consultation, was not mentioned). The Prime Minister at a later date emphatically rejected any suggestions that a new agreement might be necessary and refused to make a statement, except to say that, 'the Government are satisfied with the existing understandings which, as recent events have demonstrated, work well'.[8]

This study, it is hoped, has made it clear that it was never envisaged in the 1950s that American forces in Britain would be used by the United States (with British permission) for purposes outside NATO. The 1952 formula also spoke about a matter for joint decision between the two *governments*. The Libyan episode has shown that, even allowing for plenty of time (six days), 'government' only means a handful of top politicians and not the Cabinet. Sir Geoffrey Howe agreed that he was consulted[9] along with the Secretary of State for Defence, George Younger, who, the day before the raid told listeners on Radio Clyde:

My colleagues and I are very dubious as to whether a military strike is the best way of doing this. It is liable to hit the wrong people. It creates tensions in the area.[10]

A distinct lack of support was also notable from the Chancellor of the Exchequer, the Chairman of the Conservative Party and the Home Secretary. In spite of the fact that the 'go-ahead' for the raid was officially given by Mrs Thatcher to General Walters on 12 April, Sir Geoffrey Howe continued to discuss sanctions against Libya on 14 April with other EEC members. This reveals a distinct lack of unified 'government' support, not to mention the growing awareness that the actual raid employed many tactics of the terrorist: stealth, surprise and, unfortunately civilian casualties – with the exception that this act was somehow 'legalized' by Article 51 of the UN Charter.

What of the raid itself? Was it imperative to use British bases? The 'Pave-Tack' system fitted to the F-111Fs operating from RAF Lakenheath were also fitted to the US Navy A-6Es operating from carriers in the Mediterranean. They were not therefore 'unique' to Britain. The supposed accuracy of the system, enabling a surgical strike to be performed upon terrorist targets only, must be questioned. Navy and Air Force pilots were briefed not to drop their ordnance unless they had a positive identification and a perfect approach on their low-level run-in to the targets. Some aircraft crews were not able to meet these stringent requirements, and did not drop their weapons in the target areas. Five F-111s and two A-E6s did not complete their assigned bombing missions. Fatigue was undoubtedly one of the causes since the strike aircraft were refused permission to overfly France and were thus obliged to fly some 2500 nautical miles around the west coasts of France, Spain and Portugal – the route across France would have reduced the one-way distance to 1300 nautical miles. This meant, in flying hours, a 13–14 hour mission instead of a 6–7 hour one.

The argument that the US Navy alone could only have carried out the raid by leaving them 'tight on assets' appears unconvincing when two-thirds of the Navy attack aircraft left behind on the carriers were not used to strike Tripoli or Benghazi. A Pentagon official, Robert D. Sims, would only observe that the mission, as carried out, 'was the best way to do it'.[11] There was also an internal political aspect to the raid: after the Navy-only raid in Libya the month before, the Air Force now wanted a piece of the action; and the fact that the Defense Department budget was under consideration, and here was a chance to show how well money was being spent on bases, weapons and aircraft, was doubtlessly not overlooked.

If, as one is entitled to conclude from the evidence available, the *real reason* for the use of American bases in Britain for the Libyan raid was political, not military, there must be deep concern that the Cabinet was not involved, either in the consultation or in the decision as a whole. The Libyan episode has made a clear case for the renegotiation of the 1952 formula so that both sides comprehend it fully, and further, that the use of the bases is restricted only to obligations arising out of the North Atlantic Treaty. Where there is time for a 'joint decision' then it must be at Cabinet level, not just at Heads of State level. Where there is not time for consultation, it can no longer be assumed that the United States will act in the United Kingdom's best interests. A strong case can be made for utilising a dual-key system whenever possible, by which active participation is required to activate the weapon. Although Britain and other allies were offered a dual-key system on Cruise in 1979, and it was subsequently turned down, this should now be reviewed. Objections that a dual-key system would be too time-consuming to implement and would compromise the deterrent value of the weapon could be answered by the withdrawal of all Ground-Launched Cruise Missiles (GLCMs) from Britain, since their military value and place in NATO strategy are unclear.

The Libyan crisis has acted as a catalyst for debate about the future role of the American military presence in Britain. The Labour party have renewed their pledge to seek the withdrawal of all 'nuclear bases' in spite of a warning by Ambassador Charles Price in London that this could force a general re-appraisal of the United States forces' future in Britain (perhaps a subtle reminder that Britain is virtually dependent on the US for much of her intelligence and communication). Many of the questions concerning the bases have to do with wider concerns – about the state of the alliance, about the evolving European voice on defence issues, about growing fricton between more moderate European governments and the Reagan administration and, in Britain's case, about the dilemma of either being good Europeans, or, responding to the historical ties of the 'special relationship'.

These are not issues to which there is any one simple answer, but the time has come to face the problems and, in particular, the issue of whose interests the US bases are serving.

Introduction

During the Second World War, a huge system of bases was built world-wide by the United States of America in order to defeat the Axis powers. The Eighth Air Force and United States Strategic Air Forces in Europe became active in 1942, later to be renamed United States Air Force Europe (USAFE) in 1945. The period between June 1942 and December 1945 saw 165 installations in the United Kingdom being used by combat units of the United States Army Air Force. Amongst these installations were three air squadrons, nine commands, four air divisions, thirty-three wings, 116 groups, and 449 squadrons (including maintenance and supply).[1] After the war many of the bases were dismantled including most of those in the United Kingdom. However, they were soon to return – and in a capacity unprecedented in this country.

The aim of this study is to trace the postwar development of the United States defence bases in the United Kingdom. It is not intended to be an exhaustive military history, and reference to the technical aspects of the basing will only be made where relevant. Of more interest is the background of the decision to station US forces in the United Kingdom, and the subsequent effects upon British and American defence policies. The period 1945–54 constitutes the bulk of the study: it was during these years that the crucial agreements were made governing the use of British bases by United States forces in an emergency. These years also witnessed the rapid growth of the American presence, from a few bombers in East Anglia to a vast network of bases and facilities covering the United Kingdom.

The United Kingdom's location has proven to be critical for the deployment of many sections of the US military forces. Apart from providing bases for bombers and nuclear submarines, the United Kingdom has also proved crucial for providing an 'infrastructure' for US forces overseas. This includes communication and intelligence centres, command headquarters, storage for nuclear and conventional weapons and logistical support. What started off as a thirty-day visit by two B-29 squadrons to Britain has developed into a substantial US force of 30 000, occupying a large number of bases and facilities over the course of thirty-seven years.

The questions that are raised by the bases, at first seen as a natural offshoot of the 'special relationship',[2] centre upon the extent to which

1

the United States bases make the United Kingdom more of a target, and therefore perhaps less safe, than it would otherwise be without such a presence. The answers to these questions are necessarily a matter of individual judgement; yet without claiming to have direct answers, this study aims to provide the necessary tools for such a task. The problems that are addressed revolve around the diplomatic and political consequences of Britain's playing host to US forces: what are the precise terms of the US military presence in the United Kingdom? Have these terms, on the whole, reflected United States or United Kingdom interests? Moreover, has the balance between these interests changed over time, so that the relationship could be seen as unfair to one party or the other? Are the means for controlling the US bases adequate? Has the presence of a large number of foreign forces been a source of friction? As a sovereign state Britain has a right to terminate the arrangement: should the government do so for the security of the United Kingdom?

The approach to the issues raised by US bases in the United Kingdom will be a broad analysis of the developments that led to the establishing of the bases; and, largely by way of chronological account, the significance of these bases to the United States and to British defence policies will be examined.

The United States is not, of course, unique in maintaining a substantial overseas base network. Britain also maintains numerous overseas bases. The prevalence of basing arrangements around the world raises similar questions and concerns, no matter who is the host or sending state; the adequacy of the agreements governing a foreign military presence in a sovereign state, the legal status of foreign forces to a host state, and the extent to which one or the other's interests are being served or endangered by the presence of bases. What is of particular interest in the case of US bases in the United Kingdom is that 'as a permanent peacetime arrangement this system is truly unprecedented'.[3] Britain alone amongst the countries hosting United States bases has apparently been content with a 'gentleman's agreement' which governs the huge American military presence; never before have two major powers entered into such an agreement during peace time and not stipulated more precise terms, especially as regards what remains still an indeterminate length of stay. It is therefore surprising that the role of the United Kingdom as host to US forces has not merited more academic attention and which has dubbed Britain as 'America's unsinkable aircraft carrier'.

The United Kingdom has traditionally occupied a central role in the

US military involvement in Europe, in part springing out of the Second World War intimacy and the resultant special relationship. Winston Churchill, in his speech in Fulton, Missouri, in 1946, spoke of the need for continuing 'instruments of co-operation' between the two countries in the postwar era, when the thread of a common language and the threat of Communism pulled the countries together. It was against a background of international tension, culminating in the first real crisis of the Cold War – the Berlin blockade, that United States and British military chiefs agreed that the presence of US strategic bombers or bases in the United Kingdom would have a beneficial effect on the general situation. The original presence was small, consisting of two squadrons operating from specially enlarged runways in East Anglia. On 28 July 1948, the Secretary of State for Air, Arthur Henderson, announced that these units were not visiting Britain under a formal treaty but under 'informal and longstanding arrangements between two air forces for visits of goodwill and training purposes'.[4] Within a few months it became evident that something far more substantial was planned.

Although the United States Navy, Army, Military Airlift Command and various intelligence agencies have been involved in American operations from the United Kingdom in the postwar era, the main focus will be upon the United States Air Force (USAF). NATO relies heavily upon air power in both conventional and nuclear options. The USAF's commitment to NATO's defence has always been heaviest, in part because air power is more capital-intensive than manpower-intensive, and 'just as nuclear weapons were once viewed as a cheap way to balance Soviet conventional strength, air power is often viewed as a man-power substitute'.[5]

Current attitudes towards both the United States and their overseas bases appear to be confused. On the one hand, it could be argued that there has been a re-birth of the 'special relationship' under President Reagan and Mrs Thatcher, whose views on economic, political, international and military matters show a shared interest. Yet, against this relatively close harmony at the level of heads-of-state there is a general public distrust of United States leadership and mounting opposition to the US bases in particular. Paradoxically, a majority of British citizens supports continued participation in the NATO alliance, while a majority is also against the deployment of US cruise missiles.[6] Public opinion concerning the US nuclear bases appears to be influenced by political climate when, at time of crisis, feelings swing against their presence and, at times of relative calm, there is a more general acceptance of their presence in the United Kindgom.[7] This apparent public unease about the US bases has not found any reflection in postwar governments, under which there has generally been an acceptance not only of the US bases but also of the arrangements governing their use in an emergency. There have, however, been direct clashes of interest between the United States and Britain when the bases have been used for purposes distinct from Britain's national interests, with little or no effort at consultation from the American government. There has been very little published[8] to explain these apparent contradictions and consequently, the general awareness of the nature and role of US bases amongst the British public is often quite low. What has been published is often highly polemical or confined to one small area of concern; literature on the cruise debate and the well publicised views of the Greenham women, for instance, could furnish a library in itself, but there has been little attempt to step back and take an overview of US bases in the United Kingdom. Whilst the study is not designed to answer all the complex problems that have arisen, it is intended to offer a constructive approach to assessing the American military presence in the United Kingdom.

The subject is approached by means of a roughly chronological account, covering the development and the problems associated with US bases in the United Kingdom. The historical approach to the bases also considers many outside events that influenced the direction and use of US bases in the United Kingdom. The requirement for US bases overseas sprang from a general foreign policy which, soon after the Second World War, identified the Soviet Union as the West's chief enemy; and the bases in the United Kingdom formed part of a wider tapestry of world-wide bases under American control. Britain was to assume particular importance because of her strategic location and her close political identification with the United States. The historical narrative thus traces a relationship that has been unique in its intimacy, with the bases in turn symbolising that closeness.

So often in the history of the US bases in the United Kingdom it has been outside events which have prompted change: it was ostensibly the Berlin blockade that was the catalyst for the arrival of B-29s in East Anglia; it was the Korean War that prompted Prime Minister Attlee to negotiate an understanding with the President regarding the use of the bases; Thor missiles were deployed in Britain in response to shortcomings in the US nuclear arsenal; and the Yom Kippur War brought about a major reassessment of American bases in general.

Similarly, the significance and functions of the US bases are often illuminated more by historical 'flashpoints' or crises than by the available public documentation. For instance, the chance shooting-down of a RB-47 reconnaissance aircraft during 1960 revealed the extent of US reconnaissance operations from United Kingdom bases. The disagreement between the British and American governments during the 1973 Middle East War highlighted the nature of the consultation procedure – or lack of it – for use of United Kingdom bases by United States force. In addition, the reaction of the Soviet Union to the US bases in the United Kingdom is constructive. Ever since the arrival of US B-29 bombers in East Anglia during 1948, the face of Europe has, to the Soviet mind, looked hostile and threatening, particularly since the US had a nuclear capability in Europe long before the Soviet Union had a similar device.

The questions surrounding the US bases have been addressed in specific, but limited, ways. This study aims to approach the issue at several different levels. The Soviet reaction to the various base developments in the United Kingdom is documented where possible. The legal problems raised by the presence of a large number of US servicemen in a foreign country are also touched upon, as are the sociological problems arising out of the presence. But the main focus of the study must be upon the political problems that have arisen more generally out of international incidents, and upon those political events specifically affecting Anglo–American relations, especially as they apply to military bases. The study is, in short, an attempt to gain an overview of the US presence in the United Kingdom as it affects both governments and populace.

The study can be split into two halves. The first section covers the years 1945–54 and concentrates on the development of the bases, culminating in the agreements between President Truman and Prime Ministers Attlee and Churchill. Following the agreement there was a period of consolidating the US presence until it reached its peak in the mid-1950s. The 1950s are also important for the dawning of the missile age and the first deployment of US missiles in Britain in 1957. This early period can be thought of generally as being marked by close Anglo–American relations (with the notable watershed of Suez), and as a period of consolidation and development for the bases. The second part of the study, from 1957 until the present, covers a period of change in the American attitude to Britain. During that time, the United Kingdom was increasingly dealt with as part of Europe; and opposition within the UK became noticeable not only to the vague agreements but to the US bases themselves, which now held a growing arsenal of nuclear weaponry that would culminate in the deployment of cruise missiles, causing a serious reappraisal of the overall role of American bases in Britain's defences.

Chapter 1 will attempt a definition of the term 'base'. There is no generally agreed definition of a base, and this in turn has led to considerable confusion. There have been, for example, exaggerations of the US military strength overseas when even the smallest relay transmitter has merited the term 'base'. Whilst a hard and fast definition of a base is difficult, it is constructive to distinguish between main operating bases, support bases and facilities. Chapter 2 will cover the years 1945–48, when the background of the wartime special relationship set the stage for top-level military discussions between General Carl Spaatz and Air Chief Marshall Lord Tedder, designed to alleviate concerns about Europe's vulnerability during the early Cold War years. The discussions resulted in an agreement to make available 'certain bases' for US bombers in time of emergency, including support of US atomic operations. Chapter 3, covering the years 1948–50, has as its main focus the Berlin Crisis, which was the pretext for placing bombers in Britain – a move long contemplated by respective military chiefs. Much confusion surrounded the issue of the length of stay of US bombers in East Anglia during the Berlin Crisis. The first public comment was that the bombers were in Britain 'for a short period of temporary duty'.[9] During 1950, the US presence was formalised by the Ambassador's Agreement, which apportioned the division of the cost of construction for a number of US bases, and gave the British the right to terminate the arrangement.

The US bases in Britain were becoming an increasingly urgent political problem and, by the early 1950s, the outbreak of the Korean War opened up possibilities of the US bases being used for a struggle outside the NATO area. The demand by Parliament for an agreement that states what the bases could (and could not) be used for, forced Clement Attlee to visit President Truman. Chapter 4 covers the course of the meeting and subsequent agreements, as well as the confirmatory agreement reached between Prime Minister Churchill and President Truman on 8 January 1952. The precise interpretation of the resultant communiqué was to prove a constant source of controversy and is currently at the centre of a dispute surrounding the operational deployment of cruise missiles.

Chapter 5 will examine the rapid growth of the US military presence in Britain between 1950 and 1954. At the centre of the expansion of the

US base network in the United Kingdom was the Special Construction Programme, that provided for the expansion of the primary air bases from five in June 1949 to forty-three by June 1953. The growth in the number of US bases was mainly a response to the increasing importance that the UK was assuming in US war planning. The expanded base network was also to affect British defence policy, as increasing reliance was put on the United States for a sizeable proportion of Britain's air cover. During these years, the Strategic Air Command (SAC) started reconnaissance operations from UK bases, forming part of an increasingly elaborate Anglo–American intelligence network. The intimacy in the defence field, of which the bases were the best example, was not always mirrored in other areas of Anglo–American relations; and of particular note was the lack of atomic research collaboration as Britain struggled to make her own atomic bomb. Chapter 6 will provide a break from the chronological narrative by looking at the sociological, economic and legal status of US servicemen in the United Kingdom.

The most spectacular changes (explained in the second part of the study) were the deployment of Thor missiles in Britain and the opening of a major US submarine base at Holy Loch. Although Thor formed only a small part of the overall American military presence in the United Kingdom, its arrival coincided with the growth of organised pressure groups, in particular the Campaign for Nuclear Disarmament. United States bases in the United Kingdom were henceforth a political issue that would regularly erupt in Parliament.

The role of the US bases was to change in 1964 with a major US project that aimed for a substantial reduction in American overseas commitments. The Seventh Air Division, under SAC command, was deactivated when widescale deployment of ICBMs in the United States and growing political protest against the United States military posture in Europe made a retreat to the United States for bomber units, with deployment to their overseas bases in time of emergency, a desirable alternative. The Vietnam War also induced a feeling of isolationism amongst many Americans; there seemed little reason for keeping troops in Europe when little was done to help the United States in Asia.

The late 1960s and early 1970s were a stormy and uncertain period for US bases in the United Kingdom. The Mansfield Amendments demanded major US overseas force reductions. After several major disputes, Britain began to side more closely with European interests, while the American bases were rarely out of the national newspapers and were the focus of demonstrations and even resentment. The study ends with the most recent, and perhaps most controversial development of United States bases in the United Kingdom during the period following the decision to deploy cruise missiles at Greenham Common and Molesworth.

The need for an examination of the precise nature and role of the US defence bases in the United Kingdom has become urgent for three reasons. First, the day in which the United States could manage the NATO alliance has passed. There are now identifiable interests that are European and not necessarily American – the European commitment to Brandt's '*Ostpolitik*' and the general process of detente was one such example and another was supplied by the notable clash of interest over the Siberian gas pipeline project. Secondly, the United States can no longer set alliance strategy for Europe's defence. Economic and political constraints within the United States makes the defence of Europe increasingly dependent on a combined European effort, a fact that many European countries have been slow to accept; but an increasing lack of concern towards European sensibilities in NATO strategy has led to pressure groups and 'peace' demonstrators demanding a greater say in European defence (although the creation of the Nuclear Planning Group (NPG) and the Independent European Planning Group (IEPG) have gone some way towards meeting this demand). Lastly, the immediate postwar period saw America clearly paramount in the military sense. The realities of military power forty years later suggest that the United States should accept an altered role as *primus inter pares*, with a greater tolerance for diversity in the European defence effort.

1 Defining 'Bases'

What is a 'base'? The notable absence of a generally acknowledged definition means that the arguments become unclear and subject to political bias. Historically, basing has been tied up with the related ideas of a protectorate, military occupation or even with a colonial presence. Occupations have turned into basing arrangements, as in Czechoslovakia from 1968 onwards. The differences between these situations and the contemporary meaning of bases in the United Kingdom are as follows. First, the forces are in the United Kingdom by agreement. Second, they have a defined and limited role and have no authority over civil society. Lastly, Britain retains territorial sovereignty over the base areas (enshrined in the Ambassador's Agreement giving the British government the right to terminate the arrangement).

An example of the possible confusion over the meaning of the term 'base' arose in a series of questions during June–August 1980 in the House of Commons. Bob Cryer, MP, asked the Secretary of State for Defence to list the number of bases operated in 'whole or part by United States forces in the United Kingdom'. Francis Pym replied:

> The United States Air Force has main operating bases at RAF Alconbury, RAF Bentwaters, RAF Fairford, RAF Lakenheath, RAF Mildenhall, RAF Upper Heyford, and RAF Woodbridge and standby deployment bases at RAF Greenham Common, RAF Sculthorpe and RAF Wethersfield. The United States Navy has a base at Holy Loch. The United States Forces also occupy a number of sites, including RAF Molesworth, which are used for purposes such as housing, storage, logistics, administration and communications.[1]

Bob Cryer asked two further questions on 7 July[2] and 8 August[3] enquiring if there were any 'US bases, facilities, housing, storage, logistic support, administration or communication sites' not included in the previous reply. The list of bases and facilities supplied by the Ministry of Defence rose to fifty-three in July and fifty-six in August. The careful definitions supplied by the Secretary of State for Defence were soon muddied. Duncan Campbell, an investigative journalist, wrote that the 'list of *bases* now swelled from 12 to 53' and that 'after three attempts, the Ministry of Defence had managed to find 56 US bases in Britain. We have found 103'.[4]

Third Air Force Main Operating Bases

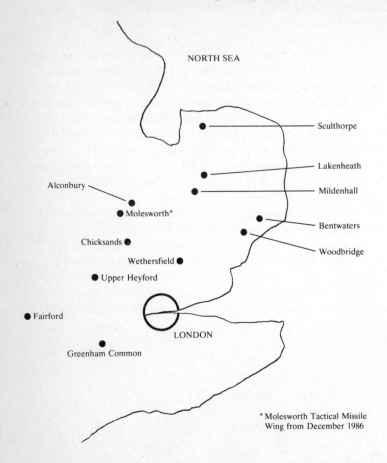

* Molesworth Tactical Missile
Wing from December 1986

The question initially sought the number of 'bases' and later, bases and 'facilities'. To ignore the division and count anything from a fuel pump, to a radio transmitter, to a major strategic base like RAF Upper Heyford as a 'base' is misleading. To avoid such confusion, and to account for the difference between Campbell's 103 and the figure of twenty-five supplied by the US Embassy in Grosvenor Square to the author, a more precise definition is necessary. Naval and air bases can, as a rule, be divided into three categories. First are the main or permanent operational bases. These comprise major bases which are fortified and garrisoned with sufficient force to be held against a major attack until relieved from the continental United States. Examples in this category would be the main bases at Upper Heyford, Alconbury, Lakenheath and Mildenhall. They are also distinguished by size, with over one hundred permanent personnel. Second, there are the limited operational bases used chiefly for reconnaissance, or having specific functions like satellite communications, microwave communication links or ammunition stores. Examples in this category would include Barford St John, Menwith Hill, Bovingdon, Welford and Winkfield, to name but a few. The limited operational bases provide the strategic bases with invaluable information or logistical support, and more often than not, the rationale for their (often shrouded) presence are those permanent operational bases in the first category. Third, there are the emergency or standby bases, such as Boscombe Down, which American aircraft could use in time of emergency; similar port facilities exist for the United States Navy (USN) at Southampton.[5] These bases are now more commonly known as 'co-located' bases for use only as agreed in time of emergency.

The main focus of this study will be upon the permanent operational bases which will be viewed as part of a general system of national or collective security. Mention of the various facilities that support these main bases will be made only where it is felt that they have significantly enhanced the American military presence in the United Kingdom. The definitions should not be considered as hard and fast since many bases have changed their function and relative importance over time, in response to varied demands. The number of permanent operational bases, hereafter referred to as 'bases' unless specified otherwise, has varied little over the last twenty years since the Strategic Air Command withdrew the Seventh Air Division from Britain.[6] The USN bases are subject to slightly different criteria, as a great number of submarines can operate from, but not necessarily be 'based' in one location. Since communication facilities constitute such an important part of the sea-borne nuclear force, these have been incorporated in the definition of naval base. There are now generally acknowledged to be five major US naval bases in the United Kingdom.[7]

The lack of a generally agreed definition of 'bases' does raise important problems. While the definitions above serve as a rough guide to US bases in the United Kingdom and their relative importance, the definition is of limited use outside the confines of this study. If the definition of base were applied to Norway it could be concluded that there were no US bases in Norway. This would, however, overlook the vast array of US 'facilities' that exist in Norway, such as part of the NADGE radar system which is a 3000 mile long chain of radar and associated air defence systems. It could also be claimed that the facilities were not specifically American but that they safeguard the sea lanes in the North Atlantic.[8]

Difficulties of definition also arise when we talk of 'defence bases'. The early advocates of a world-wide base network or a string of fortified bases, saw it as a way of off-setting the *future* power and aggressive intent of the Soviet Union and perhaps China. A Russian naval admiral, objecting to American plans for overseas bases in *Pravda* in September 1946, declared that bases as far flung from America as Okinawa or Iceland could scarcely be called 'defensive'. Two documents were to give legitimacy to the concept of defensive retaliation, but said nothing about defence bases. The United Nations Charter and the Atlantic Pact gave birth to a wider scope of mutual interests that had to be defined. The earlier Cairo Declaration had committed the United States to the principle of territorial non-aggrandisement, a principle later cemented into the United Nations Charter (Chapters 11–13). It became possible to defend American interests under the guise of the UN flag. The trusteeship principle was qualified in the UN Charter by a special dispensation for 'strategic areas' in trust territories, which placed such areas under the jurisdiction of the Security Council (with its veto provision) instead of the Trusteeship Council. This, as Hans Weigert observed, 'made it possible for a great power to control strategic bases short only of outright annexation.'[9] The strategic bases could masquerade under the guise of collective security, as permitted under Article 51 of the UN Charter.

The second reason for talking of 'defence bases' applies to the United Kingdom as a signatory to the Atlantic Pact. Under the Atlantic Pact the United States and Canada entered into a military agreement for the defence of Western Europe. It was stressed at the time that this was a purely defensive arrangement and formed part of a wider containment policy to halt the spread of Communism. Under the Pact, members agreed to provide military forces according to their means. Article 5 declared:

> The Parties agree that an armed attack against one or more of them in Europe or North America shall be considered an attack against them all; and consequently they agree, that if any such an armed attack occurs, each of them . . . will assist the Party or Parties so attacked by taking forthwith, individually and in concert with the other Parties, such action as it deems necessary, including the use of

armed force, to restore and maintain the security of the North Atlantic area.

The question of the defensive nature of the US bases has been clouded more recently by NATO's stance on 'first-use' of nuclear weapons. From NSC-68 (see note 8 on p. 223) onwards, the proposal for a policy of no-first-use of nuclear weapons was rejected on the grounds that it could be interpreted as a sign of weakness, and that to agree to a 'no-first-use' policy would weaken NATO's deterrence posture. There has, however, always been a careful distinction between the initiating of war and the use of a surprise first-strike after the war has started. First use only applies to an on-going war where NATO could maintain escalation dominance rather than a sudden 'nuclear bolt from the blue'.[10] This principle was verified in June 1981 at the Bonn NATO Summit, where it was pledged not to use any nuclear weapons except in response to an attack.[11] Various surveillance and reconnaissance operations mounted from Britain have also been perceived by the USSR as atagonistic and provocative.

The perception of the intent on overseas bases is obviously dependent upon the viewer's perspective. To one Russian observer, bases on foreign territory were not only instruments for the maintenance of neo-colonialism but served 'aggressive purposes' and were 'incompatible with the principles of peaceful coexistence of states with different social systems and constitute an international crime'.[12] From the American standpoint, the US forces in Europe serve four objectives: they play an important role in deterrence, they make a significant contribution to Europe's defence and in the event of a conflict would pose a formidable fighting force; they play a vital political role in America's relations with Western Europe; and they maintain a military balance as a counterpoise to the forces maintained by the Warsaw Pact.[13] The US forces are not just defending West Europe's interests, they also defend their own interests. Michael Heseltine made the symbiotic nature of the arrangement clear recently when he said, 'individual countries in Europe could not hope to defend themselves successfully against the weight of an attack they might face without the support of all their allies . . . the ultimate security of the North American members of the Alliance rests on what happens in Western Europe.[14]

The United States forces in the United Kingdom are impressive taken by themselves, but at their height they represented only a fraction of US military power deployed on this side of the Atlantic. In

1952, only about 10 per cent of the American servicemen in the European area were stationed in Britain.[15] The expansion of the American military forces in the Mediterranean and Europe was far greater than the expansion of forces in Britain. By the peak of US military deployments in Europe in 1954, the forces in Britain represented slightly less than 10 per cent of the total European and Mediterranean deployments. Over the years many of the US deployments in Europe were to diminish in response to political and economic factors but Britain, because of her traditional association with United States' interests, has proved to be America's most valuable military base and political ally.

2 Visits of Goodwill and Training Purposes

AMERICA'S POSTWAR BASING REQUIREMENTS

The background to plans for a postwar system of American defence bases can be traced back to President Roosevelt's idea of an International Police Force. Roosevelt's idea was taken up in a Joint Chiefs of Staff (JCS) study prepared in December 1942 with Great Britain itself as one of the policemen. Similar ideas were proposed by Colonel George F. Schulgen, providing for a World Security Force consisting of 'fifty heavy bomber bases at mutually supporting base areas determined by the location of the world's energy resources'.[1] Roosevelt expressed a very strong interest in postwar basing and saw the policing concept of bases as central to future world security. Even at this stage it was obvious that it would be a long-range air force that would be the guarantor. Britain and the Soviet Union were to take care of their own spheres of influence. Although the idea was seriously entertained Congress 'shied away from explicit endorsements of such a force, and in public Roosevelt hid behind vacuous generalities'.[2] It became clear at the Joint Staff Planners Conference (JSPC) of January 1943 this 'international police force' with the A-bomb as its backing was intended to be the backbone of the new international order. The JCS drew upon the four policemen concept in its first postwar base plan, JCS 570/2, which Roosevelt signed in November 1943 (known in some circles as 'the base bible'). The plan envisaged a regional division of responsibilities, largely influenced by Roosevelt's belief that the American public would not support the stationing of large forces abroad after the war.

The Army Air Force (USAAF, later changed to USAF) did not entertain any notions of locating forces in Europe after the occupation period. Some, like Admiral King, were concerned about this attitude. Admiral King cautioned that 'to limit the location of bases for national defense puts ammunition in the hands of isolationists'.[3] The requirements for national security and international peacekeeping appeared complementary to many American military leaders because 'they equated the interests of the United States with those of the rest of the world'.[4]

General 'Hap' Arnold, while tacicitly supporting JCS 570/2, was similarly concerned. He cautioned against the limited bases concept, arguing that 'we must meet attacks as far from our own orders as possible to insure against any part of the United States mainland being visited by a sudden devastation beyond any Pearl Harbor experience'.[5] General Arnold believed that it was necessary to have a strong postwar base system but warned of any premature attempts to base bombers in Europe. In a letter to General Carl Spaatz, Arnold cautioned against Spaatz's suggestion for any addition to the projected 'Occupational Air Force'.

> The acquisition by the United States of permanent air bases in several European countries is a subject filled with dynamite. It appears to us here that any action taken at this time by the United States to procure post-war air bases in Europe would be premature . . . it is the expressed policy of the United States to withdraw from Europe as soon as practicable, leaving possibly a token force in Germany to carry out our armistice decisions. I believe that planning for permanent post-war air bases in Europe is inadvisable.[6]

There was some vagueness as to how long American occupation forces would remain in Europe. The President estimated occupation forces would remain 'one year, maybe two' and that four policemen might maintain order in Europe by the quarantine method. At the Tehran conference there was little attempt to follow up comment by Stalin expressing willingness to see the United States hold bases in Europe and play a peacekeeping role.[7] The plans for a post-war base policy were further complicated by inter-service quarrelling, and by August 1945 there were three sets of papers amongst the various planners: the Strategic Survey Office, the Joint Planning Staff (JPS) and the Joint Post-War Committee. General Arnold, trying desperately to achieve an overview, came out with the general impression that 'the number of bases we are asking for will bankrupt the nation'.[8] Admiral Leahy of the USN claimed that the Army alone were asking for forty-five bases; Admiral King said the Navy wanted at least fourteen – this was without AAF bases.

After General Arnold's warning, General Spaatz's staff officers confined their work to recommendations for air bases to support the occupation of Germany; nevertheless this still demanded at least short-term occupation of some European air bases. In response, Spaatz forwarded the Periphery Base Program to the State Department. This called for American forces to be stationed in Germany and

Austria, with a ring surrounding them in Italy, Denmark, Norway and France. The official policy regarding the United Kingdom was to close down the wartime bases as soon as practically possible. Again, this was based upon the mistaken view that Britain was to be one of the policemen.[9] The AAF asked the State Department to secure approval for five Periphery Bases, but there were worries about the possible effects on the scheme of demobilisation.[10] In a letter from General Arnold to Secretary of Defense Marshall, Arnold had warned that 'rapid demobilization was incapacitating the Army Air Forces'.[11] By the following spring hasty demobilisation had undercut the Air Force's ability to act in Europe and elsewhere. The recommendation for five B-29 groups to go to Europe was later cut to three upon General Eisenhower's advice. This was resisted strongly by the AAF, as was a proposal to reduce the support fighter groups from ten to seven. The only measure that met with any degree of unanimity was that 'all negro troops should be withdrawn from Europe'.[12]

The inability of various parts of the services to agree upon a concrete figure was to typify the muddled policy-making over the next two to three years. In May 1946 the decision was made to scrap the Periphery Base Program. The decision was largely the result of strong objections from Secretary of State Grew, who argued that to obtain bases in Scandinavia would invite the Soviet Union to seek similar base rights in that part of the world. Alongside this consideration there was a lack of suitable personnel and very heavy bomber (VHB) bases, plus the realisation that bomber bases in Germany would be vulnerable to Soviet attack. The main reason lay with France and Italy: negotiations for bases in these two countries were, at the State Department's request, to be conducted at the military level, largely because negotiations through diplomatic channels might prejudice other negotiations for base rights. The French Air Ministry in December 1945, setting a precedent for Italy, insisted that negotiations should take place at the diplomatic level and thereby effectively ended the Periphery Base idea.[13]

There were no considerations in the Periphery Base Plase regarding the probable mission of the B-29's, the best strategic locations or the political implications involved.[14] Many in the State Department saw the size of the Air Force in Europe as adequate without further additions and found it 'difficult to understand how control of Germany could be used as an excuse at this time for negotiating base rights for any type of aircraft'.[15] The limited range of the heavy bombers (HB) then in Germany was of great threat to Russia, whereas proposals to station VHB groups in Germany by the American War Department did pose a threat, a fact quickly realised by France and Italy. Any attempts to negotiate bases in France or Italy for VHB units would be construed by the Soviet Union as the formation of a military alliance with a pointed threat.

Certain points became clear as a result of the failure of the Periphery Basing Program. First, the defence of the United States required strategic bomber units to be located east of the continental United States as soon as possible. Secondly, the bases that had been contemplated for VHB use were unsatisfactory from strategic and tactical viewpoints. The logical outcome was that 'retention of VHB units in CONUS [Continental United States] until properly located permanent bases are secured and constructed would better staisfy the strategic concept of protection of the United States than would use of the present bases'.[16]

The Air Force decided to base strategic units in the United States under the new Strategic Air Commands (SAC)[17] control and rotate them to various theatres for training and flight acclimatisation. The plan appealed mainly on economic grounds, since it could guarantee a presence in Germany without the need for expensive maintenance of long-stay crews and bases. The 'rotational' plan was optimistically seen as a temporary measure since the introduction of long-range aircraft would mean minimum reliance on overseas bases. It was hoped that the B-36 bomber would provide a long range intercontinental striking force, which in turn would eventually be replaced with long-range jet powered bombers or even missiles. The initial SAC plan was to rotate units through three strategic overseas areas – the North Atlantic, the North Pacific and the Far East – which would in turn provide the 'surest and most expedient solution to training SAC units in operational form, to or through the three areas where they are most likely to be deployed'.[18] Shortly after its formation on 21 March 1946, SAC was also given responsibility for developing an atomic striking force. Within fifteen months of its creation, it was sending bombers on their first rotational tours of six weeks' duration, beginning with nine B-29's being deployed to Giebelstadt in Germany.[19] It was, however, still assumed at this stage that Britain would join the United States as one of the policemen and no public mention of basing American military units in the United Kingdom has been made.[20]

The main motive for pressing ahead with a further attempt at obtaining overseas basing rights, after the failure of the Periphery Basing Program, was that of national security. The Air Force continued to be the most vociferous advocate for bases and anything up to a 105-group postwar Air Force was mentioned. The Air Force's demand for an extensive base system was backed up by two criteria; that the bases must ensure that 'all possible routes to [the United States] are protected via overseas basing of defensive fighters', and that bases must be 'close enough to all, potential enemies so that bombers could reach targets within the strategic heartland of an adversary'.[21] Contrary to the stated need for bases to carry out America's self-appointed 'policing role, the main concern appeared to centre on worries about national security. The Joint Strategic Survey Committee (JSSC) concluded that the United States did need substantial overseas forces, because 'defensively, the further away from our own vital areas we can hold our enemy through our possession of advance bases, the greater *our* security'.[22] Brigadier-General George A. Lincoln, Directorate of Plans and Operations, War Department General Staff, who directed the first serious attempt to draw up plans for the initiation of strategic air operations against 'the enemy', was nonetheless frank; 'we shall have to intervene militarily in Europe or Asia because we certainly don't envisage getting set back on our heels where the military operation[s] are going to start in the United States'.[23]

American postwar base requirements were first compiled in November 1943 by the JCS. A requirement for thirty-three bases was outlined, with none in Europe.[24] A second study of base requirements in May 1945 also omitted any European bases, and no strategic plan was presented to support the lists of requirements.[25] It was only with the start of strategic planning that the United Kingdom began to assume importance in American thinking. The first postwar plan in March 1946 was called PINCHER, followed a year later by a variant, BROILER. They both assumed a Russian attack on the United States or her allies. Although sparse on operational details, these plans realised that the United Kingdom would be a valuable location from which to launch a strategic air offensive. At the same time as American strategic planning began to grasp the potential value of the United Kingdom as a strategic air base, there were those in Britain who, for differing reasons, saw distinct advantages in playing host to visiting American bomber groups.

Since the end of the wartime basing of American air force units in the United Kingdom, General Carl Spaatz had kept in regular touch with the British Air Marshal, Sir Arthur Tedder. Both had confided their concerns about the growing Russian forces and the weak state of

Europe economically and militarily. Prompted by these concerns, which were exacerbated by demobilisation, Spaatz and Tedder 'wondered what would happen if the United States found it necessary to deploys its long-range B-29's to Europe. Not a single British airfield was equipped to handle them. To correct this, they decided informally that the RAF would prepare four East Anglian bases to receive B-29's – just in case'.[26] It was with these thoughts in mind that Spaatz travelled to England in June 1946 to discuss basing arrangements with Air Chief Marshal Lord Tedder. The discussions were most likely aimed at a temporary arrangement. John Greenwood, a noted air historian of this period, argues that the United States Air Force 'counted on the development of advanced air weapons not only to facilitate the accomplishment of its missions but also to reduce its overseas commitments'.[27] The long-range plan was to place all strategic forces in the United States to 'reduce their vulnerability and to have them constantly ready'.[28]

THE SPAATZ–TEDDER TALKS

The talks between General Spaatz and Air Chief Marshal Tedder in June-July 1946 were thus prompted by concerns about the extremely low state of air effectiveness in Europe and a feeling that 'the ground situation presents a serious threat to us . . . the Russian ground Forces are capable of over-running almost immediately the US Occupied Zone. Such action by Russia would leave us the alternatives of extricating or losing our occupational Forces. This presents a difficult problem with regard to basing VHB groups'.[29] Since Italy and France had already been approached for the Periphery Basing Program and had forced an American back-down over 'political difficulties', and because Germany was too near a hostile frontier, the United Kingdom was the logical alternative. During the search for suitable VHB bases in the Periphery Basing Program, it had been concluded that 'all bases currently contemplated for VHB use are totally unsatisfactory.' Whilst the United Kingdom could offer no suitable bases, her strategic location was a good deal safer than Germany and the background of the wartime special relationship would form a more receptive political lobby.

The Spaatz–Tedder talks were held on 25–28 June and 4–6 July, and were attended also by various American theatre commanders. They resulted in Spaatz obtaining tentative agreement that the RAF would prepare four or five East Anglia bases by mid-1947 for the use of American bombers in time of emergency. The agreement, known as the Spaatz–Tedder agreement, also ensured that the United States 'obtained RAF cooperation in the modification of certain bases for the support of atomic operations'.[30]

Ironically, just four months before the Spaatz–Tedder agreement, *The Times* carried a small report announcing that 'The last Flying Fortress bomber under American control in this country will take-off from Honington airfield . . . its departure will mark the end of the US Eighth Air Force in Britain'.[31] Few suspected the American Air Force would reappear so soon. The briefing material for General Spaatz's trip to Britain in June outlined the potential importance of the United Kingdom as a strategic base for deployment of the atomic bomb. Brigadier-General Everest of the USAAF recommended in Spaatz's brief that 'highest priority should be given to moving the 58th Wing to England'.[32] It was also recommended that 'construction should be initiated without delay to provide bases in the United Kingdom for receiving the first five VHB groups. *At least two bases should be prepared for handling the atomic bomb.*' The brief report then concluded emphatically that the 'defense of the United States does require strategic bomb units to be located East of the Continental United States. In fact, to insure the maintenance of US prestige and power, bases should be selected and manned immediately'.[33]

In accordance with Air Chief Marshal Tedder's consent to the recommendations, Colonel E. E. Kirkpatrick, of the Manhattan Project arrived in England on 17 August 1946. (The 'Manhattan Project' was the code name for the A-bomb development programme controlled by General Leslie Groves). Kirkpatrick was armed with personal instructions from General Spaatz to General Bissell at the US Embassy, London, to supervise the construction of assembly buildings, aprons and loading pits that fitted the dimensions of the early 'Fat Man' bomb design.[34] By early 1947 atomic bomb assembly and loading facilities were in existence in the United Kingdom and the Marianas, to support possible atomic bombing operations in Europe or the far East.[35] These actions were to set the patterns for future Air Force or Strategic Air Command war planning, because the bases in the United Kingdom would remain at the centre of Strategic Air Offensive plans until the late 1950s. The selected bases for SAC rotational training tours were at Lakenheath, Mildenhall, Scampton, Marham and Bassingbourn, all in East Anglia. With the exception of Bassingbourn, all of these were to be B-52 bases by Mid-1950. Setting a precedent for later base agreements, the Spaatz–Tedder agreement was made between top military personnel with no public awareness nor any debate of the issues and the potential results of such a momentous decision. Remarkably the Spaatz–Tedder meeting happened when the United States was generally reluctant to get involved in Europe apart from the occupation of Germany. Spaatz realised sooner than many of his political counterparts the economic, and therefore military, weakness of Britain.

The actual tours to Europe by SAC rotational units started in July 1947. In spite of the mutual security that the Spaatz–Tedder agreement engendered, relations in other areas were not as intimate. In particular, there was an adamant refusal by American authorities to share atomic information with the United Kingdom – a tool that was later to be used to gain further concessions from Britain. Although the Spaatz–Tedder agreement gave Britain the benefit of the small United States nuclear arsenal, it gradually emerged at the beginning of 1947 that Britain wanted to develop her own atomic bomb. The decision was not so much the outcome of the 1946 McMahon Act (which effectively ended Anglo–US atomic co-operation), as it was a symbol of independence and political status in the international community. Air Chief Marshal Lord Tedder, replying to an American suggestion that Britain might rely on the United States for the maintenance of a nuclear striking force, voiced a general feeling when he warned that this would 'involve a close military alliance with the United States in which Britain would be merely a temporary advance base, would involve complete subservience to United States policy and would render Britain completely impotent in negotiations with Russia or any other nation'.[36]

Under the Spaatz–Tedder agreement, facilities for atomic operations would shortly exist in Britain; it seemed logical to initiate plans for possible use in an emergency. The PINCHER series of studies was the first. These first war plans suggest both over-estimation and over-reliance upon the early B-3 bombs, of which nine were available in July 1946. Two years later there were 133, with thirty-three B-29 SILVER-PLATE bombers (the codename for those bombers converted to carry out atomic missions). Since at least two British bases had been prepared for handling the atomic bomb as an outcome of the Spaatz–Tedder talks, it signified a vast change in American perceptions of Britain's military strength and role in the postwar world. Gone was the naive belief that the maintenance of world peace 'will depend upon mutual cooperation among Britain, Russia and the United States'.[37]

By 1947, and with the growth of the first detailed plan for war involving atomic weapons (known as BROILER, part of the PINCHER series), a new attitude was being shown towards the United Kingdom. The realisation of Europe's economic and military vulnerability led the United States to reluctantly consider itself, at least temporarily, as Europe's defender. A JWPC study proclaimed that 'the defense of the British Isles for use as an Allied base of operations and for exploitation of their industrial potential, must be the minimum strategic objective in that area'.[38]

The appeal of United Kingdom bases was considerable. From bases in East Anglia B-29 bombers could cover all of Western Europe and reach three vital idustrial areas: Moscow, Donbass and the Ploesti regions. Britain also had a highly developed base system left over from the War, requiring slight modifications to bring them up to VHB standard. The British Isles were seen as necessary for mounting and staging any operations in north-western Europe. Without the British Isles, 'Allied capabilities would be reduced to a sea blockade and extremely limited air attacks from Iceland and the Azores'.[39] Plans for growth were also evident when the JWPC reasoned that since there were a total of forty-two US HB groups and seventy-five RAF HB type squadrons stationed in England during the Second World War, there was, in their eyes, 'no reason to suppose that the same number of VHB groups cannot be equally well supported'.[40]

There were problems with UK bases. The limited range of the B-29 deployed from the United Kingdom made its bombing radii less effective, in terms of targets covered, than would deployment from France or Italy. JWPC 432/5 showed a graphic map of 'Bombing Radii of Action'[41] for the B-29 from its East Anglia bases and others worldwide. The range according to their estimates was 1500–1700 miles with a 15 000 pound bomb load. From bases in England, Egypt, India, China and Okinawa, the JCS plan PINCHER illustrated that an air atomic offensive was beyond the capability of the USAAF, as several of the twenty targeted cities were up to five hundred miles beyond the operating range of the B-29. Flying from East Anglia, the B-29 could hardly reach Moscow, and Kirov was out of the question except on a one-way mission. JWPC 432/6 was also generous in its assessment of the Soviet military threat; indeed, so serious was the threat perceived by the Allies that the report concluded that 'the principal critical offensive effort against the USSR must consist of an air offensive, utilizing the atomic bomb to the fullest extent, for the purpose of destroying the Soviet war making capacity.[42]

Evidence of a lack of co-ordination between plans and resources became evident since there were no SILVERPLATE bombers based in Europe until the summer of 1949, and it was not until mid-1950 that the majority were of the modified configuration. The reputation of the B-29 as the 'atomic bomber' was most important. This was illustrated when six B-29's of SAC flew to Rhein-Main Airfield in November 1946, and then visited the free countries of west Europe. It was with their reputation as atomic bomb carriers that 'SAC B-29's unmistakably demonstrated support for the countries visited'.[43]

The Spaatz–Tedder agreement was the first major breakthrough in the reintroduction of American forces into postwar Britain. Rather than approach governments and risk rebuttal and the endangering of other negotiations, as happened in the Periphery Basing Program, it was agreed between Spaatz and Tedder that the matter would be handled as routine; it would attract 'no special attention', and an officer familiar with the 'special equipment' (Colonel E. E. Kirkpatrick) would report to General Bissell, the Military Air Attaché, at the American Embassy in London. There was also a tacit understanding that there would be further discussions regarding 'a certain type of activity'. Lord Tedder was quick to assure Spaatz that these 'requirements' would be met 'without any difficulty'.[44] The agreements were kept quiet, and there was a complete lack of comment from press and government alike regarding plans for the reintroduction of US bombers to Britain in an emergency, with atomic capability. Spaatz had informed Tedder that the AAF had planned the deactivation of the 305th and 306th bomb group (heavy) by October 1946 and the deployment of one VHB group would take place, at the earliest, in spring 1947, following the reinforcement and lengthening of runways in East Anglia to handle VHB's. Tedder expressed concern that the interval between the proposed departure of the HB's and the arrival of the VHB's at least six month's later, would give rise to claims that the United States was 'increasing markedly its military potential in Europe', and thus threaten any chances for stability in Europe. It was therefore agreed that there should be 'no interruption in the assignment of bombardment units to the [European Theatre of Operations] ETO'.[45]

The real importance to the United States military of gaining a base in Europe can be seen by the measures that would have been taken in the event of the Spaatz–Tedder talks stalling or breaking down. One of the ideas circulating around Washington, DC, at this time was that a reminder to the United Kingdom about some kind of return on the European Recovery Programme or the crippling Lend–Lease bills might not be amiss. Lucius Battle, who was then Special Assistant to the Secretary of State, suggested that 'because of the financial aid Europe had received there was a sense of obligation to do something for us – there was also a sense of closeness'.[46] These sentiments had certainly been expressed with regard to Britain by others in the administration. A letter from John McCloy to Acting Secretary of State, Dean Acheson, in September 1945 said that 'the fullest degree of reciprocal aid should be continued to be furnished by Britain so long as US forces are required in their territory. This aid should include civilian labor, subsistence, real property and strategic installations such as airfields.' (The letter also had a memorandum attached listing future base 'requirements'.) John McCloy then mentioned that the 'Empire is going to have a very difficult time obtaining the exchange necessary to meet amortization or interest payments on loans. I would think that either in settlement of existing lend–lease accounts or possibly in connection with any further credits which may be given, the British themselves would be well advised to accept this form of repayment rather than one which involves foreign exchange'.[47] Likewise, there had also been a strong recommendation from General Ira Eaker for a paper that would outline what the US Air Forces required from the British as 'part of our bargaining power for the British delegation now here asking for a loan of US funds'. The Assistant Secretary of War for Air, Lovett, also mentioned 'concessions' in a memorandum, where specific mention was again made of military and air rights at the strategic bases now under Britain's jurisdiction, and of the idea of 'support by Britain in the securing of air bases or air rights in any locality in the world which, though not under British jurisdiction, is nevertheless subject to their influence or indirect control'.[48] The absence at this stage, of any mention of charges covering the financial aspects of SAC's rotational tours to East Anglia, suggest that the British government was aware of such pressure and that a *quid pro quo* was reached.

The Spaatz–Tedder agreements coincided with the first postwar joint Air Plans prepared by the JCS. The agreement had given the SAC rotational units a presence; the War Plans were to provide a role for the American presence in Britain during an emergency.

POSTWAR AIR PLANNING

During 1947 the JWPC informed the JPS that the PINCHER series was sufficiently advanced so that they could now proceed with a joint war plan for the initial stages of a war that had been forced on the United States during FY 1948. The PINCHER series had met with strong criticism, particularly from the Air Force, which objected to the apparent subordination of air power to ground and sea forces. Colonel Alvin Leudecke, a key Air Force planner, wrote to Brigadier-General Frank Everest, the Air Force representative on the JWPC, that 'it seems that the same old thinking of World War II is coming up again with the result that Air power is treated as an adjunct to Ground and Sea power'.[49] Much of the inter-service disagreement arose over the role of the atom bomb.

In the USN, Admiral Chester Nimitz, the Chief of Naval Operations, thought that references to any kind of planning involving atomic bombs should be kept to an absolute minimum, particularly as they might not be employed at all or even outlawed by something like the Baruch Plan. In the Air Force, General Spaatz saw 'the bomb' deployed in its air role as the deciding factor in a war with the Soviet Union, where it would also help to offset their acknowledged numerical superiority.

The problem remained of how to utilise the air bases in Britain in case of emergency – be it conventional or otherwise. On 16 July 1947 the JWPC concluded that the PINCHER series, though not complete, had progressed far enough to justify preparation of a Joint War Plan, covering the initial stages of a war beginning some time in the following three years. The JSP agreed and in late August directed the JWPC to start Joint War Plan BROILER. Amongst the underlying assumptions of the plan were that 'atomic weapons would be used by the United States' and that 'the United Kingdom and Canada would be allies of the United States'.[50] The importance of overseas base areas also tended to emphasise the relative role of the Air Force; this can be seen in the basic strategy in BROILER, which was 'to secure in North America, the United Kingdom and the Cairo–Suez area and to launch a strategic air offensive against the Soviet Union'.[51]

Through successive modifications or new War Plans, the United Kingdom was to occupy an increasingly important position in American planning for the conduct of war in the western hemisphere. The first long-term war plan entitled CHARIOTEER appeared on 20 November 1947. This planned for a war against the Soviet Union in 1955 and assumed 'the loss of Western Europe and the need for a massive atomic strategic air campaign launched from peripheral bases'.[52] The great disparity between the Soviet Union and European ground forces was seen as the underlying reason for this assumption. The apparent utilisation of bases in the United Kingdom in the short-range plan, and their non-availability in the long-range plan, was puzzling unless it was assumed that the United Kingdom's strategic location would spare her the fate of continental West Europe and that she would continue to operate as a peripheral base. In later variants of the BROILER-type plans like 'MAKEFAST', three base areas were outlined for the launch of the strategic air offensive. The British Isles and Okinawa were the first two and the last varied between the Cairo–Suez area and Karachi. Long before the 'formal' arrival of the B-29s in England in response to the Berlin Crisis, the East Anglia bases assumed a central part of America's war strategy.

Only with reservations the JCS approved BROILER (in its final form it was somewhat inappropriately named FROLIC). Admiral Leahy was quick to point out that USN approval did not necessarily indicate approval of the use of atomic bombs. Admiral Denfeld also expressed reservations about the plan but conceded that only as an emergency plan was it acceptable. It is difficult to tell if the naval reservations were lodged in genuine protest on moral and strategic grounds, or if it was pique at watching the Air Force under Spaatz's guidance walk away with America's prime strategic weapon. There was also a marked gap between professed US foreign policy objectives announced in the Truman Doctrine and successive war plans which seemed to abandon Western Europe to the Soviet Union with little struggle and retain Britain merely as a strategic air base. It was not until the advent of the National Security Council (NSC) that strategic war plans were more closely allied to foreign policy and political considerations. BROILER was eventually transmitted to the services in a shortened form known as HALFMOON in July, only to be renamed a month later as FLEETWOOD. HALFMOON, the first cut version of BROILER, was approved by planning officers from the United States, Canada, and the United Kingdom in Washington DC in April 1948. Whilst HALFMOON was more specific about the scale of forces involved, it was assumed, like BROILER, that the strategic air offensive would begin about a fortnight after the initiation of hostilities (or D + 15 days), with medium bombers of SAC flying from the United Kingdom, Cairo–Suez and Okinawa. At D + 15 days the bombing effort was to be fairly evenly distributed, with two groups operating from the United Kingdom and Okinawa respectively, and one from Cairo–Suez. By D + 12 months the strategic bombing force was to grow to a total of one heavy bomber group flying from bases in the US, and ten other medium bomber groups from overseas – five from Cairo–Suez, three

from the United Kingdom, and two from Okinawa.[53] Soon after
HALFMOON was approved the Joint Strategic Planning Group (JSPG)
realised that the Egyptian bases could easily be overrun. It was
concluded that 'in the final analysis English bases offered the best
prospects for launching a massive air offensive, though other areas
would also be used as available'.[54]

Several faults with the plans became immediately apparent. The
plans, and many to follow, like MAKEFAST and its revision EARSHOT,
relied upon the somewhat cavalier assumption that atomic weapons
would be used in a war. This was in part because President Truman
'had never given defense leaders firm guidelines on future use of
atomic weapons'.[55] There were also questions about how seriously the
war plans should be treated. The plans were in no sense definitive and
changed with such rapidity that operational training for implementation of a plan was virtually impossible. The plans could be seen as a
device to justify, before Congress, excessive appropriations by the
services and particularly by the Air Force which was anxious to prove
that *it needed* the 'bomb'. The various plans illustrate two significant
points. First, the atomic trust was to be placed in the Air Force for
many years to come. Secondly, the United Kingdom was to be crucial
in implementing any short or long term war plan. Certainly at this stage
every single war plan was unworkable because of the limited number
of atomic weapons stockpiled, and because of the number and limited
range of available bombers. When General Curtis LeMay was directed
in 1947 by the Deputy Chief of Staff, Lieutenant-General Ira C.
Eaker, to prepare a contingency war plan, the sombre conclusion was
that about twenty-five 'bombs' were available.[56] (FLEETWOOD, the
official war plan in late 1948, envisaged a strategic offensive utilising
every available atomic weapon at the time, 133).[57] The JCS was
counting on nearer to three or four hundred such devices to have the
desired impact – likewise, even given the bombs, there were few
SILVERPLATE bombers available. John Greenwood estimates that
'only sixteen of forty-six SILVERPLATE B-29s modified during the war
were available to operational units, while another eighteen were
stripped of equipment and in storage. Six of the sixteen VHB groups
were activated with aircraft; three had no aircraft and the other seven
were not activated'.[58] The Armed Forces Special Weapons Project
(AFSWP), which supplied the technical teams responsible for constructing the atomic bombs, did not expect to have enough crews to
assemble even one hundred bombs simultaneously for another three
and a half years.

Having established the need for an overseas base network, the gradual truth dawned upon the Air Force that 'SAC could not deliver even fifty atomic bombs on twenty selected cities in the USSR, the blow necessary to paralyze roughly half of Soviet industry. The American threat carried a hollow ring'.[59] The American administration was meanwhile pursuing an expansion of ground forces rather than air groups. Confusion seemed rife and none of the plans gave any adequate assistance to Western Europe.

The Spaatz–Tedder Agreement and the subsequent rotational tours marked a spirit of goodwill that allowed the American military to negotiate for many other base rights in the Empire or Commonwealth. It was largely Britain's attitude, co-operative or obstuctionist, that determined the establishment of an American system of overseas bases. However it soon became clear, with the gathering of the international storm clouds over Berlin, that what the United States had in mind regarding the length of stay of forces in Europe was different from what was indicated in the Spaatz–Tedder Agreements.

THE BERLIN CRISIS

The Berlin Crisis of 1948–9 was to provide the pretext – not the cause – for the reintroduction of American military forces to Britain on a large scale. Although it is true that 'in the face of the Berlin blockade, the US deployed long-range B-29 strategic bombers to four East Anglian bases',[60] it is inadequate to argue that 'USAF units are, in effect, an outgrowth of the days of the Berlin airlift'.[61] To those more intimately involved in the military process, the deployments were the outcome of the Spaatz–Tedder Agreement where less conspicuous training 'visits' had already taken place.

In response to the worsening situation in Berlin, USAF initially planned the deployment of two medium bomber wings to the UK, for a period of thirty days' temporary operational training (TDY). Significantly, the official Third Air Force History made the claim that these bombers under SAC command '*did* have atomic capability'.[62] The same historical monograph then claimed that 'the presence of the B-29s with atomic capability was a subtle reminder of what could happen if Russian aggression went out of hand'.[63] Atomic-capable can be taken as meaning that the bombers were able to carry out nuclear missions but did not actually carry atomic bombs. Not only does contemporary research make the presence of an atomic capability in Britain unlikely, but even if there were such a capability there is no historical evidence that it was a decisive factor in bringing an end to the crisis.

What was the point of deploying B-29's to Britain? Was it, as US Secretary of Defense Forrestal suggests in his diaries, a way of getting a 'foot in the door?' Was it an early attempt at nuclear diplomacy, or did the lack of a suitable conventional response leave the deployment of bombers to Britain as the only other choice? Even if Stalin did perceive a veiled nuclear threat, it is not certain that the response would necessarily have been to back down.

The Berlin Crisis provided the opportunity to deploy a substantial number of bombers on British territory – this much is fact; but beyond this, when considerations of length of stay, the nature of the bombers and their intended mission are taken into account, the picture is far from clear. In response to the gathering storm clouds over Berlin, Secretary of State Marshall instructed the US Ambassador in London to offer to send to Europe three groups of heavy bombers, 'as a political gesture and a token of United States interest in the defence of Europe'.[64] Permission to rotate bomber groups to Britain was requested on 28 June by Ambassador Douglas. The decision to go ahead with the airlift had already been taken, and before Britain was approached, the Secretary of the Air Force Symington had informed Forrestal that the US Air Force had available (within twelve hours), for reinforcing Europe, one fighter group, three medium bomber groups with thirty B-29s in each group, and three additional medium bomber groups at a later date. These plans were made upon the assumption that 'maximum support would be furnished by the Military Air Transport Service and that all units would be deployed in the United Kingdom, where they could be supported with the assistance of the British'.[65]

Marshall's initial proposal made through Ambassador Douglas was welcomed as Britain had no effective heavy bomber force. Bevin himself had impressed upon the American administration that there should be no rush to negotiate, but that they should indicate their position by stepping up the airlift and deploy B-29s to Britain. The request from Douglas was agreed to with astonishing speed. The same day the request was made, the Foreign Secretary replied to Ambassador Douglas in London that 'we can agree in principle to such an arrangement . . . we think that the agreement should be made subject to subsequent discussion on the administrative and financial implications'.[66] The decision to accept the US proposal was made by the Committee of Ministers on Germany. This was a more restricted group that the Defence Committee, consisting of the Prime Minister, Bevin, A. V. Alexander (Defence), Herbert Morrison (Leader of the House), and the Chiefs of Staff. Shortly before the decision was taken to accept Douglas's request, it was pointed out by Sir John Kirkpatrick that the USAF already had the informal authority to rotate medium bomber groups to the United Kingdom under the Spaatz–Tedder agreement and that 'we seem committed to the proposal in principle, a fact of which the Prime Minister does not appear aware'.[67]

The quick acceptance by the Committee of Ministers on Germany of the American request was due to several reasons: fear of Russian expansionist aims in Europe following the successful Communist coup in Czechoslovakia, the imminent withdrawal of Russia from the Berlin Kommandatura, fear of an American retreat into isolationism that characterised the interwar years, and last, but not least, the Spaatz–Tedder agreement effectively making any other decision improbable. General Lucius D. Clay, who was the US Military Governor in Germany, warned that 'America's presence in Berlin was the symbol of her commitment to defend Western Europe against the march of communism, and that any faltering in this commitment would be disastrous'[68] – such statements implied that any failure of America's allies to toe the line could also be disastrous. The acceptance of the proposal, with such apparent ease, came as a surprise to Secretary of Defense Forrestal and Under-Secretary of State Lovett, so much so that 'Mr Bevin was asked by Secretary of State Marshall if he had fully considered its implications'.[69] It would appear that the British government had considered the implications of a *temporary* presence, but few knew exactly what the Americans had in mind regarding the future use of bases.

To meet what Margaret Gowing has called 'the first acute crisis in the Cold War', the precise arrangements for the visit of the bombers were *ad hoc* and unclear. No precise objectives were agreed to between either government regarding the duration or nature of the stay. The idea to deploy bombers to Britain was probably that of Secretary of Defense James Forrestal. As early as 22 June, one day before the Russian total blockade of Berlin began, Forrestal had suggested as a 'countermove' to Russian provocation or aggression the transfer of bombers to bases in Britain, within striking distance of Russia. In fact some bombers had already been deployed to Germany under the HALFMOON Joint Emergency War Plan. Forrestal saw the sending of B-29s to Britain as important for three reasons, which he outlined in his diaries. It would be seen as an action that would 'underline to the American people how seriously the United States views the current sequence of events'. It would also give the Air Force experience 'in this kind of operation' and 'accustom the British to the necessary habits and routines that go into the accommodation of an alien, even though an allied power'. Lastly, he saw it as essential to move bombers to Britain as soon as possible and then set about formalising the arrangement:

> We have the opportunity *now* of sending these planes and once sent they would become somewhat of an accepted fixture whereas deterioration of the situation in Europe might lead to a condition of mind under which the British would be compelled to reverse their attitude.[70]

In Forrestal's list of reasons, Berlin was not mentioned directly, but he saw the forward basing of bombers as a precedent for future intervention in Europe to counter Russian aggression. The idea of transferring B-29s to advance bases in time of emergency – 'the atomic equivalent of gunboat diplomacy' – was not new with Berlin. Some weeks previously, Forrestal had urged that the administration send some bombers and their crews to Greece, then in the midst of a civil war, for training purposes. 'While thus not unaware of the move's diplomatic significance in the case of Berlin, he also thought the forward basing of bombers was a practical decision long overdue in the nation's preparations for war.'[71]

There were some of the US administration who feared that the move might only provoke the Russians further. It was for this reason that the transfer of bombers was delayed from June until mid-July.[72] The US Army, in particular, under General Bradley was in favour of B-29 deployments as well as of sending a convoy up the Autobahn to 'put things to the test' and to 'bomb . . . the Soviet troops manning the blockade and also Soviet Airfields in East Germany'.[73] On 15 July, the National Security Council (NSC) agreed, 'subject to reservations by the Secretary of the Army, that the Secretary of State and the Secretary of Defense should recommend to the President that the United States proceed with the dispatch of B-29 bombers to the British Isles'.[74] On the same day it was announced that B-29s would leave for RAF bases in Britain.[75] *The Times* announced this momentous occasion with a rather unmemorable paragraph that carried no suggestion of the massive involvement to come:

> Two B-29 medium bomb groups (60 in all) have left their bases in the United States and are en route to bases in England for a short period

of temporary duty. The movement of the planes is part of the normal long range flight training programme which was instituted more than a year ago by the Strategic Air Command.[76]

The 'short period of temporary duty' was to be the first of numerous rotational units of bomber groups. The periods of temporary duty were, over the years, to amount to a permanent presence. Various leaks to the *Washington Post* were picked up by the *Daily Express* on 4 September with its headline about the re-opening of 'Great Wartime Bases' for use over 'a number of years'. This caused great anxiety in the Foreign Office and Government; no public statement concerning the American presence had yet been made to negate such stories. According to Foreign Office documents, the announcement was delayed for two reasons. There was no telling 'how long the emergency would continue' and, secondly, there was little or no idea 'what the United States really had in mind'.[77]

Shortly after the arrival of the two bomber groups in July, a high-level military decision was made to the effect that the USAF visit would be of a longer duration than the originally-planned 30–60 day temporary duty. It was with the advent of this decision that the nature of the USAF's stay in the United Kingdom changed. The Third Air Force Historical Office explained that from this time on plans and programmes were being 'formulated in terms of a greatly extended time element'.[78] From the British documentation for the early days of the Berlin Crisis, there is no record of any 'high level decision' regarding a stay longer duration for USAF units. The overall picture seems to have been one of confusion. Arthur Henderson, the Secretary of State for Air, wrote to the Foreign Secretary that 'it is not clear from our papers how long the aircraft were intended to stay' except that reference is made to 'arrangements with the RAF regarding a 90 day visit'.[79] A month later, after the arrival of the bombers, the question still remained unanswered.

After the arrival of two bomber groups in July, a further request was made by Ambassador Douglas to station a third group in Britain. The third group would be transferred from Germany, where it was felt that the air bases were too close to a hostile and dangerous frontier. The Foreign Secretary, following consultations with the Minister of Defence and the Secretary of State for Air, agreed to the transfer; the third group of B-29s moved to Britain in August. A second significant addition to the United States military presence in Britain was also made in July when an agreement was made between the respective military officials to re-open Burtonwood as a USAF depot to provide support for the Airlift. Within a few days of the agreement eleven USAF officers all 116 enlisted men were working round the clock to restore Burtonwod to its former wartime glory as 'one of the greatest air maintenance depots in the world'.[80] The first few men were soon joined by others bringing their total of 2500 at the height of the crisis. *The New York Times* commented that 'this unprecedented setting up in Britain of a major military installation in time of peace with the wholehearted approval of the British government is but part and parcel of a major – though unemphasised – shift of the United States air power into Western Europe during the past six months'.[87] The number of American military aircraft in Europe had risen from 175 to 466 during this period. At the same time, US Air Force personnel in Europe had increased from 5000 to 18 000 – of whom roughly one-third were to be based in Britain by winter. The agreement between American and British military personnel to re-open Burtonwood was made in much the same spirit as the lend-lease or destroyers–bases deal during the war; legalistic issues were brushed aside in the face of necessity.

The presence of B-29s soon created demands from MP's for more information regarding the visit of the American bombers. The Secretary of State for Air, Arthur Henderson, made a statement which coincided with a joint announcement released by the British Air Ministry and USAF explaining that the two squadrons (sixty aircraft) of B-29s were here for a 'short period of temporary duty', and that this was part of the 'normal long-range flight training programme instituted over a year ago by the United States Strategic Air Command'.[82] The pressure for a further explanation regarding the nature and duration of the stay by John Platts-Mills led to a further statement a few days later by the Secretary of State for Air:

> Units of the USAF do not visit this country under a formal treaty but under informal and long-standing arrangements between USAF and RAF for visits of goodwill and training purposes. The B-29s at present at RAF stations are here to carry out long-distance flying training in Western Europe. It has not been decided how long they will stay.[83]

In spite of the non-commital tone of the government's position and the US government's belief that the visit would lead to something longer-term, it seems that the British government saw the role of the bombers only in the context of the Berlin Crisis. In a Cabinet memorandum it had been understood that the 'intention was that all three groups of aircraft should remain in the United Kingdom so long as the crisis continued'.[84] Bevin was quick to see that, although bombers were undoubtedly a welçome presence in Britain, to give them 'permanent peacetime bases involved quite new principles'.[85] In spite of the concern voiced in some quarters about the implications of an extended stay, Britian was still weak in both the military and economic contexts. It was the sober recognition of this fact that led to a notable trip to Washington, DC, in October by the Chancellor of the Exchequer, Sir Stafford Cripps. The Chancellor confided to Forrestal that 'Britain is placing its main reliance on the development of fighter aircraft to insure the security of Britain. Britain must be regarded as the main base for the deployment of American power and the chief offensive against Russia must be by air'.[86]

The United States, it would appear, was already regarding Britain as the main base for the deployment of its power, and in particular, air power. Shortly after the Berlin Crisis and Czech coup, the JCS passed a motion[87] which established a requirement for the indefinite continuation of the right to base and maintain air groups in the United Kingdom. In August 1948, scarcely a month after it was created, the American Third Air Division at Marham was made a permanent unit under SAC's control. In November, four months after the first B-29s arrived, the 'USAF intimated to the RAF that they would like a permanent presence in Britain'.[88] The presence of B-29s in Britain did not escape the polemics of the Soviet press, which commented; 'Thus with the obliging consent of the Labour government, which is ignoring the interests of world peace, the American militarists are turning Britain into a base for their aggressive plans in Europe.[89]

Many have argued that the presence of atomic-capable aircraft in Britain was decisive in the outcome of the Berlin Crisis. Walter Millis, amongst others, made the assumption that the B-29s were atomic-capable and that Truman had taken a strong line and would use these weapons if need arose.[90] However it was not until September, after the bombers had arrived, that it was agreed between Truman and Marshall that General Norstad should be sent to England with a letter to the British Chiefs of Staff saying there were 'certain matters' the American Chiefs of Staff wished to discuss. The object was to obtain the acquiescence of the British to the 'construction of certain necessary buildings, or huts, for the housing of the components of the bomb at two airfields [Sculthorpe and Lakenheath] . . . the importance of this decision to us is that it will indicate whether or not the British mean business because the equipment of these fields obviously carries with it the inference of the purpose for which they will be used'.[91] Of course, 'bombs' could have been transported from the United States to the UK during the crisis, but this would seem a risky and foolhardy action in the midst of a major international crisis. There was also fear amongst senior American military officials that such negotiations during a crisis might lead the British government to take advantage of the situation to renew 'their importunity on a wider exchange of information leading to the manufacture of the bomb'.[92]

Whatever the rights or the wrongs of this question, it is fair to assume that the B-29s were intended to have a symbolic effect. In spite of the veiled threat, the Soviet Union did not lift the blockade following the deployment of B-29s and they maintained their effort for ten months thereafter. Seemingly, the Russians 'were not outwardly influenced by the ninety B-29s'.[93]

The fact that the Soviet Union chose not to *escalate* the crisis, and not to interfere with the air corridors is significant, and was probably due to the presence of B-29 bombers in Britain as a reminder of the potential military might of the United States.[94] Avi Shlaim wrote that it was not coercion but deterence which was the 'vaguely conceived objective of the move: deterring the Russians from escalating in response to the airlift . . . it is appearances and images rather than reality which constitute deterrence'.[95]

The next chapter will look at the growth of the American military presence in the United Kingdom, from its initial limited presence of three groups to a major overseas Air Force. The Spaatz–Tedder Agreement, that had provided for rotational tours of American bombers to Britian in time of emergency, was soon to be superseded by a more extensive agreement that, in effect, gave the Americans a permanent military presence in the United Kingdom. The Berlin Crisis marked the beginning of a reliance on an American military presence in the United Kingdom, whilst the United States administration had taken the opportunity to introduce bombers into Britian during the first acute crisis of the Cold War. The ramifications of the decision to deploy B-29s to Britian were to extend far beyond the Berlin Crisis which occasioned it. Even by the time the Russian blockade of Berlin was eventually lifted, the bombers had become, as Forrestal predicted, 'somewhat of an accepted fixture'.

3 Consolidation: Part 1 1948–50

THE BASES AFTER THE BERLIN CRISIS

By September 1948, at the height of 'Operation Vittles', there were ninety B-29 bombers at seven RAF stations and the former supply and maintenance depot at Burtonwood. The permanency of the units stationed here was in doubt in spite of their growing numbers. The Secretary of State for Air stated in the House of Commons, 'it has not been decided how long these arrangements will continue'.[1] However, when Arthur Henderson was further pressed to give an assurance that these arrangements would not continue beyond the duration of the airlift, he refused to do so. This refusal was a portent of what was to come, and by June 1953 the Parliamentary Secretary to the Minister of Defence announced that there were 45 000 US military personnel in Britain[2] – compared to some 11 500 in July 1950.[3]

There were, in addition to the US Air Force, significant US Navy personnel in the United Kingdom. Their exact function was vague but in a memorandum from the American Secretary of Defense to the Secretary of State it was estimated that 'our Naval personnel under command of Commander USN East Atlantic and Mediterranean now based in the United Kingdom total approximately 74 officers and 540 enlisted men. In addition, naval personnel afloat under this command frequently spending extended periods of time ashore in the UK total approximately 440 officers and 9000 enlisted men . . . the combined totals of US military personnel presently located in the United Kingdom or shortly to arrive therein (USN and USAF), including forces afloat, will appproximate 15 726 officers and enlisted men'.[4] This chapter will examine the growth of American bases in the United Kingdom following the Berlin Crisis, up to the Ambassador's Agreement which heralded a permanent American military presence.

Between 1948 and 1950 Britain became America's 'airstrip one' (a phrase first used by George Orwell in his novel *Nineteen Eighty-Four*)[5]. (Ironically enough, George Orwell had originally wanted to call his book 'Nineteen Forty-Eight', the year in which the American bombers arrived in Britain.) The resolution of the Berlin Crisis focused British attention on the intended future use of the East Anglia bases by American bombers. Anxieties in British governmental circles were aroused by an early CIA report which assumed that, in the event of a Soviet attack, 'the Western Powers would undertake immediate counteraction, including maximum employment of US air power, using the atomic bomb at least against Soviet targets'.[6] It was realised that the position of the United Kingdom following a Soviet occupation of the European continent would be critical. If on the one hand the United Kingdom was occupied by Russian forces or completely neutralised, US capabilities for counter-action through naval and air operations would be severly limited. If, however, the bases in the United Kingdom remained tenable for American naval and air operations, it was obvious that 'substantial' continuing damage could be inflicted upon the adversary.

The American Emergency War Plans had all assumed that the atomic bomb would sooner or later be used in a strategic air offensive; the question of the use of atomic bombs owned by the Americans was 'terrifyingly real and was already a matter of urgent concern to the Chiefs of Staff'.[7] The strategic employment of atomic weapons had not been discussed between the Americans and British, and the British Chiefs of Staff had absolutely no guidelines concerning the probable American deployment of atomic-capable bombers from our shores. It was not until the creation of the Seventh Air Division under SAC to command strategic air units in Britain, that the JCS 'made an allocation of atomic weapons to the defense of Europe'.[8]

The possibility of atomic weapons being used from the United Kingdom's shores opened up a central anxiety within the British government over the question of control of such operations. The problems of the control of America's nuclear stockpile was also occupying many minds in the US Congress.

The situation was further muddied by the revelation of the existence of the Quebec Agreement to a Joint Congressional Committee in May 1947. The wartime agreement reached between Roosevelt and Churchill effectively stated that there had to be a 'consent' between the parties before use of 'the bomb'; it was viewed with astonishment and incredulity by many American officials. The revelation of the Quebec Agreement was not, however, a complete surprise to the American administration. Some senior personnel in the administration, like Dean Acheson and General Groves (of the Manhattan Project), definitely knew of its existence because an abortive attempt was made by Acheson to change it in 1946.

THE QUEBEC AGREEMENT

The Quebec Agreement, or, to give it its proper title, 'Articles of Agreement governing collaboration between the authorities of the USA and UK in the matter of Tube Alloys' (a wartime codename for atom bomb research and development), had been signed by Roosevelt and Churchill, with Canada as a non-signatory party. It was agreed on 19 August 1943 that the United Kingdom should be admitted to the Manhattan project as a joint partner. In the second clause it was agreed 'we will never use this agency against each other' and most importantly 'we will not use it against third parties without each other's consent'.[9] The agreement then went on to promise that neither would communicate any information about Tube Alloys except by mutual consent, and that the British Government would have to recognise that any postwar advantages of 'an industrial or commercial character' arising out of 'Tube Alloys' should be dealt with on terms specified by the President to the Prime Minister. A Combined Policy Committee was established to administer the agreement. This agreement effectively meant that any future American nuclear arsenal would be subject to a veto by Britain, something that might have been agreeable in 1943, but was not in 1948.

Dean Acheson had argued against the acceptability of the Quebec Agreement primarily for strategic reasons, but the official line of argument was political. It was argued that the agreement imposed a restraint upon the President's power as Commander-in-Chief to act freely in the national interest and it was therefore deemed unconstitutional. At the end of 1945 there were moves afoot to change the agreement, with a recommendation to the Combined Policy Committee that a new document should be prepared to replace the Quebec Agreement '*in toto*'. The new proposal in its first clause recommended that the governments of the US, Canada, and the United Kingdom 'will not use atomic weapons against other parties without *prior consultation* with each other', thus aiming directly at Clause 2 of the Quebec Agreement which had expressed atomic weapons would not be used without each other's *consent*.[10] The meeting between Truman, Attlee and Mackenzie-King of Canada in November 1945, and subsequent meetings, failed to persuade Britain to give up her veto right.

A more serious threat to the Quebec Agreement was posed by the McMahon Bill then in passage in Congress. This bill – completely disregarding the wartime commitments to the British and Canadians which were anyway of uncertain duration – strove to make technical collaboration on atomic energy between the countries impossible. This became the case when the Bill passed into law in June 1946, resulting not only in a severe knock to Anglo–American relations but leaving Britain alone in her expensive quest for the bomb. The McMahon Act had been prompted on the one hand by consistent troubles over allocation of raw material and the administrative clumsiness of collaboration and, on the other hand, by growing American fears for security that were confirmed by the discovery of a Canadian spy ring in February 1946 which included a British scientist, Nunn May. While the McMahon Act obviously made part of the Quebec Agreement inoperative it left the whole question of consultation over the use of the bomb unclear.[11]

A fresh onslaught on the Quebec Agreement took place a year later. On 12 March 1947 Truman spoke before a Joint Session of Congress. His historic address concerned the gravity of the world situation, with particular reference to Greece and Turkey where Britain was unable to meet her obligations. The agreement reached at Quebec was a well-kept secret from most. Vandenberg, Connally and Bourke B. Hickenlooper were members of the Committee on Foreign Relations as well as of the Joint Committee on Atomic Energy. 'Better than most of their Congressional colleagues, they were aware of the ties linking the US and Britain. But as they heard Truman speak on March 12, they did not know that in 1943 at Quebec, Roosevelt had agreed with Churchill that neither country would use the atomic bomb without the consent of the other'.[12]

Exactly a month later, when Acheson appeared before the Joint Congressional Committee, US representatives first learned of the agreement. Hickenlooper and Vandenberg were 'shocked and out-raged'. Hickenlooper wrote to the Secretary of State Marshall in August protesting that 'the present agreement, in view of all the circumstances, is intolerable'.[13] Senator Vandenberg, as Chairman of the Senate Foreign Relations Committee, saw the Quebec Agreement as 'astounding' and 'unthinkable';[14] and he felt a tremendous responsibility, as chairman of perhaps the most prestigious and influential committee in American politics, to change the agreement. Hicken-looper even went so far as to declare to Marshall that he 'would be unable to support American economic aid to Britain unless the situation was rectified at once'.[15] The American administration wanted desperately to drop the second clause, and a cable to London in December 1947 assumed there could be no objection since 'so long as the present collaboration between the two countries continued, the clause was otiose'.[16] Meanwhile, in Washington DC, a package was being prepared proposing the exchange of limited technical atomic information for the nullification of the veto clause in the Quebec Agreement, which Vandenberg saw could be a 'source of desperate embarrassment'.[17]

THE '*MODUS VIVENDI*' (JANUARY 1948)

The new package, or *modus vivendi* as it became known, looked attractive to the British at first. The *modus vivendi* was to be an agreement between the United Kingdom and the United States on the future of their respective atomic energy programmes. There was also to be, most important from the British perspective, exchange of technical information covering nine specific areas, including natural uranium, reactors, metallurgy of plutonium, detection of nuclear explosions and nuclear cross sections. The *modus vivendi* was also meant to signify the beginning of greater atomic co-operation with the Dominions, while another clause related to closer American and Canadian collaboration. This package was in exchange for the nullification of the Quebec Agreement and in particular Clause 2 and Clause 4. The *modus vivendi* was also envisaged to have beneficial effects spilling over into other fields of Anglo-American and Canadian relations. The major disadvantage to Britain was the surrender of some of her uranium claims.[18] The exchange of information was seen as restoring faith in the Anglo–American relationship and in atomic collaboration which had effectively stopped by the McMahon Act. That Act had halted collaboration in the nuclear field with two exceptions: these were non-military nuclear information and raw material, which in effect worked to the advantage of the US. The struggle to build an atomic bomb without collaboration from the United States was seen as wasteful of both time and resources. It was hoped the *modus vivendi* would alleviate this; in return Britain would lose her veto right over the use of Britain as a base from which to launch a strategic offensive utilising the atomic bomb. However, when collaboration on atomic projects did resume, it was found that British development had kept up with the United States.

In effect the *modus vivendi* asked Britain and Canada to surrender both their accumulated uranium stocks in excess of that needed for current industrial projects, and their 'veto' right on the use of the bomb. In exchange, the United States would assist others in the development of atomic energy for industrial purposes. The United States was primarily interested in securing a greater share of uranium and then the removal of the veto. The proposals went before the Combined Policy Committee on 10 December 1947, with the burden of the American position falling on Acting Secretary of State, Robert Lovett, assisted by Forrestal and Lillenthal (of the AEC). Lord Inverchapel was head of the negotiating team for the Britain and Hume-Wrong, a diplomat, for Canada. Amonst the British advisers was Sir Gordon Monro, who asked about the wartime agreements on the bomb. Lovett replied that the 'bomb agreements should be swept away rather than continue to exist as a source of misunderstanding and controversy'.[19] Negotiations continued until 7 January 1948 when the final agreement was ready. It consisted of three parts: a technical co-operation agreement, information exchange and an agreement on ore allocation. The first clause of the *modus vivendi* dealt with the British veto, declaring that 'all agreements between the three governments or any two of them in the field of atomic energy shall be regarded as null and of no effect',[20] with a few exceptions that are not relevant here.

John Cockroft and Sir Roger Makins of the Foreign office and David Peirson of the Ministry of Supply proposed that the agreement should take the form of a general declaration of intent, which was a form of agreement that the President could conclude without reference to Congress, and would not come under Article 102 of the United Nations Charter. This was extended as a working or temporary arrangement and, as Margaret Gowing puts it, a means of 'co-existence pending a permanent settlement'. The *modus vivendi* was agreed to by the Combined Policy Committee on 7 January 1948, but was not officially signed; instead, in keeping with the style of other agreements, Lovett, Inverchapel and Wrong declared their intent to abide by the document. The agreement allowed the CPC to continue as the organ for dealing with atomic energy problems, and amongst its functions was the allocation of raw materials (mainly uranium and thorium). Within a short period of time the item dealing with the exchange of information on atomic reactors was deleted, the information from American scientists proved to be innocuous, and the United States gained considerably. Under the *modus vivendi* Britain gave uranium *before* receiving technical information and so got little of the latter. The most serious flaw was without doubt the 'surrender of the British veto on the American use of the atomic bomb, without even substituting the word "consultation" for the word "consent", as had been proposed in 1946'.[21]

The timing of the *modus vivendi* gave cause for alarm with the ensuing Berlin Crisis and the arrival of the B-29s only a matter of months away. Scarcely three years later there was the threat of the American use of an atomic bomb during the Korean War. It was only with this threat that the full effects of the *modus vivendi* were realised, when the possibility of British bases used for a cause out of NATO area arose. The surrender of Clause 2 of the Quebec Agreement, seen as intolerable by the American administration, was seen in Britain as a reciprocal exchange for the American surrender of Clause 4, which recognised that the postwar advantages – industrial and commercial – of atomic energy were to be dealt with in terms specified by the President to the Prime Minister. The *modus vivendi* also relieved the United States of any raw material shortages in their nuclear development programme, by alloting to Washington the entire Congo (uranium) output for 1948, and giving it an option on any of the following years' output not required by Britain.

Opinions upon the result of the *modus vivendi* differ. Sir Roger Makins (now Lord Sherfield) felt that 'Peirson was anxious for agreement and was interested in a raw materials agreement. The raw material deal was made with Groves by which there was a division of available raw material and Britain was never at any time short of raw materials. The technical information helped but didn't lead to any immediate development of collaboration. However, scientists talk together and it is difficult to quantify how much information was exchanged and its value'.[22] But was this limited technical information worth the surrender of the veto? Margaret Gowing expressed surprise that 'in view of the potential issues of life and death that were involved, neither officials nor Ministers showed any concern or interest in the surrender of Britain's veto, or right to consultation on the use of the bomb'.[23] This was particularly surprising because it was not only the right of consultation on the use of the bomb from British bases that was surrendered but use of bombs anywhere. One possible explanation for the apparent apathy on this crucial question was that many probably did believe that if B-29s were to visit Britain it would only be for 'temporary duty' and 'visits of goodwill and training' – the arrangements for such a visit were made six months after the *modus vivendi*. Few, apart from those intimately involved in the military process, had any idea of the length of stay envisaged when the B-29s arrive in Britain during the Berlin Crisis. Arrangements for the use of the atomic bomb were to be regarded as hypothetical until the outbreak of the Korean War.

No matter how seriously the Americans took the initial right of consent in the Quebec Agreement, 'it gave Britain at least a contingent right to consultation before action was taken that might lead to her own annihilation. Now Britain had no claim to consultation'.[24] The *modus vivendi* had no set term and, as Margaret Gowing concludes, the aim of the agreement was the greater defence and security of the United States as secured by the acquisition of additional uranium and the negation of any consensual agreement on the use of the bomb. Lord Sherfield has argued that the agreements were negotiated in an atmosphere of 'complete trust'[25] – a trust that must be seen as surprising in the light of previous US–UK atomic relations. The next two years were to challenge severely this trust as the *modus vivendi* ended any 'formal sanction that Britain might have enjoyed over the use of US atomic weapons from their new strategic bases'.[26] The *modus vivendi* was a sad example of British trust of the United States good intentions taking the place of hard bargaining. The agreement saw the surrender of the first of Britain's key bargaining chips in the post-war politico-economic *realpolitik* with the US. The second was to be Britain's strategic location for bases.

TEMPORARY DUTY?

In March 1948, four months before the official arrival of the American bombers, the USAF and the Air Ministry had initiated a survey of airfields in the United Kingdom to determine 'those capable of sustaining operations by US Air Force strategic bombardment type aircraft'.[27] Shortly after the arrival of the first medium bomb group in the United Kingdom, service-level discussions with the Air Ministry took place outlining 'requirements' for airfields in the United Kingdom. JCS 1952/10 claimed that 'during the course of these discussions the following agreements were reached:

a) Airfields at Marham, Lakenheath and Sculthorpe were to be immediately available to the US Air Force as required.

b) In view of the vulnerability of the above airfields, four airfields in the Oxford area, presently requiring certain improvements, would be made available for US Air Force strategic bombardment units in the event of hostilities.

c) Three other airfields capable of supporting limited MB (medium bombardment) operations would be made available in the event of hostilities.[28]

If taken seriously, the implications are disturbing, since this would mean that the United Kingdom was effectively committed to an expansion of the American base network during the Berlin Crisis, an expansion that the government did not know about and of whose duration no mention was made.

British records show that, as part of post-Berlin Crisis war plans, the USAF put forward a request to develop four Midlands airfields early in 1949. After the deliberations of a Defence Committee in London it was decided to tell the American authorities that improvements could be undertaken only if the government were reimbursed.[29] Although the Defence Committee agreed *in principle* to the development of four airfields there was still no formal Cabinet approval for permanent USAF bases in this country – a point Bevin was at pains to make clear to the British Ambassador in Washington:

I explained to Mr Douglas [the American Ambassador] that the fact was that the British Cabinet has never yet accepted the principle that there should be a permanent American base in Great Britain. What we had done was to allow the B-29 groups to be brought here as a protection during the difficult time arising out of the Berlin blockade. But there had never been a decision taken by the Cabinet regarding the permanent location of American bombers in this country; neither had we ever reported the question to Parliament.[30]

During the Berlin Crisis several new war plans and reports had been in the planning stage, and they saw the light of day soon after the Crisis. The first post-Berlin Crisis war plan was TROJAN, approved by the JCS on 28 January 1949. This plan was in turn an update of FLEETWOOD and an annexe outlined the proposed atomic offensive, including a broad range of industrial facilities in seventy Soviet cities – Moscow and Leningrad included. The delivery of the strategic air offensive was again to rest on forces flying from the same bases as stipulated in HALFMOON.

During deliberations on the military budget for FY 1950 it became increasingly clear that the current strategy was unrealistic, bearing in mind the forces likely to become available under stringent spending ceilings. The JCS issued a new directive to the Joint Strategic Plans Committee (JSPC) on 26 April 1949 and, due to continuing inter-service squabbling and delays planning conferences with Britain and Canada, the outcome of the JSPC study called OFFTACKLE was only approved on 8 December 1949. OFFTACKLE was a new development for two reasons. It was the first strategic plan to be based on guidance from the National Security Council, which meant, in effect, that planning was more in touch with what was going on politically and economically. NSC 20/4 stated that 'we should endeavor to achieve our general objectives by methods short of war' and in spite of the fact that war might grow out of 'incidents between forces in direct contact', it would result because the Soviet Union might be tempted to 'take armed action under a miscalculation of the determination and willingness of the US to resort to force in order to prevent the development of a threat intolerable to US security'.[31]

Like other plans, OFFTACKLE was based on the assumption that war would be the result of aggressiveness of the USSR or its satellites. But unlike its predecessors the strategic offensive was not just 'directed against' the Soviet war machine and its infra-structure, but aimed at 'destroying them'. OFFTACKLE was far more specific about the role of the United Kingdom which in turn supported the USAF demand for more bases. JSPC 877/59 was emphatic about the importance of the UK as an air base and stated that 'of all the operations in Western Eurasia, first priority is given to that of securing the United Kingdom against invasion' and to that of defending it against air attack to the degree necessary to 'insure its availability as a major base for all types of military operations'.[32] It was contemplated that the United Kingdom would have six main functions in any future war or emergency. It would first and foremost be the major base for a strategic air offensive. Second, the United Kingdom would also serve as a base for air operations, and as a potential base area to secure air supremacy over Western Europe. The United Kingdom would also serve as a base area for a build-up leading towards an invasion of the European continent, as well as being a base area to support such an invasion. In addition, (and this was the first time that a naval support role had been mentioned for the United Kingdom's USN contingent), it was 'a naval base area from which to protect the sea lines of communication' which were vital to the above operations. Lastly, it was somewhat vaguely to 'assist in the provision of essential British requirements'.[33]

The deployment patterns also show the importance of the United Kingdom in American strategic considerations (D-Day was assumed to be during FY 1950).

The emphasis on the United Kingdom was explained partly by the

Table 3.1   OFFTACKLE base deployments[34]

Base area	D-Day	D+12 months
Zone of the Interior (i.e. US)	1 heavy group	2 heavy groups
United Kingdom	2 medium groups	5 medium groups
NW Africa	—	3 medium groups
Okinawa	1 medium group	1 medium group

fact that no bombers had been allocated this time to the Cairo–Suez area, abandoned as the launching-point of a strategic offensive largely because it was felt to be beyond the capability of US forces and therefore better left to the British. The OFFTACKLE plans, like others, had as its main failure the weakness of the United States in ground forces, as they 'necessarily limited initial offensive operations to air attack'; this also meant that the United States 'could do little to aid the Western European nations in defending their territories',[35] despite the newly concluded North Atlantic Alliance. Soon after, the short-range War Plan OFFTACKLE was presented to the Weapons System Evaluation Group, who in turn presented the JCS with a memorandum with the pointed title 'Inadequacy of Bases Provided for Strategic Air Offensive'. Their report added one extra medium bombardment group to the OFFTACKLE numbers for the United Kingdom. However, the report then went on to state:

> there are inadequate bases provided in Great Britain to deploy the six medium bombardment groups and one reconnaissance group as contemplated in current Strategic Air Command emergency plans. This inadequacy is caused by the vulnerable location of presently assigned bases, Sculthorpe, Marham and Lakenheath. The vulnerability of these aerodromes is aggravated by a lack of dispersed hardstands for B-29 or B-50 airplanes.[36]

The WSEG memorandum rightly pointed out that there were also no arrangements existing between the executive heads of the two governments to ensure the availability of the three bases, of the supply depot at Burtonwood, or of the headquarters of the 3rd Air Division (Provisional) established on 16 July 1948. A preliminary approach to the British government for American bases in the Midlands area, at Upper Heyford and Brize Norton, met with a refusal largely because it would jeopardize RAF operational effectiveness and the government would not authorise the expenditure of funds required for reconstruction of the aerodromes to meet the requirements of the B-29 or B-50.

The recommendation was that this matter should be taken up on the highest governmental level. The JCS headed by General Eisenhower was annoyed by the interference of the British government in what had hitherto been a military affair.

Attempts at negotiating base rights through military channels had so far foundered on the question of who paid for what. JCS estimates prepared during January 1949, when the Berlin Crisis and Operation 'Vittles' was still active, estimated that the total cost of improving the four Oxfordshire airfields would be about $31 million. The Secretary of Defense decided to submit the question to the NSC on 17 March 1949 to determine 'whether or not the development of four airfields in the Oxford area of the United Kingdom was in the national interest'.[37] The NSC then referred the subject to the JCS and received affirmation on 27 March 1949 that the construction of these four airfields was in the United States' national interest.

NSC 45 set forth for consideration the necessity of at least four more air bases, of medium bomber standard, largely to avoid the growing vulnerability of the East Anglia bases. The new bases were to be 'in the heart of the British defense system.'[38] The funds which were needed for the development work on the four Oxfordshire air bases during FY 1950 amounted to £7 million, according to RAF estimates, with the total cost estimated to be £7 717 000 (or $31 million). The British Treasury declined an Air Ministry proposal that £1 800 000 be included in the budget for the fiscal year 1950 to finance the base development. This was done on the grounds that:

> the British government could not support an appropriation of funds for USAF requirements without agreement between the Government of the US and UK as to the source of funds. It is the opinion of Ambassador Douglas and of General Johnson, Air Force Commander in the UK, that no favorable action may be expected from the British government without pressure from high quarters in the US.[39]

Following the WSEG and NSC advice, the Secretary of State directed the American Ambassador in Britain (Douglas) to undertake negotiations with the British government. Informal discussions were held but 'the Ambassador refrained from opening formal negotiations with the British pending information as to what proportion of the construction funds the US government would be willing to provide'.[40] Rather surprisingly, the Secretary of Defense suggested to the Secretary of State, seeing that negotiations were at an impasse, that perhaps the British should bear the complete cost of the proposed building project. If that was not possible, the American government would offer to defray the dollar cost (in other words dollars which would have to be expended to obtain equipment and materials available only outside the United Kingdom).[41]

Other ways were employed to bring pressure to bear on the British government for additional bases. For instance, the newly-formed North Atlantic Treaty Organization of April 1949 was open to favourable American interpretation. The NATO members were pledged to Article 3 by means of 'continuous and effective self help and mutual aid, to maintain and develop their individual and collective capacity to resist aggression.' The NSC was quick to claim that it was clearly understood by all parties that mutual aid meant the 'contribution by each party consistent with its geographical location and resources of such mutual aid as it can reasonably be expected to contribute in the form in which it can most effectively furnish it'.[42] Similarly, a whole spate of reports emphasising the Russian military preparedness appeared during the first six months of 1949. A report by an Interdepartmental Working Group in the United States was typical of such reports stressing the Russian 'preponderance of immediately available military power on the Eurasian continent and a consequent ability to resort to war at any time as a means of imposing its will in that areas.' The report also stressed that the principal deterrent to aggression 'is the superior war potential of the United States'.[43]

Negotiations toward additional bases in the United Kingdom were spurred on by a report that an American Air Force WB-29 (weather reconnaissance plane) on routine patrol from Japan to Alaska had picked up signs of radioactivity on 3 September 1949. The radioactivity 'slightly exceeded the intensity necessary to constitute an official alert'.[44] It soon became clear that the Russians had successfully conducted an atomic test and it was realised that the official American War Plans and CIA estimates had been wrong. The President's advisory Committee on Military Training had estimated in 1948 that the Soviet Union would not have an atomic bomb for 'at least' three years.[45] The Finletter Commission[46] estimated it would be four and a half years before the Soviet Union could launch a nuclear attack against the United States.

The explosion of a Soviet nuclear device intensified American fears of 'the Soviet threat' and the Americans responded to the explosion with a sense of foreboding and increased atomic weapons production, research into new applications of atomic energy and the search for the new 'super' bomb (or fusion bomb). George Kennan, in his Memoirs,[47] recalls that in 1949–50 many in Washington believed that the Soviet Union would start a war as soon as they had amassed a sufficient nuclear arsenal. In contrast, J. Robert Oppenheimer recalled that Truman refused to believe that the Russians had an atomic or hydrogen bomb until 1953.[48]

THE AMBASSADOR'S AGREEMENT (APRIL 1950)

The unwelcome news that the Soviet Union also had an atomic bomb created concern in Britain, because the lack of Soviet long-range bombers capable of striking the United States and of aircraft carriers meant that Britain would be a prime target once the Soviet Union had a larger stock of atomic weapons – while at the same time 'the United States has a requirement for an indefinite continuation of the right to base and maintain air groups in the United Kingdom'.[49] Such anxieties led the Foreign Secretary, Ernest Bevin, to express concern over the *ad hoc* nature of the American military presence in the Cabinet. 'While he welcomed the presence of US bombers in the UK at the present time . . . he was anxious to see the present peace time arrangements put on a more definite basis'.[50] Such sentiments, combined with the recommendations of NSC-45 in the United States, which had advised the opening of discussions towards the selection of more secure installations behind the London Fighter Defence and Radar Screen at Brize Norton, Upper Heyford, Fairford and Greenham Common, were to lead to the Ambassador's Agreement.

American negotiators were anxious to establish some kind of financial arrangement for the proposed base expansion, since USAF war-planning was outrunning the slow pace of negotiation for the Midlands airfields. Project BOWERY and its later version, LITERARY, had already provided that in an emergency certain personnel and equipment would be evacuated from the continent to the United Kingdom. In order to meet the requirements of the USAF plan, the Third Air Division initiated three major projects:

DOUBLE-QUICK: removal of B-29s from East Anglia bases to other locations where they would be less vulnerable to enemy attack.

VALISE: a safety precaution should hostilities start before DOUBLE-QUICK was ready. This plan stipulated that after aircraft had deployed their initial mission they would deploy to the West Coast of England and Northern Ireland.

SPEEDWAY: this involved the selection and preparation of all sites along the East Coast of England for SAC jet-fighter operations.[51]

The problem was twofold. First there was the matter of acquiring the facilities; and second, there was the problem of financing the construction to bring the airfields up to B-29 operating standard, which involved extended runways, additional taxiways, housing and hard-standing.

The first joint high-level meeting in the United Kingdom had been held on 15 October 1948, at which the Air Ministry stated that in addition to Lakenheath, Sculthorpe and Marham, authority had been granted to turn over four more airfields. The Air Ministry stressed that their authority was limited to only four additional bases. Proposed fighter operations, then being considered by USAF planners, would take place on the 'vacated' East Anglia airfields. The British Joint Staff Mission in Washington was also kept fully aware of the developments and co-ordinated top-level thinking for the Air Ministry with the USAF. The agreement by the Air Ministry, in principle, to an extension of the American presence led the USAF to develop the extended stay concept. Meanwhile, with such a vast expansion of facilities planned, the problem of securing adequate funding assumed major proportions. In a memorandum for Stuart Symington, Secretary of the Air Force at this time, General Johnson stated that 'it would seem that the RAF should make these expenditures for capital improvements which will be of permanent benefit to the RAF upon the termination of our tenancy'.[52] The British Defence Council, headed by the Prime Minister, and of utmost importance in the control of governmental expenditure for military purposes, made it clear that it did not object in principle to the idea of USAF having additional airfields – if the cost would be borne by the United States.

The crux of the problem was that neither the USAF nor the RAF had sufficient funds for the construction at the four Oxfordshire airfields. The possibility of using Economic Cooperation Administration funds was dismissed for technical reasons. The problem was well summarised in two messages, the first from the American point of view, and the second from the British Joint Staff Mission in Washington:

Basically the difficulty is that both organizations are short of funds, since their budgets did not provide for this bomber operation, and are trying to avoid as much expense as possible.

The financial aspects of these understandings are a matter for settlement between our governments at high level, but we are certain that only construction work essential for the work of the B-29s is likely to be authorized.[53]

The British attitude was undoubtedly coloured by the precarious economic condition at that time, along with a grudging acceptance that sooner or later they would have to assume some of the burden of the construction work. The US government seemed to rest their argument on the vagaries of the American presence, and as the length of their tenancy was of somewhat uncertain duration they were unwilling to foot the bill without a guarantee of a more permanent presence in the United Kingdom. The commander of the Third Air Division, General Leon Johnson, wrote to the Ambassador in London that the British were prepared to go ahead with the construction, 'considering at all times that the United States Government would pay for it.' General Johnson argued forcibly that the British government should finance these construction costs because the USAF 'duration of tenancy is indefinite and further because of our unusual status in the United Kingdom'.[54] At this juncture, on 11 May 1949, President Truman referred the problem to the State Department, and the Secretary of State was then instructed to undertake negotiations with the British government over funding for these bases. Once again the British Defence Council made no objection to building the fields, provided the United States government would stand the complete cost. The British Defence Council in Washington decided that whilst the Midlands airfields were perhaps desirable they were, under British War Plans, not necessary. Other projects like the airfield at Abu Sueir occupied a higher priority in British minds.

The situation was exacerbated by a restatement of the United States government position, arguing that the approval of Congress would be necessary for such military expenditure abroad and that this would be impossible without either an agreement over the length of stay at the fields or a determination of the recovery of residual value, should the USAF occupancy be terminated. Issues were further confused at the ABC (American–British–Canadian) Joint Planners Conference in Washington in September 1949. The conference outlined the USAF Emergency War Plan, to supersede the old plan TROJAN. The facilities required for the new Plan included 'some thirty airfields in the United

Kingdom, nine of which are required to accommodate B-29 type aircraft'.[55] The obvious discrepancy between the requirement for nine bases in the emergency war plan and the original demand for four medium bombardment bases caused consternation. Bevin stated in response to this new plan that he would not endorse the project for the four Midlands airfields, because American requirements 'are not firm' and 'presumably the United States Air Force requirements will be on an increasing scale in the future'.[56] In fact, a Top Secret 'requirements list'[57] at this time exceeded the nine bases discussed in the ABC Conference, and gave a hint of the future American military involvement on British shores. The memorandum by the JCS for the Secretary of Defense listed 'rights required' country by country. The rights required in the United Kingdom were military operating air bases suitable for sustaining medium bombardment and/or strategic reconnaissance operations, and they were listed as Brize Norton, Fairford, Upper Heyford, with the fourth Midlands airbase named as Chelveston. In addition, the three existing East Anglia bases at Mildenhall, Sculthorpe and Lakenheath were required to support F-51 fighter operations or additional bomber operations in an emergency. Military operating air bases were required specifically for sustaining jet fighter operations at Woodbridge, Manston and Carnaby. Bases were also required for 'sustaining air line of communication operations for the Military Air Transport Service (MATS) and JAC' at Nutts Corner in Northern Ireland, Prestwick, Stornoway, Valley and Heathrow. Bases were also needed for 'air depot' activities at Burtonwood and Alconbury. Last, there was a vague requirement for the 'right to supplement British effort to maintain stockpiles and prepare and develop communications, ports, harbor, base, training, and logistic facilities *and airbases* as may be necessary for the employment of US forces contemplated in NATO areas'.[58] The true picture seemed to call for *at least* seventeen bases and facilities in the United Kingdom, as the minimum to carry out US Emergency War Plans. The British Treasury, however, continued to insist that we could not undertake any further substantial financial commitments without endangering our economic recovery.

The situation remained unchanged until early 1950. On 6 February the first move towards formal negotiations was made by Air Chief Marshal Slessor, Chief of the Air Staff, who informed Hector McNeil, Acting Secretary of State for Foreign Affairs in the United States, that although the American bombardment groups were only to be in Britain for the duration of the Berlin Airlift, 'both the British and

American governments recognised the mutual advantages of continuing the groups here, and that the British must proceed to make available the fields required in the Midland areas'.[59] Air Chief Marshal Slessor pushed the Cabinet to arrange negotiations for 17 March and foresaw 'little difficulty' with the Defence Ministry or Foreign Office, perceiving the real problem as the Treasury. The start of official discussions on the four Midland airfields was announced by Air Chief Marshal Slessor in a personal letter to General Vandenberg, which apologised for the long time 'in getting going.'

A formal meeting was scheduled at Ambassadorial level for 18 March. The cost for the four airfields in the Midlands area was estimated at 31 million dollars, with the 'possibility' that the US might pay external dollar costs to the amount of about 4 million dollars. Apart from the problem of financing the airfield development, the Americans had the problem of how to soothe, as one official put it, 'the British fear based on the knowledge of our current emergency planning that the B-29 bases are only the beginning and that there will be an *ever increasing demand for airfields in Britain*'.[60] If, as was anticipated, the British felt unable to meet the sterling cost (of just over £7 million), then the services of the US Aviation Engineer Battalion were to be offered, and according to General Johnson's estimates this could reduce sterling costs to almost half of what would be initially proposed. It was also believed by General Johnson that the $3.7 million American share could be furnished without Congressional action.

As anticipated, the British negotiators turned down the initial proposition and Ambassador Douglas, following General Johnson's suggestion, offered the services of the Aviation Engineer Battalion. Only then did the Treasury begin to take an active interest in the Midlands project. Aidan Crawley, the Parliamentary Under Secretary of State for Air in charge of the British side of the negotiations, replied to the Ambassador a week later that 'we can see no insuperable difficulty about the work being done by the battalions in this country,[61] although he disputed the American estimate that 66 per cent of the contribution would be American if the battalions were included and suggested it would be equivalent 'to perhaps 30 per cent of the cost'.[62] The letter continued by recommending a reduction in the scope of construction, which would pare an additional million pounds. Ambassador Douglas refused to countenance a reduction in scope, stating: '. . . I believe to accept them might jeopardize the whole plan of the United States Air Force operating from the United Kingdom.

We both know that this is a joint effort that must not fail'.[63]

Crawley did acquiesce in the American refusal to consider a major reduction in scope. The formal arrangement was known as the Ambassador's Agreement and was concluded between 15–20 April 1950, when both the USAF and Air Ministry agreed to accept various responsibilities in the development of the bases in the Midlands. The final agreement consisted of an exchange of letters between the US Ambassador, Louis Douglas and Aidan Crawley, representing the United Kingdom. The basis of the Ambassador's Agreement was in the extension of the four Midlands bases at Upper Heyford, Brize Norton, Fairford and a fourth to be named. The United States agreed to provide the services of the Aviation Engineer Battalion, with the task of performing 'all work within their capability'.[64] The Air Ministry was to provide, during the period of construction, the cost of maintenance on the base and free accommodation for the Aviation Engineer's personnel. It was also agreed in principle that the four airfields would be raised only to the level of minimum wartime operational standby, reducing the cost to about £6 million – which the Treasury had to find. An informal agreement was also reached regarding the duration of the American presence: this merely assured the British of the right to terminate the arrangement.

The Ambassador's Agreement was remarkable as much for its omissions as for its contents. The agreement did not, for instance, set a specific time-limit on the 'visit'. But the American delight was scarcely concealed: 'Thus after many months of activity, formal agreement was finally reached on what turned out to be the first phase of a tremendously large expansion of the original USAF plans for operations in the United Kingdom'.[65] The Ambassador's Agreement only related to short-term concerns, and the costs incurred by an extended stay of the USAF were eventually to reopen the vexed question of finance. Crawley made it clear to Ambassador Douglas that if any 'similar project were to arise in the future, the United Kingdom would not be in a position to contribute appreciably to the cost'.[66] The price-tag for the construction programme was agreed in the Ambassador's Agreement to be $6.6 million for the American contribution of Aviation Engineers' labour. The United Kingdom was to pay $10.4 million in materials and contracting, thus totalling some $17 million for the project.[67] The 928th Engineer Aviation Group, consisting of three battalions, established their headquarters at Brize Norton, and the Third Air Division issued construction orders for the Midlands bases on 11 August 1950.

The British reaction to the Ambassador's Agreement was generally favourable. The Minister of Defence had said a month before the Agreement that it was 'desirable to persuade the Americans to keep their air forces in the United Kingdom', and he 'proposed that our representatives should press them to pay for the cost of the facilities they required. In the last resort he felt it would be right to make some concessions.' Attlee had also declared that 'from a military point of view we had a great deal to gain in encouraging the Americans to base their air forces in the United Kingdom in peace time'.[68] Ernest Bevin, as Foreign Secretary, was the only one to sound a cautionary note; whilst he welcomed the presence of US bombers in the United Kingdom, he was anxious to see the arrangements put on a more definite basis. He was particularly anxious about two problems: first, how we should secure our right to bring arrangements to a close; secondly, what would happen if the United States conducted active operations from United Kingdom airfields before the United Kingdom was at war.[69]

The Ambassador's Agreement answered the first of Bevin's anxieties by giving the British the right to terminate the arrangement if it is no longer considered to be in the interests of common defence. The second concern, left unanswered by the Agreement, was soon to take its place in the political arena when the Korean War broke out. Concern was also felt since there were now SILVERPLATE type B-29s in the United Kingdom, and there was a nagging fear amongst the Chiefs of Staff and Bevin over what might happen if there was an atomic offensive or exchange involving American forces in Britain, and if the issue was either outside the NATO area or not of a specific threat to Britain's national security.

IMPLEMENTATION OF THE AMBASSADOR'S AGREEMENT: THE AMERICAN MILITARY PRESENCE GROWS

Soon after the Ambassador's Agreement, the Third Air Division was notified by its headquarters in Washington[70] of the plan to base jet fighter squadrons in this country. The first squadron was expected in the autumn and would initiate a system of rotational training similar to that adopted for the B-29 groups. This would mean that the United States would have been fighters and bombers continually in this country, and that these units would co-operate with the RAF and other Western Union countries in defence and training exercises. The outbreak of the Korean War was, like the Berlin Crisis, to act as the pretext for the urgent strengthening of American Armed forces in the United Kingdom, with the addition of one fighter group and an increase in the number of medium bombardment groups from one to three. The fighter group was introduced to 'gain invaluable time and experience in integrating our forces with the British air defense system. Further, it would materially increase the fighter defense capability of the United Kingdom'.[71] The increase of the medium bombardment groups was seen as 'reducing by approximately one-half the time required to carry out their initial strategic air offensive missions under that required if starting from continental United States'.[72] The Department of State was advised of Presidential approval on 8 July and thus informed Ambassador Douglas that the Medium bomber groups to be deployed were the 93rd and 97th, and the fighter group, the 20th. The increased presence was symbolic of the UK's more general reliance upon the United States, a fact stressed by the US Office of Public Affairs:

> Despite a serious postwar decline in political and economic strength and a greatly reduced capacity to defend itself, the United Kingdom occupies a key position in world strategic planning . . . much of British foreign policy is meaningless without active US support, which is the cornerstone of postwar security plans.[73]

The enlarged American military presence also absorbed some of the scarce facilities of the British fighter command, including two fighter squadrons on alert during daylight hours, a radar screen adequate to warn against a daylight attack coming from the continent and one regiment of British 40mm guns at each of the four Midlands airfields. It has been agreed as part of the Spaatz–Tedder agreement that Britain was to have primary responsibility for the defence of the American bases. The scale of American involvement became public knowledge when the Prime Minister was asked about the 'strength and nature' of equipment of foreign armed forces on British soil. The Prime Minister hastily replied that the only foreign forces were American and that 'there are about 1500 US Naval personnel in this country (including the headquarters of the Commander in Chief, US Naval Forces East Atlantic and Mediterranean) and about 10 000 USAF personnel, comprising three medium bomber groups with headquarters and administrative units, these forces are equipped with about 180 aircraft'.[74]

The expansion planned by the United States in Britain had its critics on both sides of the Atlantic, who saw it as having problems of its own. For instance, thoughts in some American circles were turning to the next generation of aircraft, like the B-36, which would have an intercontinental range; valuable if there were any difficulty with existing arrangements. Thomas Finletter, the Air Force Secretary, in a letter to Secretary of Defense, Louis Johnson, outlined the dangers of the enlarged presence in the United Kingdom to the United States:

> We are dependent at this moment almost entirely on the availability of UK bases for the launching of our strategic countermeasure.
>
> Now I haven't any real doubt but that the UK will come along if we get engaged in War. But the question is when. I do not like at all the fact that we are almost entirely dependent on the UK as to whether we can launch our strategic countermeasure.
>
> . . . I think I know the British well enough to know that they will come in; but I also know them well enough to know that some-times they can be very slow; and this strategic countermeasure is something which cannot afford to hold itself up while the British Cabinet is debating about things.[75]

Finletter saw the eventual solution in the diminishing of American reliance on overseas bases, as bombers with intercontinental range, which could be staged through Alaska or operate directly on the two-way flights from the United States, entered service. At this time the B-36 constituted less than 10 per cent of the total air striking power, the rest being B-50s and B-29s in the medium bomber category. Air refuelling was possible with the B-50, giving it an intercontinental range; but this was hazardous and, according to Finletter, 'the refuelling operation will not work'.[76] Thus, for the immediate future at least, there was a very heavy reliance on medium bomber forces operating from intermediate bases, and the 'only ones which can be relied upon are in the UK'.[77]

Finletter was not alone in his sentiments. An earlier report for Secretary Johnson had suggested that the general nature of the plans for the strategic air offensive, and the fact these plans depended largely upon the availability of air bases in Britain, would make it 'imprudent to rely solely upon the availability'.[78] SAC, aware of this problem, prepared alternative plans to provide for the contingency of non-availability of UK bases. These alternative plans contemplated operations from North African bases and the Azores in lieu of the United Kingdom. The principal North African base requirements were in French Morocco, with lesser requirements in Tunisia–Tripoli and Egypt. Dharan in Saudi Arabia was indicated as an important post-strike staging base. However, the plan met with considerable opposition from the military and was eventually rejected when it was decided that 'adequate base facilities do not exist in the areas indicated. Therefore, the Strategic Air Command alternate plan today is not feasible'.[79]

Unease with the basing arrangements was detectable in the United Kingdom also. Although the American presence was generally welcomed, there was a feeling of uncertainty surrounding the working arrangements for the use of British bases. The Ambassador's Agreement had also sidestepped the question of length of stay, when it declared that 'airfields in the United Kingdom would be available for use by the United States Air Force so long as both Governments considered it desirable in the interests of common defence'.[80] In a letter written in April 1950, with which the American ambassador concurred, Aidan Crawley had made it plain that he felt there was no need to put the matters referred to in the letter which constituted the Ambassador's Agreement into a formal agreement. In spite of this, many felt that there was a need for a formal agreement or guarantee which would guard British interests; and demands for such an agreement were to lead to attempts by both Attlee and Churchill to secure a more formal understanding with President Truman.

Apart from attempts to secure an agreement about the use of American strategic bombers operating from British bases, planners in Britain from the beginning of 1950 were trying in vain to obtain information about the Strategic Air Plan as a whole. The lack of explicit information on such vital plans, understandably, caused unease in the United Kingdom. Such unease was exposed in government circles once again when it transpired that all the B-29s had been modified to carry the atomic bomb, with virtually no public awareness of this.

The Pentagon Plan of 1950 also made the problem of control and use of the bomb from UK territory topical. The plan was that Britain would produce plutonium, which the United States would turn into weapons to be transferred to Britain. British Embassy officials in Washington were quick to warn London that delicate questions would arise. The plan foundered due to apparent lack of mutual trust. The United States wanted to be sure that in the event of a major war Britain would actually use atomic weapons transferred to her and would not hesitate to do so even in the face of retaliation. The State Department, in a directive to the President on 30 November 1950, pointed out that whilst they would not hesitate to order the use of atomic weapons in a war against Russian aggression, they would in effect reduce their stockpiles by transferring weapons to British control. The implications of such an directive for the basing arrangement was obvious: Britain could, under no circumstances, be allowed any kind of say in the use of American nuclear weapons. Fear of America losing any of her nuclear stockpile by transferral of weapons made their deployment from United States bases in Britain the obvious alternative.

The British Chiefs of Staff tried since 1948 to discuss with the Americans the arrangements for the strategic use of atomic weapons. These efforts always met with a rebuttal from the Americans and the COS remained ignorant of plans to use atomic bombs from British bases. At the end of 1950, British official concern about consultation over the use of the bomb from American aircraft stationed in Britain became less hypothetical and more a reality, as the likelihood of a nuclear strike in the Far East increased. Concern in political and military circles in Britain was concentrated on Korea and Truman's threatened use of the bomb in Korea. Andrew Pierre talks of the 'excellent working relationship that evolved after SAC bombers were first based on British bases in 1948',[81] but the next few months were to prove an exception to this rule when Truman reportedly threatened the use of the bomb in Korea without consultation, and in February, Klaus Fuchs, a naturalised British atomic spy who worked at Los Alamos, was arrested.

British relations with Europe were not all that could be desired either. A telegram from the US Ambassador to France to the Secretary of State sought assurances from the American administration that British 'desolidarization' from the continent was economic only and did not extend to military or strategic concepts, and that the United States for her part 'has not abandoned the idea of the defence of the continent in favour or retiring to bases in England and Spain in the event of war with Russia'.[82] The question of West European integration also posed a severe challenge to Britain's leadership role in Europe. The United Kingdom was in a difficult position, not having either fully entered into plans for European organisation, not having stayed out of them. Britain seemed to welcome the integration process in principle, from the Coal and Steel Community to plans for a Defence Community, but the British role was one of 'limited liability than of full partnership'.[83] The United Kingdom, while accepting integration as a scheme to liberalise trade patterns within Europe, would not join West European countries in political and economic union largely because of the fear of a fundamental realignment of interests away from the Commonwealth and sterling area. Britain was also committed to a Western and pro-American military alliance – and the almost casual and unquestioning acceptance of the presence of American bombers was symptomatic of this.

President Truman's statement that the use of the bomb in Korea was being considered emphasised the possibility that British bases used by American forces could very well embroil Britain in a cause outside the NATO area, and moreover, be a test of the extent to which we were prepared to toe the line.

Attlee, in the wake of this incident, received over one hundred signatures of complaint from Members of Parliament within twenty-four hours of Truman's threat being made. The Prime Minister immediately declared his intent to fly to Washington, DC, to confer with Truman personally, to clarify the arrangements for the use of American bases in the United Kingdom.

4 The Agreements: 1950–2

THE KOREAN WAR AND THE THREAT TO USE THE BOMB

At a press conference on 30 November 1950, President Truman had
been asked questions about the situation in Korea, which had taken a
turn for the worse with the Chinese intervention. One reporter asked,
'Will we take whatever steps are necessary to meet the military
situation? Will that include the A-bomb?' The President replied that
this would include 'every weapon that we have'. There then followed
the ambiguous exchange that was thought to imply active consideration of a nuclear strike in the Far East:

> [Question]: Mr. President, you said 'every weapon that we have.'
> Does that mean that there is active consideration of the use of the
> bomb?
>
> [The President]: There has always been active consideration of its
> use.[1]

Aware that ambiguity existed, the President, later on that day,
instructed Charles Ross of the White House Press Office to issue a
clarificatory statement saying that 'consideration of the use of any
weapon is always implicit in the very possession of the weapon'.[2] The
President made it clear that by law only he, as Commander-in-Chief,
could authorise the bomb's use and that 'he had not authorised its
use'.[3] In spite of the clarificatory statement, however, the damage had
been done, and the ambiguity over the statements was understood as a
threat to use the atomic bomb. Many contemporary writers seem
certain that the threat was real and called for the most urgent
consultation with the President by Attlee.[4]

The threat was taken seriously for several reasons. There had been a
feeling of general unease amongst senior officials in Britain concerning
American rights and the use of A-bombs, but there were 'fears that a
letter on the subject might cause suspicion and offence'.[5] The question
was apparently submitted for ministerial discussion which had laid
down that 'matters should be left as they stood, on the grounds that in
practice this issue could hardly arise unless British policies had
diverged so far from those in the United States that American use of
the airfields would have to be reconsidered anyway'.[6] The threat, or so

it was understood, to use nuclear weapons in Korea made that ministerial decision unsatisfactory. In spite of Charles Ross's pacificatory words, panic spread when, the day after the press conference, Truman sent a note to Congress asking for an additional $16.8 million for defence and a little over $7 billion dollars for the AEC to produce 'more fissionable material and atomic weapons'.[7] The beginning of the Korean War in July 1950 was crucial because it was the first major conflict involving both superpowers by proxy, and it was far from clear what would happen and whether the war would escalate into a major superpower conflict. The first successful atomic explosion by Russia in August 1949, the seizure of power by Communists in China in October, NSC-68 in April 1950,[8] and finally the invasion of South Korea in late June 1950, made all aware of the dangers of a conflict involving the superpowers.

There were also fears surrounding the long-range plans for war made by the JCS in 1949, christened DROPSHOT. The plan was prepared for an imaginary response to a Soviet offensive in 1957, but the date was largely unimportant and it was, to use the JCS words, a 'flow sheet for Armageddon'. DROPSHOT had as its basic objective the imposing, with America's allies, of US war objectives upon Russia by destroying the Soviet Union's will and capacity to resist by 'conducting a strategic offensive in Western Europe and strategic defensive in the Far East'.[9] The United Kingdom was again an important base for 'offensive operations', but there was a pragmatic realisation that it would only be available for a limited amount of time. Other was plans promulgated in connection with DROPSHOT had estimated 'forty A-bombs would knock England to her knees and 120 would destroy her, and SAC believed they could depend upon British bases for only 60 days'.[10] This, alongside a move in July 1950 by the JCS to reinforce American power in the West, caused consternation among British ministers and officials. The JCS had urged that to reinforce American power, non-nuclear components of atomic weapons should be stored in Britain; 'then only the nuclear cores would have to be sent if the situation grew worse . . . the President agreed to the transfer'.[11]

The statement by Truman that the use of the bomb in Korea was being considered gave British officials a focus for all their anxieties, and it was a chance for Attlee to raise more general issue about consultation on the use of the bomb; a subject which the Americans had hitherto refused to discuss. The British position ragarding the American bases for the ensuing discussions was that nuclear devices should not be used without consultation, and preferably not without agreement with Britain and perhaps others as well. However, amongst the recommendations made to the President by the State Department for the Attlee discussions was the proviso that there would be no commitment made restricting the freedom of action of the United States. Also, the recommendation was that the American desire not to use the bomb 'be stressed'.

In Britain it was decided that in spite of the revision of Truman's earlier press statement, urgent action was 'necessary in order to allay public anxiety'.[12] It was agreed at a Cabinet meeting that Attlee would announce his intention of going to Washington when he spoke in a foreign affairs debate later that night. The crux of Attlee's mission was hammered out in Cabinet discussions and agreed upon as follows:

> The impression should not be given that the only purpose of the visit was to discuss the use of the atomic bomb. That question would, however, be discussed and the responsibility for deciding on the use of the atom bomb would have to be defined. A decision on this importance could not be left to the commander in the field or even to the United States government along.[13]

Concern was not merely confined to the Labour Party. Churchill, Eden and Butler talked of the need for assurance that events in Korea would not propel the world into a major war. Attlee flew to Washington on Sunday 3 December, arriving in Washington the following morning. He was accompanied on the flight by Field-Marshal Sir William Slim (who succeeded Montgomery as CIGS) and various Foreign Office Far Eastern experts. The Prime Minister's visit of December 1950 was also significant in the wider context of Anglo–American relations. It was a symbolic visit because, to use Kenneth Harris's words, it was 'the last great attempt to recreate the kind of special relationship based on equality which had existed in the early days of the war'.[14]

THE ATTLEE–TRUMAN MEETING (DECEMBER 1950)

The decision for the Prime Minister to go in person was prompted by the gravity of the situation and protestations of MPs, but also because the Foreign Secretary was by now a sick man and he retired soon after, in March 1951, only to die a month later. A contemporary observed that Bevin's 'spirit and determination has begun to slip by then . . . he would come and go and had a tendency to go to sleep'.[15] After Attlee's arrival in Washington, six meetings between Truman and the Prime Minister were held. Amongst those who participated as advisers to the President were Secretary of State Dean Acheson, Secretary of the Treasury Snyder, Secretary of Defense Marshall, Secretary of Commerce Sawyer, General of the Army Omar Bradley, the Chairman of the JCS, Chairman of the National Security Resources Board, Stuart Symington and W. Averell Harriman. On the Prime Minister's team were the British Ambassador Oliver Franks, Field Marshal Sir William Slim, the Marshal of the RAF Lord Tedder, Sir Roger Makins, R. H. Scott of the Foreign Office and Sir Edwin Plowden, Chief of the Economic Planning Staff.

In the Cabinet Room of the White House, Truman spoke with Attlee of the A-bomb and its possible use, whereupon the President reminded Attlee that the 'Governments of the United Kingdom and the United States had always been partners in this matter and that he would not consider any use of the bomb without consulting the United Kingdom.' Attlee, anxious to get such an agreement in writing, was told by the President that 'it would not be in writing, since if a man's word wasn't any good it wasn't made any better by writing it down'.[16] Attlee was not a man to back off lightly. Dean Acheson noted that Attlee 'never relaxed for a moment his determination to establish a British veto over American strategic action, particularly in the case of the bomb'.[17] True to form, the next day (8 December), Attlee was back on the attack. During discussion, Secretary Lovett recalled that the Quebec Agreement had provided that the atomic bomb would not be used against a third party without mutual consent. As will be recalled, members of the Joint Congressional Committee on Atomic Energy had urged that the provisions concerning 'consent' be abrogated, which in effect the *modus vivendi* did on 7 January 1948. There was therefore, at the time of the talks, no formal governmental arrangement concerning the use of United Kingdom bases by American forces, merely those worked out between the RAF and Third Air Division, and the Ambassador's Agreement. Attlee still had control of nuclear weapons on British soil on his mind, and it was while General Collins was preparing reports and maps of the latest fighting in Korea that the President took the Prime Minister into the privacy of his study. Acheson wrote that he thought they had gone off for a personal chat, but the essence of the discussions was revealed when Attlee re-emerged from the study: 'We've had a good talk about the bomb. We want to say in the communiqué that neither of us will use the bomb without prior consultation with each other.' Dean Acheson recalls his reaction in his memoirs:

> I remember the silence. We were horrified. It seemed that Attlee had raised the matter as soon as they were alone. . . . Attlee said he thought it could do no harm for the President to affirm that he would not use the bomb without consulting his allies. He wanted this for political reasons back home. The President agreed'.[18]

There was some anger and confusion at what appeared to be a reversion to the pre *modus vivendi* situation, but the President was now emphatic that no commitment, of any sort and to anyone, limited his duties and powers under the constitution to authorise the use of atomic weapons – if he believed it to be necessary for the defence of the country. Dean Acheson suggested a programme of keeping in close touch with the Prime Minister in all world situations that might threaten violence or hostilities. This was in essence the final formula that Sir Oliver Franks produced. During subsequent conversations with F. W. Martin of the British Embassy, Gordon Arneson of the State Department observed that the 'official United States position as agreed by the President and as accepted by Prime Minister Attlee was set forth in the penultimate paragraph of the joint communiqué, no more no less'.[19] The communiqué, some six typed pages long, in its penultimate paragraph concluded:

> The President stated that it was his hope that world conditions would never call for use of the atomic bomb. The President told the Prime Minister that it was also his desire to keep the Prime Minister at all times informed of developments which might bring about a change in the situation.[20]

The draft communiqué[21] said nothing of this, only a far vaguer commitment that the military capabilities of the United States and the United Kingdom should be increased 'as rapidly as possible.' It was largely at Attlee's personal instigation that the later paragraph was included; it was, nonetheless, a far cry from the 'consultation' promised in Truman's private office. The stern resistance to any such attempts to commit the President to consultation can be put largely at Acheson's door.

Just before he died, Acheson reminisced about Attlee and the December visit. He commented that he thought Attlee was 'most astute and in fact almost too astute . . . what he was trying to get the President to do, was to agree that we would not use an atomic weapon without the agreement of Britain. This was at one time in the Quebec Agreement – we were perfectly willing to talk about consultation, but to require the agreement of the British before this would be used was a silly thing to do because it might have to be used at once. If you got notice that incoming missiles were coming, you didn't have time to go sending cables around asking for agreement. This is what he later on did achieve in a private talk with the President. *And, we had to unachieve that*.[22] Acheson was resolute in his insistence that there could be no agreement that would limit the President's power. By the same logic, the President could make no commitments that would impinge upon his power to authorise the use of the atomic weapon. This essentially political objection was to be used whenever the British tried to obtain a more specific commitment to consultation. Sir Roger Makins, now Lord Sherfield, who was one of the negotiating team who accompanied Attlee said in retrospect that 'people agitating for formal treaties are agitating for something that is not on the cards . . . it is inconceivable that the Quebec Agreement could be negotiated again'.[23]

The British record of the Attlee–Truman discussions was different and they believed that the President *had* affirmed the gist of Attlee's requests, even though it depended on no written agreement and did not appear in the formal communiqué. There was, apart from the communiqué no agreed record of the meetings and the Americans refused to accept the British record of discussions because it contained references to 'consultation' procedure for the use of the bomb. The talks on the use of the bomb, and in particular their use from RAF bases by American bombers, appeared to be largely fruitless once more, with the promise of the President to the Prime Minister apparently discarded. The fear that had existed before Korea that an issue of this importance could become a matter for rushed and *ad hoc* last-minute discussions was still felt by the Chiefs of Staff and Foreign Office alike. The communiqué also did little to satisfy the demands of those who were still insistent upon a formal agreement, with specific information, on the role of the Third Air Division (soon to become the Third Air Force) and the newly-formed Seventh Air Division under USAFE and SAC control respectively. In spite of apparent dissatisfaction from some quarters, Attlee seemed reassured at the outcome of the meeting but he refused to divulge to the House the full details of what had been agreed. He told the Cabinet, upon his return on 12 December, that 'the President has assured the Prime Minister that he regarded the atomic bomb as in a sense a joint possession of the United

States, United Kingdom and Canada, and that he would not authorize its use without prior consultation with the other two governments save in an extreme urgency – such as an atomic attack on the United States which called for immediate retaliation'.[24] Attlee's impressions of what *he* had agreed to were precisely what Acheson thought he had 'unachieved'. Perhaps Attlee was taking Truman at face value, bearing in mind that the President had said 'if a man's word isn't any good it's not made any better by writing it down'. The American negotiating team were evidently using a more hard-style diplomacy where the printed word, or, in this case, the communiqué that disregarded much of the discussion, was all-important. Attlee later went on to make his satisfaction known to the House of Commons:

> it was in this spirit and against the background of the wartime partnership that I was able to raise the vital question of the use of atomic weapons and it was in the same spirit and against the same background that I received the assurances which I consider to be perfectly satisfactory.[25]

The understandings that Attlee saw as 'perfectly satisfactory' do not appear in the final communiqué, which itself only promised that the Americans would not use the bomb without informing the British: consultation was not even suggested.

The communiqué as a working document was seen in action when, on the last morning of the Attlee visit, the Under Secretary of State, Robert Lovett, called upon Dean Acheson from the Pentagon saying that the radar was picking up what appeared to be incoming planes. There was a tense moment and the advice given to Lovett by Acheson was, 'Tell Attlee about it, but don't suggest any course of action'.[26] In the event, it was realised before Attlee was informed that what had been picked up on the radar screen was flocks of geese heading across Canada. Lucius Battle summarised the agreement reached between Truman and Attlee perfectly when he said their results were 'somewhat ambiguous where both sides interpreted it as best he wanted and both sides couldn't guarantee full consideration. Frankly I suspect [the agreement] had been left deliberately fuzzy'.[27]

Following Attlee's announcement to the House of Commons about the consultations on the atomic bomb, Churchill was incensed to 'discover for the first time'[28] that the second clause of the Quebec Agreement, concerning 'consent' before use of the bomb, had been surrendered. He was also convinced that it would be in the national interest to publish the agreement. Churchill felt so strongly on the subject that he decided to write to the President himself, asking him to agree that atomic weapons should not be used from British bases without prior British consent. Margaret Gowing observed that 'Mr Churchill's belief that because he signed an agreement with President Roosevelt in 1943 he had the right to deal directly with the current President seemed extraordinary'.[29]

Apart from the agreement on the use of the bomb from our bases, many were worried about the lack of information about SAC operational plans. Bevin expressed these anxieties to Dean Acheson on 14 January 1951. Sir Oliver Franks as Britain's Ambassador in Washington, DC, pointed out that Bevin did not want to be in the position of having Gifford[30] call him up one night saying, 'Our planes are taking off in five minutes, do you mind?'.[31] Dean Acheson was quick to remind the Foreign Secretary that the 'British people recognize that obligations will fall upon them from the part which they will have to play in any future war. They are being asked to shoulder fresh burdens in order to fulfil these obligations'.[32] Bevin claimed that it had been implied in his earlier talks with Ambassador Douglas (Ambassador to the UK 1947–50) that the British would be consulted about any plans for the use of US bombers in Britain and he then added, 'in fact that understanding has been the basis of our agreement to their presence here and to provide facilities for them as we have done . . . I cannot feel that I have discharged that responsibility while the British government has no information as to the strategic plans in support of which these aircraft might be used at very short notice nor how far this plan accords with our own'.[33] Arneson made it clear on 7 April 1951 that the only commitment, in the perspective of the American negotiators, was that laid down in the joint communiqué of 18 December 1950.

Sir John Slessor, head of the Chiefs of Staff, who was still highly dissatisfied with the current arrangements, wrote to the Director of the Policy Planning Staff (Paul Nitze) suggesting that following the joint communiqué a 'more formal agreement might be desirable' in view of the governmental responsibility to Parliament and the necessity of being absolutely clear on the use of British bases. The COS urged that since they saw the agreement as inadequate, 'it was a matter of vital importance and extreme urgency that the United States should agree to immediate joint study of the strategic use of the bomb, and to a disclosure to Britain of plans for its use'.[34] The existing situation whereby the United States could launch an attack using United

Kingdom bases, without an indication of their plans, was seen as quite intolerable.

In the United States, Senator Vandenberg was leading the congressional opposition to British attempts to gain a formal or implied commitment. The Senator had also warned his colleagues against British attempts to get 'the President on the line'. The December meeting and the private Truman–Attlee discussion was seen as one such attempt. Senator Vandenberg also urged that the United States should find out 'whether the British were prepared to deny US bases unless we made commitments'.[35] The hesitancy to make any commitment to the British on prior consultation was not merely a political argument, but was also based on the fear that there might not be enough time to consult. The American administration's argument that were the President asked if he had any agreement that prohibited the use of nuclear weapons under any circumstances, he would have to answer 'no', was met by the British reminder that the Prime Minister had to be in a position to state that the government remained in control of its own bases, even with an American presence. Nitze, who took over from George Kennan as the head of the State Department's Planning Staff, warned the Foreign Secretary that if it were necessary to publicly make the point that the United Kingdom maintained control over its own bases, it might be wise to make simultaneously the other point that the West must stand together or run the risk of being defeated piecemeal. To him it was the problem of meeting concurrently the problems raised by the issues of sovereignty and the desirability of having frank discussions, but Nitze warned, 'we could, however, make no commitment or agreement to follow a procedure which would give an aura of having given a commitment or agreement'.[36]

Many of the differences of opinion between the two countries over the bases agreement revolved around their respective faith in the bomb, and therefore any envisaged consultation procedure. The United States regarded the atomic bomb as a panacea which would rapidly halt any Soviet aggression and obviate the need for massive foreign troop commitments, which were expensive and unpopular. At this stage it was also believed that the threat of Soviet retaliation was not sufficiently widespread to be credible. The feeling in Britain was that the responsibility for the use of such weapons could not be handed over to the United States when it was not even in the 'front line', and that 'any military disadvantage of delay must be subordinated to the need for issuing an ultimatum'.[37]

In September 1951 the Foreign Secretary, now Herbert Morrison, visited Washington and expressed his concern to Acheson about the lack of information about the Strategic Air Plan and said that the long delay in the supply of information was 'most disturbing', stressing once again that it was 'intolerable that Britain should risk annihilation without being first informed or consulted'.[38] These talks were unsuccessful, leading Acheson only to reiterate the political arguments against any commitment to consultation. However, these talks did spur the United States into holding more general politico-military talks on 14 September. Attending this meeting was Sir Oliver Franks (the British Ambassador to the United States), F. W. Marten of the Foreign Office and Sir William Elliott (representative of the British Chiefs of Staff in Washington). For the United States there were Paul Nitze (Director of the Policy Planning staff), Freeman Matthews (Deputy Secretary of State for Political Affairs) and General Omar Bradley, the US Chief of Staff. The talks were significant, resulting in a recognition that:

> there must at least be consultation, and that the British must give their prior consent, before the United States used atomic weapons from Britain. The American side accepted that the use of British bases involved British sovereignty and that it was therefore natural that the United States should seek acquiescence before launching a war from them.[39]

The United Kingdom secured her objective of an expression of general intent. The American negotiators were not, however, willing to enter any agreement that would prevent their sovereign right to make war if they felt it necessary to do so. More importantly it was stressed by Nitze that the talks were to 'be without commitment – that they would merely be an exchange of views'. Matthews and Bradley concurred with Nitze that the talks 'could in no way be a commitment for the future'. Bradley added that 'we were not prepared to obligate ourselves to consult and there should be no public announcement to the effect that we had' (FRUS, Vol. 1 (1951) memo. 13/9/51).

In October, Sir Oliver Franks, who was anxious to secure some agreement on the use of American bases before the general election on 25 October, presented a draft formula to the United States concluding that the question of the use of air bases in an emergency 'naturally remains a matter for joint decision in the light of circumstances at the time'.[40] The NSC agreed that this formula could be used if required, although it was tacitly understood that this was only an emergency measure. It was Churchill who, as Prime Minister, announced this measure to the House of Commons in December 1951. Whilst it

marked a notable shift in the American position and signified a partial
return to the second clause of the Quebec Agreement, it was at the
same time vague about who was to make the 'joint decision', and it was
unclear whether this would give Britain any veto over proposed actions
by American forces from British bases.

THE CHURCHILL GOVERNMENT AND THE AMERICAN BASES

The Attlee government left office, defeated by the Conservative Party
with a majority of 26 seats, on 25 October 1951. The Attlee
government left as its legacy perhaps the most important defence
commitment made by one first-class power to another. The communiqué of December 1950 had hardly led to a conclusive understanding, either of the conditions for use of British bases by American
forces, or of any kind of joint planning. Nor were the last years of
Attlee's government notable for any serious debate about the bases.
As observed by one author, 'the granting of bases to the United States
Strategic Air Command, the Soviet atomic test, NATO and the
Korean War gave rise to leading articles in the press on atomic
questions but the debate was not really joined'.[41] With Churchill now
in power, his first task was to seek clarification of the status of United
States bases in Britain.

There was evidence of anxiety within the American State Department in the event of Churchill being re-elected. Thus on 18 October, it
had been decided to prepare a draft statement on the use of bases to
withstand his onslaught. Churchill, for his part, was obsessed with the
Quebec Agreement, and his concern was 'not so much about the lapse
of the clause which had given Britain a right of consent over the use of
atomic bombs. He believed that Britain had been unfairly treated and
forced into spending vast sums of money on her own project simply
because Attlee was "feeble and incompetent" and had not told the
Americans the facts about the wartime agreements'.[42] Churchill was an
outspoken critic of both the *modus vivendi* and the agreement reached
between Attlee and Truman. Attlee had just returned from the
meeting with Truman, only to face a vicious attack from Churchill in
the House of Commons criticising the communiqué as being in
'general terms' with no guarantee or assurance of consultation.
Churchill went on: 'I am strongly of the opinion that the Government
should make a fuller statement on this subject. This matter has become
one of very real and vital consequence to us since the decision of the

Government to afford to the United States the bomber bases in East Anglia'.[43]

The State Department's earlier anxieties were justified when Churchill opened the debate on the future of American bases in the United Kingdom in his Guildhall speech on 9 November. Churchill reminded those present:

> It must not be forgotten that under the late government we took peculiar risks in providing the principal atomic base for the United States in East Anglia, and that, in consequence, we have placed ourselves in the very forefront of Soviet antagonism. We have therefore every need and every right to seek and receive the fullest consideration from Americans for our point of view, and I feel sure this will not be denied us.[44]

On 12 November, Churchill announced his intention to travel to the United States at the beginning of January to press for consideration from America for Britain's point of view. The visit was seen by some in the United States as a chance to put pressure on the American administration to reconsider their commitments to Britain. Senator Edwin Johnson, a Democrat (Colorado) and member of the Joint Atomic Energy Committee, said that the United States ought to abandon any bases it had in Britain. 'There was no excuse', he maintained, 'for making the British people a target for an enemy attack'.[45] He also added at a later date that no consideration should be given to such bases in any study of whether the US should extend additional financial help to Great Britain, and that 'we ought not to be using England as an atomic base. If we are doing so, as Churchill says, it should be discontinued at once. There are many much better atomic bases than England where the risks are not as great'.[46] The Senator suggested Iceland, North Africa and Turkey as more desirable alternatives. Many in the military services disagreed with such views, and the importance of the United Kingdom as a prime American strategic base was re-emphasised when, at the beginning of May 1951, General Eisenhower's headquarters in Paris announced that the United States Third Air Division in Britain had been raised to the status of Air Force. It was announced simultaneously in Washington that the Seventh Air Division had been formed and was to be sited in the United Kingdom, while the higher status accorded to the Third Air Division was a recognition of its growing importance.

The new division, the Seventh Air Division, was established on 23 March with a twofold mission of 'exercising command jurisdiction over the units using the area for training on a rotational basis and supervising the preparations of a SAC forward operating area in the UK to be ready for use under an emergency'.[47] The Division was to be under the command of Major General Archie J. Old and was to be responsible for all American strategic operations in Britain, including the two maintenance and supply bases in Britain at Burtonwood (Lancashire) and Sealand (Flintshire). On 16 May 1951, the Third Air Force transferred jurisdiction of nine existing air bases, both USAFE and RAF, to the Seventh Air Division with a personnel strength of 5000 officers and men. The Seventh Air Division, with its head-quarters at South Ruislip, had jurisdiction over Bassingbourn, Lakenheath, Lindholme, Manston, Marham, Mildenhall, Sculthorpe, West Drayton and Waddington; six more air bases were transferred as they became available at Upper Heyford, Brize Norton, Fairford, Greenham Common, Woodbridge and Carnaby. The Korean War had also demonstrated to the USAF the need for fighter escort, and SAC heeded this lesson by transferring the 31st Fighter Wing equipped with F-84s to Manston, Kent, on temporary duty. This temporary duty ended when the 81st and later the 123rd Fighter Wings were stationed with the Third Air Force, eliminating the need for a separate SAC unit. SAC fighters were only used in future on exercise flights, although as soon as the fighters left Manston a small number of RB-45s of the 91st Strategic Reconnaissance Group spent a period of duty there. This was the beginning of another important phase of the United Kingdom's role as America's 'unsinkable aircraft carrier' – that of a reconnaissance base.

The overall command of US units in the United Kingdom was under General Leon Johnson – based at South Ruislip, where the Third Air Force also had its headquarters. The Third Air Force is, from the point of view of this study, particularly important because it was 'the single point of contact in dealings with the British government developing bases for both SAC and USAFE'.[48] The mission of the new Third Air Force was similar to that of the Third Air Division, namely 'to coordinate all Air Force requirements for British resources and facilities, acting as the authorized representative of the Air Force presenting these requirements to, and negotiating agreements with, the British Air Ministry'. It was also to 'plan for the implementation of Air Force Emergency War Plans as they pertain to the United Kingdom and British possessions, securing aggreements from appropriate British agencies to support these plans and coordinate with the appropriate Air Force commanding officers as required'.[49] The rhetoric of the Cold War was reflected in their mission, with talk of 'protecting what we now call Western civilization against the destructive designs of a Godless enemy . . . we are fighting for the kind of peace the Communism seeks to destroy'.[50] Since its reactivation in 1951, the Third Air Force has been an exclusively tactical command, the 7AD dealing with strategic forces.

The need for precise arrangements governing the use of RAF bases by the American forces became even more urgent in Churchill's mind when negotiations, expanding upon the Ambassador's Agreement of April 1950 between the American and British governments, resulted in the Special Construction Programme,[51] which would provide an additional twenty-six bases and facilities. The cost of this immense project was to be split initially on a fifty-fifty basis, but this changed as costs escalated. This was a far cry from the first days of 'temporary duty', or 'visits of goodwill'. Evidence of increasing military co-operation between American and British armed forces also became more widespread. 'Exercise Foil' was a large-scale exercise that illustrated this, in which 'the United States and Western Union forces cooperated with the RAF from June 25 until July 3 . . . participating in the exercise were bomber and fighter commands of the RAF and superfortress bombers of the US Third Air Division in Britain'.[52]

The ever-lengthening range of the US bombers stationed in Britain was also to present urgent problems as the possibility of a strike deep into the Russian heartland opened up the likelihood of retaliation against bases in Britain. It had been realised early in 1950 that the B-29s operational radius, of at best 2500 kilometres,[53] was inadequate faced with the advent of long-range Soviet bombers. The B-29 gave way to the B-50, which was in turn to give way to the B-27 medium-range bomber in order to acquire jet bombing capacity as missiles took over the long-range strike role. The obsolete B-29s were transferred to the RAF, and some retired. Seventy bombers saw a new lease of life under the RAF, with the name 'Washington' bomber, but they were by no means modern aircraft. In January 1951, the huge Convair B-36 visited the United Kingdom for the first time on a routine long-range navigational training flight. However the gradual introduction of longer range bombers still did not reflect any diminution in the seemingly insatiable American demand for overseas bases.

Churchill's dilemma was that of a close and on the whole successful military co-operation, against a political background that indicated far less contentment. The modern array of bombers and support facilities was beyond what Britain could reasonably have afforded without American aid and bases. Yet the political concern that was voiced was not just from within the United Kingdom. The Soviet Union watched the build-up of American bases in the United Kingdom and elsewhere with consternation. Apart from constant criticism by the Soviet press of 'capitalist encirclement', there were more constructive proposals put forward to address the problem of worldwide American base acquisition. A UN delegate, Vyshinsky, in a speech to the General Assembly, called for alternative disarmament plans that included overseas bases. Such Soviet plans met with little success, and thus attacks were regularly launched through the press on the American presence in Britain. An article that appeared in *Izvestia* is typical of Russian attitudes towards the bases:

> the British Isles are being studded with American military bases. Their construction and maintenance are costing the British government tens of millions of pounds which comes out of the British taxpayers pocket . . . the presence of American armed forces is evoking widespread alarm and protest amongst those who are alive to the grave consequences this holds out for their country.[54]

Perhaps the best informed Western journalist source for this period was Raymond Daniel, a sympathetic observer of the American base build-up, writing for the *New York Times*. He saw that, largely for political reasons, Churchill had to have a guarantee that if 'American planes are going to use British bases the British government should have some control over them, especially as any attack launched from this country would be certain to produce quick retaliation'.[55] He also voiced a feeling of confidence that what Churchill was challenging was the specific arrangements for the use of United Kingdom bases, not the general question of whether American forces should occupy British bases. Daniel observed that Churchill 'won't do anything that might cause removal of American aircraft and crews from Britian. He has made that clear already by saying that the United States Air Force will be permitted to remain here as 'long as is needed in the interests of world peace and security'.[56] The Berlin Crisis, the Czech coup, the successful Russian explosion of an atomic device, and Britain's uneasy Atlantic and intra-European relations made the arrangement necessary, not only for the general interest of world security, but also for the United Kingdom's own interests. The American presence had helped to make up for many of the shortcomings in our own defence. But against the benefits of American military aid, there was little evidence of the wartime promises for continuance and expansion of the practice of 'intimate consultation and collaboration [with the UK] in joint military planning'.[57] In many circles there was a feeling that Britain was not the equal partner, in spite of the intimate wartime collaboration and 'special relationship'; and if the 'US expects the UK to be our principal partner in strategic planning a relationship of trust and equality is a prerequisite'.[58] Churchill was quick to remind the British public of the considerable risks that were entailed by the American presence when he spoke in the House of Commons of the 'formidable step of the last government' in establishing a 'great and ever growing air base in East Anglia' for using atomic weapons against the Soviet Union in case of aggression. The Prime Minister was also acutely aware of the image of Britain as an American 'aircraft carrier', albeit unsinkable. He summarised the dual nature of the American presence when he warned that the step taken by the Attlee government 'placed us in the front line should there be a Third World War. The measure added to the deterrent against war but it might throw the brunt on us should war come'.[59] Attlee was quick to remind the Prime Minister that the previous government had agreed to the stationing of American bombers in this country as part of the Atlantic defences, and it was never intended as 'a base for the atomic bomb against the Soviet Union', nor, Attlee added, 'was it ever suggested',[60] There were actually no atomic bombs in Britain, although there were non-nuclear elements of the A-bomb and planes capable of delivering them. The UK was considered too vulnerable to make it a good risk for the stockpiling of weapons, being 1300 miles from Leningrad, 1560 miles from Moscow, 575 from Berlin and 650 from Prague.

The prevalent fear under the Churchill government was that the United States might be provoked into a preventive or retaliatory attack from British bases, which might in turn endanger our own security or embroil the United Kingdom in a conflict that was not of our making or concern. The Prime Minister's awareness of the possible dangers could be seen by his constant references to the United States' bases in the United Kingdom as 'atomic bases'. Churchill did, however, appreciate the defensive value of the American presence and sought no veto over any action jointly agreed to by NATO powers in the face of aggression. In order to allay Parliamentary concern about the use of the United Kingdom bases, and the provisions for the withdrawal of those facilities, the Prime Minister revealed the October 'Franks' formula to the House of Commons for the first time.

> The use of these bases in an emergency would be *a matter for joint decision* by His Majesty's Government and the United States Government in the light of circumstances prevailing at the time.[61]

THE CHURCHILL–TRUMAN MEETING

At the end of 1951 the Third Air Force comprised more than 20 000 personnel operating out of six fighter and bomber bases and two large supply and maintenance bases, with plans for rapid expansion. Such a force was more than originally envisaged and the arrangement had the air of being far from temporary, the risks implied in playing host to atomic bases has also grown. These factors, alongside the failure of any other approach to re-establish Churchill's cherished 'consent' clause of the Quebec Agreement, prompted his visit to Washington in person.

The announcement of Churchill's intention to hold talks with Truman in a flurry of activity in Washington and the preparation of various 'position papers'. One such paper saw Churchill's prime objective as 're-establishing the intimacy which existed between the two governments during the last war' and to 'gain greater weight for Britain's voice in Western decisions'.[62] In a prepared statement for Dean Acheson (to be presented only if raised by Churchill) on US–UK relations, an oblique reference was made to the bases in the United Kingdom:

> Our friendship and cooperation are important to the British for our support helps to conceal or compensate for Britain's diminished strength. The British sometimes attempt to make their special position more manifest to other powers than we believe desirable . . . the US is as eager as the UK to improve the relationship for greater effectiveness in the pursuit of western objectives. It is opposed, however, to making this relationship formal.[63]

Apart from the generalities of Anglo–American relations, it was also thought that Britain would broach the subject of the technical exchange of atomic information, which had been interpreted in a very limited fashion under the *modus vivendi* agreement. In this field it was evident that security weakness in Britain, sparked off by the Fuchs case, was to be used as a pretext for continuing non-co-operation.[64] It was also suspected that Churchill might raise, in connection with his desire to obtain a closer working relationship on atomic energy, the problem of 'determining the circumstances under which US airfields in the UK may be employed.' The guideline for this eventuality showed a surprising change of heart in the US administration although it remained unclear whether the new stance was presented merely as a public posture or if it accurately reflected the US administration's private views:

> As to the use of the Midlands Bases, our view is that we should frankly agree with Mr Churchill that we recognize that these bases could not be used in the event of hostilities without British consent.[65]

The guidelines prepared by Gordon Arneson, who was well aware of Churchill's reforming spirit, incorporated the State Department's general aims into position papers prepared respectively for the USAEC and Department of Defense. These private guidelines told a different story and can be summarised as first, continuing existing arrangements under the *modus vivendi*; second, to determine if new elements in the British programme offered promising areas for additional co-operation, and lastly, vigilance to assure that the United States retained her freedom to decide when and where to use the atomic bomb. The second and third Russian atomic detonations just before the Truman–Churchill meeting came as a timely reminder of the more general concerns that were to form the backdrop.

The long-awaited visit took place over two days and consisted of four meetings at the White House on 7–8 January 1952. Churchill was accompanied by the Foreign Secretary, Anthony Eden, the Secretary of State for Commonwealth Relations, Lord Ismay, and the Paymaster General, Lord Cherwell. The President's advisers included the Secretaries of State, Treasury and Defense, along with Charles E. Wilson and Averell Harriman. The United States was asked to agree to consult Britain fully before launching a general war, and to reaffirm assurances that the use of United Kingdom bases for atomic attack was a matter for joint decision. The US team was requested to agree to an ultimatum before an atomic attack was launched; Churchill also demanded to be more fully informed on details of the Strategic Air Plan. It was impossible for the British government to judge whether, in any given circumstances, they should agree to American use of bases when they did not know what the strategic air plan was as far as targets, effects and accuracy of the bombs were concerned.

As a result of the meeting a compromise was reached on the Strategic Air Plan, but not on the use of the atomic bomb from US bases in the United Kingdom, largely because President Truman claimed 'special responsibility' and powers *vis-à-vis* the strategic air plan. In the exercise of the President's powers as Commander-in-Chief, Truman was tied by considerable legislative halters, but he agreed that those countries lined up with the United States should be consulted first. Truman's Secretary of Defense argued that it was inevitable that the atomic bomb would be used in World War 3, but with no question of British bases being used for such a purpose *without* British consent. The Secretary of Defense promised Churchill a personal briefing on the Strategic Air Plan and was told as much about it as Dean Acheson knew. By the end of 1952 the COS had received much information about the strategic air plan but were unable to convey it immediately to the British Commander-in-Chief for planning purposes. The Churchill visit was also to prompt the COS to review British strategy, which in turn led to the Global Strategy Paper with its relative emphasis on nuclear deterrence.

At the end of the two-day visit on 8 January 1952, the President and Prime Minister issued a communiqué. The relevant part of the short communiqué was the last paragraph, which stated:

> Under arrangements made for the common defense, the United States has the use of certain bases in the United Kingdom. We reaffirm the understanding that the use of these bases in an emergency would be a matter for joint decision by His Majesty's Government and the United States government in the light of the circumstances prevailing at the time.[66]

The United States Government also promised to 'remain in close consultation on the development which might increase danger to maintenance of world peace'.[67] The communiqué was to mark an important stage in the development of the American bases in Britain and to lead to closer strategic co-operation and integration. This was the first time that the assurance had actually been published in black and white, and was to be the last statement concerning the use of British bases by US forces: it was still spoken of with approval by British Secretary of State for Defense Michael Heseltine and Margaret Thatcher, the Prime Minister, in 1985. It has, however, proved somewhat conspicuous in its vagueness and the phrase 'a matter for joint decision' was to be a continuous source of contentious interpretation. Many British observers understood the phrase to mean a return to the consent clause whereby it represented a veto. To many Americans it was not, and was never intended to be, a veto.

INTERPRETATION OF THE COMMUNIQUÉ

The interpretation of the communiqué is central to the understanding of the American presence in the United Kingdom. Like the Truman–Attlee record, it is far from clear from the United Kingdom's records what was agreed. The record does however help to colour the British interpretation of what was meant by 'joint decision'. According to the British records, President Truman stated to Churchill and Eden on 7 January, the first day of the meeting, that 'he was just as reluctant as

His Majesty's Government to see atomic weapons used . . . nevertheless, this feeling would not prevent his taking the decision if and when
it proved to be necessary. In any case, those countries lined up with the
United States should be consulted first'.[68]

There was a general overall feeling of disappointment that 'nothing
more concrete had come out of the talks,' but it was generally felt that
the 'Anglo–American partnership had been strengthened'.[69] By
getting an agreement in black and white, Churchill believed he had
quietened British fears that by some precipitous attack the United
States was going to expose the United Kingdom to Russian atomic
retaliation. The guarantee of course was not new; it had been made to
Clement Attlee in the discussions with Truman, but having it in writing
was deemed somehow to give it extra validity and strength. However,
in the light of the British belief that they had gained a concession with a
contingent right to consultation or even consent, the American view of
the meeting and resultant communiqué were again at odds. In the
House of Representatives resolution number 514 was introduced in
February with the express intent of gaining full transcripts and
information about the Churchill–Truman meetings, along with information relating to any agreements made by the President of the United
States and Prime Minister of Great Britain during the recent conversations. Jack McFall, Assistant Secretary for the Secretary of State,
replying to this request on behalf of the State Department, explained
in a letter to the Hon. James P. Richards, Chairman of the prestigous
Foreign Affairs Committee in the House, that 'the talks were informal
and conducted primarily on the basis that the Governments of the
United States and the United Kingdom might reach a better understanding of each other's positions on the various problems facing both
nations throughout the world today. *The talks were not in any sense
negotiations toward final and binding decisions on the part of either
Government participating*'.[70]

The American press reaction to the talks were lukewarm. On the
one hand, Neal Stanford of the *Christian Science Monitor* commented
that 'it cannot be said after these talks that Washington does not
understand London's problems – and vice versa'. A more pessimistic
editorial in the *Washington Post* commented that 'the best that can be
said of the Truman–Churchill meeting is that they apparently restored
warmth and frankness which had been sadly lacking in the later years
of the Labour government'.[71] Raymond Daniel of the *New York Times*
commented from London that 'the impression among diplomats here
was that the conversations left United States–British relations just

about where they were before, if the communiqué . . . must be taken at face value.' Daniel also observed that '*The Times of London* and indeed some well informed diplomats were especially interested in the last sentence . . . observers here said that sentence could be more important than all the rest of the communiqué . . . some realists held that they might be nothing more than window dressing'.[72]

Many American commentators thought that the communiqué should relieve fear amongst Englishmen that America might start a war. It was the fear of being involved in a proxy war that made the interpretation of the phrase 'a matter for joint decision' crucial. Current definitions serve as a sample of the variety of interpretations that have been given to the phrase over the years. To some, the meaning of the communiqué is self-evident. Caspar Weinberger sees the communiqué as 'speaking for itself' and he saw no point in 'elaborating on words that are perfectly clear'.[73] To Lucius Battle, who was senior aide to Secretary of State Acheson, the phrase 'matter for joint decision' was 'extremely vague and ambiguous'.[74] Dean Acheson himself was dismissive of the talks when he told a secret congressional committee that the communiqué did not constitute an agreement in the international political sense. Some, while acknowledging ambiguity in interpretation, denied the validity of the British understanding of the phrase. James Schlesinger was one such protagonist who saw the Churchill–Truman communiqué as having 'a considerable latitude for interpretation but there was no such intention of a veto'.[75] Schlesinger was at pains to point out that when the agreement was made it was presupposed that American nuclear leadership was virtually absolute, and concern had not built up 'that America is not as skilful as Europe would like to think.' He also saw that the effects of time upon the interpretation of the communiqué was important:

> Because of the unique relationship that existed between the US and the UK, a degree of intimacy that has receded somewhat, it was assumed that there would be close discussion. Some element of the special relationship is still here but then it was presupposed that there would be consultation.[76]

Vagueness was an integral part of the working arrangements for the communiqué, so that on the one hand America would not feel tied and on the other the United Kingdom would feel it had a guarantee. Acheson had been concerned about a veto that removed American independence in regard to issues of war and peace. Over the years base rights were defined in various ways to give the host country greater or less influence on base use. There has always been, to a greater or lesser extent as the above sample illustrates, a degree of uncertainty. Sir Roger Makins (now Lord Sherfield), who was taking over as British Ambassador in Washington at the time of the Churchill–Truman agreement, cautioned that 'binding agreements dealing with matters of national security are very difficult to come by and perhaps not wholly to be relied upon'.[77] The latitude of interpretation has been largely responsible for the duration of the agreement.

The change of President from Truman to Eisenhower saw the first of many 'reaffirmations' on the use of the bomb from United Kingdom bases. Eden advised Truman that it would be important to obtain a reaffirmation of what Truman had said the previous year about the use of the bomb and that he would hope that 'our communiqué at the end of this visit would reaffirm what the agreed communiqué of last year said about the use of our air bases by the United States'.[78] Accordingly two meetings were held, the first at the State Department in Washington on 6 March 1953. Present at this meeting on the British side were Eden, Sir Roger Makins and Sir P. Dixon. The State Department was represented by Dulles, Arneson and O'Connor. Eden, in his capacity as Foreign Secretary, asked for similar assurances from President Eisenhower as those given by President Truman to Attlee and Churchill. Eden made it clear that the UK was not demanding complete consultation across the board:

> If the United States were the object of a surprise atomic attack, no doubt would they feel free to retaliate in kind without consultation. We in the United Kingdom would similarly feel free to retaliate in such circumstances. But in the even of the United States proposing to take the initiative, we considered that they ought to consult us just as we would consult them.[79]

Dulles, it appears, was under the impression that the British were asking the United States to publicly commit themselves to consultation with regard to the use of the atomic bomb generally. When it was made clear that the British were only asking for a statement about US bases in the United Kingdom, with no statement mentioning the atomic weapon, Dulles foresaw no difficulty. The use of the atomic weapon was to be taken up in discussion between Eden and the President personally. Eden was worried that the British Isles were particularly vulnerable to atomic attack, so that if the United States were to use atomic weapons from bases in Turkey, the Soviet reaction might well be to attack the United Kingdom. It was for this reason that Eden felt it vital that Britain should be consulted before use of the bomb was considered.

The meeting between Eden and Sir Roger Makins with President Eisenhower and General Bedell Smith took place on Monday, 9 March. The President made it clear that the idea that the atomic weapon was of a different character from other weapons was all 'outmoded thought', particularly not that the United States had so many of them. He deprecated any attempt to deal with them in isolation saying, 'I suppose you want me to consult you before I dropped a blockbuster anyway'.[80] The President was just as adamant as his predecessors in resisting any attempts at binding promises of consultation, arguing that in his view of the constitutional position it would be 'treasonous' to give a binding assurance of consultation with Britain in all circumstances before use of the bomb. It would presumably, by the same logic, be treasonous not to consult if time and circumstances permitted. The President refused to discuss any specific forms of commitment and the communiqué at the end of the talks simply repeated the formula agreed to by Churchill and Truman; he did add that he 'preferred to think not in terms of constant consultation before their premeditated use'.[81]

The surrender of the Quebec Agreement and the 'consent' clause was not easily forgotten while Churchill was in office, and six years after the *modus vivendi* he was still claiming that Labour abandoned it, as he did in a debate on the hydrogen bomb on 5 April 1954. Although there was much criticism of Churchill's decision to turn a non-partisan debate into a highly partisan one, it helped express a sentiment that was by no means unique to Churchill. This feeling was that the whole issue of 'consent' or 'consultation' was inexorably bound up with national pride. An American observer who witnessed the debate commented that, 'Behind these motives there may lie a sense of frustration and injured pride shared by many people in the UK, that world leadership now lies with Washington and that the UK cannot sway the course of events in the post-war world'.[82] The outcome of the Eden–Eisenhower talks were typical of subsequent attempts to reaffirm or even change the 1952 agreements – but the agreements made between Churchill and Truman were to remain unchanged until the present.

Interpretations were to change but for many American officials the consultation issue was laid to rest, as stated by Andrew C. Mayer, a specialist in national defence:

The President alone has the basic authority to order the use of nuclear weapons. This authority, inherent in his constitutional role as Commander-in-Chief, may be delegated to subordinate officers in the chain of command *virtually without limitation.*

The President's authority to the use of theatre nuclear weapons . . . is similarly unlimited. While the US government has agreed to consult with other NATO allies before using nuclear weapons in the NATO area, *this obligation is limited to situations where time and circumstances permit.*[83]

From the American standpoint the European NATO members were a collection of 'middle sized and small sovereign states whose disparate interests make it difficult in many instances to gain the consensus required for action'.[84] This was to be illustrated dramatically in the Middle East War of 1973 when American forces worldwide were put on alert. As time has passed, the agreements made in 1952 have not become any clearer, as shown by the Cruise missile debate. In the House of Commons on 12 May 1983, Prime Minister Margaret Thatcher was able to reassure all, before the arrival of Cruise missiles in Britain, that the understanding with the United States made in 1952 meant that 'no nuclear weapons would be fired or launched from British territory without the agreement of the Prime Minister'.[85] It was apparently less categorical to President Reagan, who said in the same week 'I don't think either one of us will do anything independent of the other. This constitutes a sort of veto power, doesn't it'.[86]

The next chapter traces the actual development of United States bases in Britain, with particular attention being paid to the Special Construction Program initiated at the same time as the Truman–Attlee meetings The Truman–Attlee agreement and its final version in 1952, reached between Truman and Churchill, form the backdrop to the military negotiations that led to the incredible growth of American forces in Britain. Britain, originally host to two wings of bombers for visits of goodwill and temporary duty, was to become, within the space of three years, America's unsinkable aircraft carrier.

5 1950–4: The US Presence Consolidated – America Builds Up Her Military Presence in the UK: The Developing Years

THE SPECIAL CONSTRUCTION PROGRAMME

It was during the Washington ABC (American–British–Canadian) Joint Planners Conference, held in Washington in September 1949, that specific plans for emergency operations were developed for USAF and RAF units operating out of the United Kingdom. The American version of the plans was called OFFTACKLE and the British version went under the name GALLOPER. The plan was seen as a joint USAF–RAF team operation, with most of the fighters being provided by the RAF; the bombing responsibility was generally assumed by SAC and other permanent USAF units in the United Kingdom. General Eisenhower, in his capacity as Acting Chairman of the JCS, initiated a new joint outline emergency war plan covering the first two years of a war beginning on 1 July 1949. The overall concept, as given to the JSPC, was a combination of a strategic offensive in Western Eurasia with defence in the Far East. The ABC Conference of 26 September to 4 October saw the delegates unable to agree on a specific plan; but they did adopt a strategic concept for 1950 and 1951 which was basically that laid down in OFFTACKLE, approved by the JCS on 8 December 1949. The strategic offensive during the early stages of the war 'would consist entirely of strategic air operations against the Soviet Union employing atomic and conventional bombs'.[1]

Unlike its predecessor, TROJAN, OFFTACKLE envisaged an air offensive that would destroy (not merely be directed against) vital elements of the Soviet war-making capacity. It also included as a new

86

Main Operating Locations (August 1951)

Source: *Third Air Force Historical Brief* (16 July 1948 to 31 December 1967).

objective the retardation of Russian advances into Western Europe. To accomplish these missions the JCS had adopted an ambitious target plan prepared by the Air Force, which would require 'the dropping of atomic bombs and 17610 tons of conventional bombs during the first three months of operations, to be followed by continuing attack to deliver 246900 tons of conventional weapons by D+24 months'.[2] This fearsome deluge would obviously require a substantial number of aircraft operating from overseas bases. It had been decided at an earlier date to drop the TROJAN deployment of bombers to the Cairo–Suez area, which then put more emphasis on United Kingdom bases, with American bombers increasing in strength from two medium groups on D-Day to five on D+12 months.

The increasing demand on British airfields to support the Emergency War Plan can be broken into two segments. The first was the additional construction of the four Oxfordshire bases over and above that programmed in the Ambassador's Agreement, and the second was the construction at numerous other sites in the United Kingdom; this new phase was to take place under the Special Construction Programme (SCP). The earlier Ambassador's Agreement had applied solely to the four Midlands airfields as agreed in April 1950. The SCP extended the scope of construction at these bases, and also pertained to a programme of massive expansion which involved an additional twenty-three bases and four depots. The SCP and its proposed expansion was first discussed at a meeting with the British Under-Secretary of State for Air, Aidan Crawley, on 29 July 1950. General Leon Johnson prepared a letter to Air Marshal Sir William F. Dickson, listing the major USAF requirements as they had been determined by the Third Air Division headquarters. The scope of the requirements was immense. In the letter of 3 August 1950, these major requirements were laid down as:

1. Move bomber aircraft from East Anglia to the Midlands.
2. Extend Mildenhall runway to 9,000 feet.
3. Provide 30 B-29 type hardstands at Mildenhall, Lakenheath, Marham and Sculthorpe.
4. Provide 'Specialized Equipment' storage at bomber airfields.
5. Provide housing for 3,500 at eight bases.
6. Detailed examination of Carnaby, Woodbridge and Manston.
7. Install heavy wire double fencing around bomber airfields.
8. Rehabilitation of existing World War II pipelines.
9. Provide alternate h.q. site.

10. Provide additional depot facilities.
11. Provide post-strike staging facilities outside the UK.[3]

The manner in which the SCP was negotiated was similar to that of the Ambassador's Agreement. The central questions that had made the negotiation of the Ambassador's Agreement such a protracted affair were far more straightforward in the case of the SCP. This was in part due to the experience of hammering out the former agreement, but also because the British negotiators now had a more accurate idea of USAF requirements.

The Treasury was also to prove far less intransigent than in the days of the Ambassador's Agreement. The reversal of the Treasury position was evident in a letter to the Commander of the Third Air Division, General Johnson:

> I have received Treasury authority to spend an additional £3 million on works services for the USAF, without prejudice to whatever agreements may ultimately be agreed . . . the Treasury have given us this authority now so as to ensure that there is no delay in starting the work which both you and I consider to be of immediate urgency.[4]

General Johnson, upon presenting his requirements to the USAF Installation Board, was authorised to 'proceed with commitments' and spend up to $15 million, with a further $5 million to be allocated in the near future. In fact, this was to prove the tip of the iceberg, because by 1951 the construction budget was estimated at 'over 100 million dollars, shared 50 : 50 with Britain, after some 21 million dollars worth of direct troop labour had been deducted'.[5] Upon General Johnson's return from Washington, he preseed Air Marshal Dickson for immediate action. In a second letter to Air Marshal Dickson it was made quite clear that 'prior to the development of the detailed arrangements for sharing costs of OFFTACKLE/GALLOPER, fund authorization on hand at Third Air Division could only be used for those projects required as USAF operational necessities'.[6] The letter also suggested a delineation of costs into three categories: first, those items the cost of which should be borne entirely by the USAF; second, those items the cost of which should be equally apportioned; and, last, those items that should be charged wholly to the United Kingdom. The Air Ministry replied on 6 December.[7] A letter penned by Air Marshal Dickson made the point that the costs should be analysed according to their long-term value to the RAF and to the operational function these projects were designed to serve under GALLOPER. He also pointed out that the work being carried out in compliance with the Ambassador's Agreement had considerably over-run its preliminary estimates, and it was thus proposed that the cost of the fourth field (Greenham Common) should be included in the GALLOPER programme. It was also recommended that instead of appraising each individual project, an overall split should be decided upon. A 50:50 sharing of costs was suggested by Air Marshal Dickson. Initially, it was believed that a 60:40 share would apply, in each case one expecting the other side to contribute the greater proportion. General Johnson also consulted Ambassador Holmes (Aldrich's successor as United States Ambassador) and secured permission for the extension in scope of the Ambassador's Agreement as it applied to the Midlands bases.

In the New Year, Air Chief Marshal Dickson[8] wrote to General Johnson, having conferred with the Air Ministry, and expressed his general understanding that costs of construction under OFFTACKLE/GALLOPER would be shared equally by USAF and the Air Ministry. The USAF were to receive 'credit' for such materials and engineer labour as they might provide. One reason why a 50:50 split was agreed upon for the programme in general, rather than for individual projects, was that it was known exactly how many installations would be made available by the RAF. In order to present a general picture of the 'order of magnitude of expenditure anticipated' Air Chief Marshal Dickson suggested the following general figures: £10 million for the four Midlands bases, and £25 million for the remaining bases, making £35 million for the total programme.[9] There was a slight variance between the Air Ministry and Third Air Division figures, with the estimate prepared by the Third Air Division Installations Staff being about $109 million (the British estimate of £35 million pounds was approximately $98 million. Air Chief Marshal Dickson replied to General Johnson on 25 May confirming Air Ministry agreement with the Third Air Division proposals for a reimbursement procedure, the USAF interpretation of 'credits' for United States material and labour, and the application of the arrangements to the Midlands bases.

It had taken less than nine months to reach agreement on the $100 million SCP, which was a considerable difference from the twenty months taken to finalise the Ambassador's Agreement (worth $18 million). It should be stressed that the SCP was based on fixed projects rather than on predetermined costs. The ultimate cost would be shared, rather than a predetermined cost figure, and the SCP was thus in agreement on the principle of equal cost sharing rather than the amount. The SCP was significant for two main reasons. The first was that it heralded the start of a huge expansion of the main presence in the United Kingdom. The SCP applied to eight main SAC bomber bases[10] and two depots at Burtonwood and Alconbury. Duncan Campbell estimates that the 1952 programme included a further $39 million for the development of the Burtonwood depot, and the first few dispersal bases for SAC aircraft from the main stations. These included Stansted, Essex and Desborough, Northamptonshire. In 1953 it was expected that the cost of developing UK bases would require expenditure of a further $167 million'.[11]

The SCP took place at a time when it became apparent that operational control of SAC forces deployed to the United Kingdom would be better if they had their own headquarters instead of being assigned to the Third Air Division. In March 1951 the Chief of Staff USAF directed that 'certain responsibilities and resources' be transferred to SAC Seventh Air Division which was activated in the same month. The transfer agreement was eventually reached on 17 September 1951.[12] although the Seventh Air Division was operating as a functional headquarters in advance of this agreement. The Seventh Air Division immediately took over the twelve installations the Third Air Division had been using and with the signing of the Transfer Agreement, the Seventh Air Division assumed full control of SAC operations in the United Kingdom reporting directly to General LeMay at SAC headquarters at Omaha. The agreement specified that the Third Air Force (on May 1951 the Third Air Division was renamed the Third Air Force) would retain responsibility for all tactical and logistical activities as well as depot maintenance. The Seventh Air Division was to be responsible for implementing emergency War Plans. Soon the SAC air bases were to disappear behind double fences and USAF Security Police patrolled the based while anti-aircraft batteries were put in place on the perimeters of the airfields.

The SCP formed a landmark in the history of United States bases in the United Kingdom for a second reason. It was in effect to be the last of the major British cash contributions with the bulk of the remaining base expansion being funded almost exclusively by the USAF. By September 1951, when it was time to start drawing up the FY 1953 Construction Programme, it was estimated that the total additional requirements for the USAF in the UK would amount to $173 million.[13] This made the combined FY 1951–53 programme worth almost $300 million (or about £100 million pounds).

Britain was certainly in no position to afford this kind of expenditure as the Chancellor of the Exchequer, Gaitskell, made clear to the

United States government during a trip to Washington in October. During the talks the Chancellor of the Exchequer suggested that the 'US should meet the whole capital and maintenance cost of work services for the USAF'.[14] It was also made clear that contributions like those to the SCP would be well-nigh impossible in the future. In a letter from Air Marshal Slessor to General Hoyt Vandenberg mention was also made of the United Kingdom's precarious financial situation and proposed a study to 'determine the limitations of construction capability physically possible with capital goods and labour available within the geographical confines of the United Kingdom'.[15] Hints were dropped during the Gaitskell visit about the eventual magnitude of the programme that the USAF envisaged for the United Kingdom. By the autumn of 1951 it became apparent that the original SCP estimates were rather low and that the programme would therefore overrun estimates. This, combined with the severely strained British economy, led to a re-examination of USAF–UK fiscal policies and financial arrangements already in existence. The solution to these problems was beyond the Third Air Force–RAF dialogue and would require negotiation at Congressional and Governmental level.

The complicated preliminary negotiations took place early the following year. The USAF presented the case to Congress through the Department of Defense whilst the American Embassy in Grosvenor Square acted as an intermediary between the Third Air Force and the British government. On 1 April a memorandum was presented to the State Department by the British government; it was in effect a statement that in future, if the USAF wanted bases in Britain, then they must be prepared to pay a large proportion.[16] The suggestion was that a 80:20 ratio for paying the costs should be instituted with the United Kingdom making the smaller contribution, with a maximum contribution of £17.5 million – this was its original cash commitment under the SCP. The ratio, furthermore, was to apply to major and minor programmes alike and the ratio was retroactively to apply to the SCP with an Air Ministry levy of ten per cent for 'departmental expenses'. On 10 April the memorandum was passed from the Third Air Force headquarters to Thomas Finletter, Secretary of the US Air Force, who immediately recommended sticking to the original 50:50 SCP ratio for both the SCP and FY 1953 programmes. The Third Air Force headquarters, perhaps better aware of the British financial situation than most others, had proposed that the UK government contribute another £5 million (in addition to the original £17.5 million SCP contribution) to maintain an equal ratio for the remainder of the

SCP. The trouble with the SCP was that it provided for the sharing of all costs for a specific programme of construction or modification on a base; what it did not specify was a ceiling on expenditure. A further five Third Air Force–Embassy solutions were put forward, the general objective of which was to secure the maximum flow of dollars into the United Kingdom which could continue for six months to a year, and which could be vital in determinng British solvency.

General Francis Griswold, who assumed command of the Third Air Force on 6 May 1952,[17] prepared a letter for Lieutenant-General White (Director of Installations, HQ USAF) in which he made clear the urgent need for United Kingdom bases:

> it is clear that the development of base facilities is the key to our ability to carry out the Air Force mission and must continue without interruption or delay. I understand the FY 1953 construction budget scheduled for presentation to Congress this week is being submitted on the basis of equal British participation. This is unrealistic in view of the recent British proposals submitted through the State Department to Defense . . . I urgently recommend your personal efforts to insure that USAF presentation to Congress makes clear the fact that this construction program must proceed regardless of ultimate arrangements with the British on sharing the costs or we will be forced to make major changes in mission assignment.[18]

The message was clear: the base development programme required to meet the OFFTACKLE/GALLOPER plans was being endangered by a lack of firm financial agreements. A point consistently missed, or overlooked, at this stage was that while the USAF pressed for a 50:50 ratio, the contribution made by Britain by way of rent-free land and facilities exceeded the value of the construction programmes for 1951–3. Far from American complaints that Britain was reneging or dragging our feet, it could be argued that it was in fact the British who were bearing the lion's share of the overall 'cost' facilities. Eventually, due to the exhortations of those like General Griswold and Air Marshal Slessor, it was agreed that, in the light of the possible endangering of the USAF base programme and the precarious financial situation, the 50:50 demand would be dropped.

A continuous series of meetings was held in Washington to try to solve the differences. In an effort to speed up the most critical construction work it was proposed that the Air Ministry would be assured of 100 per cent USAF liability against 'certain selected critical line items'.[19] The remaining items were to be left in abeyance to be handled by whatever arrangements could be hammered out. The next obvious problem was to decide what the selected line items were, but it was generally taken to be the SCP and a guarantee that the Third Air Force would finance construction up to 100 per cent of available funds. On 4 September the American Embassy in London received a cable with 'authority to open another meeting with the British negotiators on the subject of the unresolved construction costs and concomittant USAF–UK problems'.[20] The Embassy then approached the Treasury willing to open discussion on the basis of the 1 April memorandum advocating the 80:20 split. The meeting was rather short and the crux of the United States' position was that the 'existing agreements should be adhered to' and should apply to the actual costs of the projects rather than an original estimate. Not surprisingly, a firm British refusal to bear this cost was the result; the Americans were similarly unwilling to shoulder such a burden.

It was only after almost a year of sporadic negotiations that an agreement was eventually reached and it was to be known as the Air Base Cost Sharing Arrangement, approved on 6 August 1953 by Lord De L'Isle and Dudley VC, Secretary of State for Air and President of the Air Council, who advised the Defence Council and Chancellor that it would be beneficial to go ahead with the compromise arrangement. Unusually, for an agreement concerning American bases in Britain, there was a formal signing ceremony held on 9 September 1953. Colonel Edward Hopkins of the Third Air Force who was present at the ceremony had recommended that the formal signing be done 'in order to add stature to the agreement.' He then went on to recommend that 'there be no publicity in connection with the formal signing'.[21] The lack of comment (with the exception of *The Times*, who announced a 'new agreement on the cost of 19 UK Air Bases to be used by the US'[22] – but only in February 1954) was typical of the way such major developments on our future security went largely unnoticed. The first letter of the Air Base Cost Sharing Arrangement, which set out the terms of the understanding, was signed by Winthrop Aldrich, the US Ambassador, London. The second letter was signed for the British government by George Ward of the Air Ministry, who accepted the terms of understanding as presented by Aldrich. Under the arrangement, which represented a continuation of the Ambassador's Agreement and SCP, the British had several obligations: They were to contribute some $70 million against the USAF–UK Military Construction Programme (MCP), and we were to provide 'facilities and land' without charge and waive Administration charges (put forward in the April memorandum) completely for fiscal years 1951–2 and half for other years. In addition we were to waive any claims on 'loss, use and depreciation' of RAF equipment leased to the USAF, and waive any charges on US Aviation Engineer personnel. Britain was also to pay the cost of relocating units and materials from bases to be occupied by the USAF within an annual limit of $280 000. Lastly, we were to 'reserve RAF equipment as USAF strategic reserve in the event of emergency'.[23]

The American contributions under the Cost Sharing arrangements were nontheless substantial, involving payment of all USAF–UK MCP costs above $63 million, as well as all minor construction costs. USAF were also to pay all recurrent maintenance costs after 1 July 1951. There were also some general provisions that were mainly administrative in nature; under these the Air Ministry was to continue as the USAF agent in executing the US–UK MCP. Britain was also obliged to set aside $350 million dollars worth of construction capability for the MCP until the end of 1955, to eliminate any US liability for land reinstatement, and recognise the need for adequate financial control procedures. Aldrich in his letter expressed the fact that the bases 'constitute an important factor in our joint Western Defence Effort and that it is, therefore, in the interest of both our Governments that their construction, maintenance and utilization continues to be carried out on a partnership basis'.[24] In all, the British Treasury was expected to provide resources (labour and material) worth £95 million over the calendar years 1952–55; within this the total contribution towards the SCP was to amount to £22.5 million. Overall, the United Kingdom's contribution of facilities at no cost had resulted in the USAF securing operational bases in the United Kingdom at a much lower cash outlay than would have been possible anywhere else in the world. The United States' cash outlay for bomber bases in the United Kingdom was about 55 per cent of the total cost, and it approached 60 per cent of the total cost on fighter bases.[25] Whilst the expansion of the American bases in the United Kingdom had been made possible by the Ambassador's Agreement, the results of the SCP and MCP were to prove dramatic. The American bases rose from three in July 1948, to ten by August 1950, and by October 1953 there were twenty-seven Third Air Force bases add facilities and fifteen Seventh Air Division bases, making a total of forty-two.[26] No other overseas base area saw such a dramatic growth and this made Britain an indispensable consideration in American strategic planning. The expenditure by the United States on bases in Britain also gave long-run savings for America's economy. General Hoyt Vandenberg publicly testified that the bases had afforded savings when he pointed out that 'if no overseas bases existed, SAC would have to attain 'five or six' times its present strength in order to perform the same mission'.[27]

In addition to the economic provisions contained in the cost-sharing agreement there was also an interesting provision regarding the duration of stay of US forces. Under the provision it was understood that the facilities subject to the cost-sharing agreement, as agreed between Air Chief Marshal Sir John Whitworth-Jones and Major General Francis H. Griswold, would be 'available for use by units of the United States Air Force so long as, in the opinion of both the United States Government and Her Majesty's Government, the presence of such units is considered desirable in the interests of common defence. This arrangement will be subject to periodical review, and will in any case terminate as soon as, in the opinion of either government, collective security has been assured in accordance with the principles set forth in the Charter of the United Nations'.[28]

Aldrich finished his letter to Ward suggesting that there was 'no need for the matters I have referred to in this letter to be embodied in a formal agreement'.[29] In his letter accepting the arrangement on behalf of the British government, as presented by Aldrich, Ward stated:

> I agree that the understanding between our two governments is correctly set out in your letter and confirm that Her Majesty's Government see no need for the terms of the understandings to be embodied in a formal agreement.[30]

The Cost Sharing Agreement concluded the third, and most significant, financial agreement with the British government – the general public were completely unaware of the vast increase in the US presence that was soon to take place.

A QUESTION OF NUMBERS

The SCP and the Cost Sharing arrangements, like other agreements concerning the American bases, were worked out at the top military level, and, consequently, at parliamentary level there was often confusion regarding the scale of American military involvement in the United Kingdom. The English Speaking Union (ESU) were the first to see the problems of the huge influx of American service personnel. The ESU suggested to the Foreign Office in December 1950 that 'in view of the increasing numbers of American forces likely to be coming here', the complicated wartime machinery for the welfare of United States servicemen should be revived.[31] The Foreign Office were under the impression that 'the strength of the USAF here was unlikely to increase much beyond the numbers here at that time [December 1950]'.[32] Similarly the Ministry of Defence had little idea of the huge American expansion that was being planned. The MoD told the Foreign Office 'we know nothing to support the English Speaking Union's assumption that there will be an increase, except that an additional 1500 American troops are to come here for guard duties at the aerodromes at which the USAF is stationed. The present number of American servicemen is between 11 000 and 12 000'.[33]

In February 1951, Ernest Davies at the Foreign Office wrote a letter (approved in draft by Sir Roger Makins) to Aidan Crawley at the Air Ministry saying that some of the arguments for a return to the wartime welfare system were based on 'the mistaken impression that the number of American servicemen stationed in this country is likely to increase considerably, even if there is no serious deterioration in the internatinal situation'.[34] This sentence was apparently not commented on by the Air Ministry or the Ministry of Defence, to whom a copy of the letter was sent. On 1 August an official at the Foreign Office was told by Major-General John P. McConnell that personnel under his command (the Seventh Air Division) would number some 40 000 by 1952 and 75 000 by 1953. These figures took no account of the Third Air Force or US Navy. The discrepancy between the two sets of figures was obvious and embarrassing. The Foreign Office asked the MoD if they had anything to add to their January figures.[35] The MoD replied that US military personnel amounted to 'some 25 000' in July 1951 and that these numbers were expected to increase to about 35 000 by January 1952, after which they were supposed to 'level off'.

The confusion in the Foreign Office and the MoD suggested that little was known about plans to double the number of US personnel in the United Kingdom by July 1951 and they were also under the impression that US personnel would level off at about 35 000.[36] It was, to a senior Foreign Office official, 'very undesirable, if only from the Parliamentary angle, that there should be much obscurity about the number of United States servicemen stationed in this country and about the basis of the Anglo–US arrangement under which these US servicemen were assigned'.[37]

In spite of the aforementioned financial agreements for American basing in the United Kingdom and, in spite of the Truman–Churchill understandings, the future of the bases was still felt to be unclear. The attempts at codifying the position in the Ambassador's Agreement and Cost Sharing agreement, which said in effect that the airfields in the United Kingdom would be available for use by the United States Air Force so long as both governments considered it desirable in the interests of common defence, did little to enlighten anyone as to the future plans for the American bases in Britain, or of any eventual numbers. The SCP, which only gave an approximation of the growing scale of American involvement, did not actually discuss the question of numbers although there was a recognition that in granting Americans the use of airfields the British were *ipso facto* also giving permission for extra air and ground crews. It had been agreed in the letter from Aidan Crawley to the American Ambassador forming the Ambassador's Agreement that 'no overall agreement covering the grant of these facilities was required.' This situation was now changed for two reasons. First, the progressive build-up of strength did not seem to have been contemplated at the time of Crawley's letter. Second, the listing by the United States government of their facilities in the United Kingdom as military operating requirements under NATO procedure[38] changed the informal tone of the Ambassador's Agreement.

Where military operating requirements had started from scratch, as in Malta's case, a comprehensive agreement had been negotiated to provide them. Many military operating procedures in the United Kingdom had still not been worked out, like the legal status of the American forces and long-term finance for the bases. The agreements that did exist, apart from being vague, were not registered with the United Nations in spite of the fact that the United Kingdom had bound herself to register all intergovernmental agreements with that organisation. Various ways were found to avoid these obligations by regarding some of the agreements (like the SCP) as commercial leases and therefore not registerable with the UN, or concluding an agreement as an exchange of letters (like the Cost Sharing Arrangement). A Foreign Office spokesman cautioned that 'What we should *not* do, I think, is to take up the position that any arrangement reached with the United States government that is not suitable for registration with the UN must be left completely woolly'.[39]

The United States military operating requirements mentioned only airfields and facilities required and not the number of squadrons which it was proposed to station on those airfields. For political and practical reasons it now became necessary for the government to be kept constantly informed of the numbers of American servicemen which the American authorities planned to have on British soil at any given time, However, the uncertainty about numbers was only one aspect of a more general uncertainty which prevailed due to the general lack of comprehensive base agreements. The failure to register agreements with the UN was also puzzling when the United States saw fit to register their NATO requirements with the UN. There was, for instance, an understanding that the agreement being negotiated with Portugal over the Azores would be registered with the UN. It seemed to the Foreign Office 'very undesirable that we should lag behind such countries as Portugal in regularizing the position of US forces in British territory in some constitutional manner'.[40] The nature of the agreements was prompted partly by US inexperience in the international arena and the fact that 'in the heyday of US overseas deployments in the 1950's and 1960's there was little sensitivity to the delicate interaction of military and political factors that sustained that expansion'.[41]

The uncertainty over numbers was ended when the Third Air Force agreed to inform the Air Ministry of the numbers of USAF personnel in the United Kingdom on a monthly basis – the Air Ministry would then pass on the information to the MoD and Foreign Office. There was, however, no agreement on whether there should be advance warning about future peacetime plans. The first formal declaration of numbers was announced by the Air Ministry and the Foreign Office. USAF strength in the United Kingdom for 30 November was 31 312; the Army had a strength of 212 officers and 2966 enlisted men, and the USN had roughly 118 officers and 452 enlisted men.[42] The Army were mainly engaged in guard duty and protecting 'special stores' as well as training. The USN had a small but important role. The USN, vastly overestimating the strength of the British navy, dismantled nearly all of her short stations after the Second World War. In the United Kingdom a few facilities remained. There was a permanent mooring buoy for the station ship for COMNAVEU (the USS HAMEL) at Plymouth from April 1947 on. After the disestablishment of the huge naval base at Exeter, this left only 20 Grosvenor Square in London and the radio station in Londonderry as the 'only shore properties of any consequence still used by the [US] navy in the UK.'[43] The tranformation of the USN war-time command into a peace-time organisation was completed by 1 April 1947 whilst the decision to maintain a staff in London 'had been made long before.' Amongst the functions, stressed as 'one of the most important activities', of the US Naval Officers in

London was that of 'collecting and disseminating Intelligence, mainly from British sources'.[44]

The early 1950s saw the beginning of a process of consolidation where the now familiar infrastructure of the American presence developed in the form of ammunition depots, intelligence and communication facilities to support SAC's strategic role and the Third Air Force's tactical missions.

THE FORWARD STRATEGY

The British bases took on an increasingly important place in NATO's strategic thinking when the 'forward strategy' was adopted at a meeting of the North Atlantic Council in New York in September 1950. The adoption of the forward strategy was largely a response to the North Korean invasion of South Korea in June. The strategy involved a massive ground commitment by America to Europe. President Truman announced in September substantial increases in the United States forces to be stationed in Western Europe in the interests of the defense of that area. At the time this was thought of as a temporary measure pending a general East–West settlement or economic recovery that would permit Europeans to provide for their own defence. There was also a feeling in Europe left over from the last war that Europeans needed defending and not liberating. The forward strategy had many detractors who argued (with justification as it turned out) that the commitment would be not only expensive but would encourage Europeans to rely upon America's military presence; some argued that it was a dangerous break from the traditional American policy of non-commitment abroad unless absolutely necessary. The USAF also opposed the forward strategy involving massive commitments of ground forces in Europe, arguing that air power was the sole overseas requirement for American security. The most important rationale for the adoption of the forward strategy was the realisation, outlined by Dean Acheson, that:

> The best use we can make of our present advantage in retaliatory air power is to move ahead under this protective shield to build the balanced collective forces in Western Europe that will continue to deter aggression after our atomic advantage has been diminished.[45]

The forward strategy marked the realisation that unclear superiority would eventually be lost and thus provided no basis for long-term planning. From the mid 1950s on, as the deployment of Thor IRBM's was to show, nuclear forces did little but neutralise or match those of the other side. It was therefore to conventional superiority that American planners turned. In late 1951 opposition leaders in the Senate had expressed horror at the 'prospect of sending more troops to Europe as part of an "international army" under NATO command'.[46] But by 1952 the United States had stationed nearly half of its active military forces on foreign territory and their commitments included some forty-three collective defence agreements with various countries and the training and equipping by American military personnel of local military forces in over seventy countries.

THE BEGINNING OF REFLEX TOURS AND INTELLIGENCE OPERATIONS

Apart from the importance of the United Kingdom as a strategic base to the US, as stressed in the Forward Strategy, the bases were also gaining importance in less obvious ways in particular, clandestine intelligence-gathering involving overflights of Soviet, or Soviet-controlled, territory. In 1951 a small number of RB-45Cs of the 91st Strategic Reconnaissance Group (Medium) made their first visit to Manston, hosted by the Seventh Air Division. The reconnaissance value of Britain's geographical proximity to the Soviet Union and Eastern Europe had not been overlooked. It may be coincidence, but the first commander of the Seventh Air Division was Brigadier-General Paul Cullen who, although killed on his way to take up the command, had been one of the leading photo-reconnaissance authorities in the United States. (There is still a SAC Reconnaissance, Photo and Navigation Competition with the award being named after P. T. Cullen.)

The general role of the Seventh Air Division was rotational training on three-month tours of duty. When the extension of the Midlands airfields and the SCP were finished, SAC was to rotate entire combat wings, air refuelling squadrons and smaller units to various overseas bases. The completion of the airfields also coincided with the arrival of the first B-47 wing (the 306th) in Britain. Sometimes accompanied by air refuelling squadrons, the B-47s were to rotate from American bases to Britain using bases at Lakenheath, Upper Heyford, Fairford, Mildenhall and Brize Norton. The rotational tours involving three-month migrations of complete units to and fro across the Atlantic were to be phased out gradually over the early part of 1955. This was in part due to consent complaints from residents near the American bases of noise due to heavy flying schedules, but also due to the strain on the B-47s, whilst the cost of regularly shuttling 2000 people and their supplies also proved to be enormous. A cheaper way of maintaining a constant presence had to be found. The answer was found in the form of 'Reflex' training where smaller groups of SAC bombers were scattered around on static, not airborne, alert. The Reflex crew were required to be on continuous alert for two weeks of the three week visit to England.

The huge B-36 had also paid some visits to Burtonwood and Upper Heyford in 1951. The B-36 boasted a range of approximately 8000 miles at 40 000 feet, while the B-47 had a range of 5600 miles (or 7800 with in-flight refuelling). The B-50 called 'Lucky Lady Two' was the first bomber to complete a non-stop circumnavigation of the world with in-flight refuelling. The long range B-52, in the first of its many versions, was not available until 1956, meaning that the United States was absolutely dependent upon overseas bases. Even after the advent of intercontinental flight capabilities, bases were still essential although they were no longer vital for potential strikes against the Soviet Union. Like nearly all components of the United States basing network 'they remained important in the broader context of geopolitical confrontation between the United States and Soviet Union'.[47]

The American overseas basing network during the years 1950–3 saw an enormous expansion both in representation and scope. The huge build-up during these years when there was a heavy reliance upon short range bombers marked the heyday of American world wide-might. The vast network of American bases developed in this period acted not only as a legacy but as a self-perpetuating justification for the continued large world-wide presence. The enthusiasm for bases in the United Kingdom, which was later to be tainted by the Mansfield Lobby, was still strong. In a Senate committee, one such message of enthusiasm was expressed:

> From a military point of view, England is our greatest and strongest ally. In many respects, she is our best friend in world affairs . . . the program for building American airbases in Britain is of mutual interest to both nations and is one of the greatest forward movements to assure successful defense of the North Atlantic area.[48]

While Britain saw her destiny as being with her wartime ally, some European countries were beginning to think in terms of integration in economic and military terms. Churchill promised at the end of 1951 to associate as 'closely as possible' with the proposed European Defence Community, largely to forestall criticism of British intransigence. Britain had assumed that her postwar role would be closely allied to America's. Even before NATO there was a *de facto* commitment by Britain to an American alliance, with Britain assuming a rather exposed 'advanced' role. The United States had also assumed a moral commitment to defend the United Kingdom, exemplified in various JCS war plans, that was hardly any less far-reaching. In spite of the superficial closeness of Anglo–American relations many of the negotiations surrounding the bases were not so much about the use of our bases but concerned a wider debate about the extent to which America was prepared to treat Britain as an equal partner. During the discussions leading to the British 'Global Strategy Paper' of 1952 it was pointed out that the fall of Britain as a world power and the dismantling of the Empire had left America as the predominant influence, whose 'experience, judgement and internal political system were ill-adapted to her enormous responsibilities and her capacity to determine the fate not only of the Western Allies but of most of Asia as well'.[49] The rationale for the development of an independent British nuclear deterrent was partly a prestige symbol in the international community and a suspicion amongst the Chiefs of Staff that 'it was not possible to rely on the Americans to deal adequately with targets not of direct strategic interest to the United States'.[50]

The SAC Emergency War Plan approved by the JCS on 22 October 1951 targeted three main areas: the Moscow–Gorky area, Leningrad, and the Volga. The United Kingdom's role in the implementation of a successful strike, assuming Russian provocation, was paramount:

> The initial strike would be launched on approximately D + 6 days. Heavy bombers flying from Maine would drop 20 bombs in the Moscow–Gorky area and return to the United Kingdom. Simultaneously, medium bombers from Labrador would attack the Leningrad area with 12 weapons and re-assemble at British bases. Meanwhile, medium bombers based in the British Isles would approach the USSR along the edge of the Mediterranean Sea and deliver 52 bombs in the industrial region of the Volga and Donets Basin.[51]

Significantly, such a plan assumed that there were facilities in Britain for storing atomic weapons. The early 1950s saw the construction of Special Ammunition Stores, in effect very thick concrete igloos surrounded by earth, which were to hold the first of a sizeable American nuclear stockpile in Britain. Whilst the Special Ammunition Stores Programme was being completed and security tightened up, only the non-nuclear components of atomic weapons were being stored, so that, by D+6 days, SAC would have had adequate time to transfer the nuclear cores from their American storage sites.

THE DAWN OF THE MISSILE AGE – SUPERPOWER BASE RIVALRY

During the first decade after the Second World War, the Soviet Union was almost totally lacking in overseas facilities, corresponding to their limited air and naval capacity. Soviet propaganda during this period was directed towards the elimination of all foreign bases that were seen as part to the 'capitalist encirclement'.[52] Until 1951 the United States relied primarily upon the World War 2 vintage B-29 bomber, alongside its modified form, the B-50. The advent of the B-47 was an important milestone in US basing history. The new bomber was supplied to USAF on 23 October 1951 but was not deployed to the United Kingdom until June 1953.[53] The bomber had twice the speed of the older SAC bombers at about 600 miles per hour and its range was enhanced by the increasingly refined practice of aerial refuelling. The US 'determined a forward deployment [of the B-47] to enhance their chances of penetration and lessen their vulnerability to a Soviet first strike'.[54] The Russians had no equivalent and their early post-war bombers, like the Tupolev-4, could reach the north west of the United States from Siberia only and also, by so doing, give some four hours of time to alert the radar. A full two years were to pass after the B-47 made its first appearance in Britain before the Soviet Union was able to introduce the M-4 bombers, also with a top speed of 600 miles per hour. After this, precocious Russian missile deployments eroded the hitherto clear American strategic superiority, leading to fears of a 'technological Pearl Harbor'.

By 1956 first Russian ICBMs were being tested and a year later the launch of Sputnik led to SAC putting approximately one-third of its aircraft on ground alert and feverish American missile developments. With the advent of intercontinental missiles the need for expensive overseas bases, aside from geopolitical considerations, became increasingly difficult to justify. The Senate Committee on Foreign Relations observed in a report on overseas commitments that

'Once an American overseas base is established, it takes on a life of its own. Original missions may become outdated, but new missions are developed, not only with the intent of keeping the facility going, but often actually to enlarge it'.[55]

The emphasis on conventional overseas commitments was reversed under the Eisenhower and Kennedy administrations. Although the Forward Strategy was not scrapped. President Eisenhower was not persuaded of the need for massive conventional deployments to overseas bases; the strategy was unpopular with both the public and the Administration. Eisenhower's Secretary of State, John Foster Dulles, favoured a new policy that would give a far greater emphasis to nuclear weapons in US strategy. The culmination of the change in thinking from the Truman era was the strategy of 'massive retaliation'. The new strategy also coincided with a build-up of a range of nuclear capabilities in the American arsenal, from hydrogen bombs to smaller yield weapons designed for battlefield use. Bernard Brodie noted that nuclear weapons could no longer be regarded as 'exceedingly scarce or costly'.[56] This approach won support in Britain and had been confirmed in the British Chiefs of Staff Global Strategy Paper of 1952. Sir John Slessor, in particular, valued the nuclear armed long-range SAC bombers based in Britain; he regarded them as the 'Great Deterrent'. The 'Great Deterrent' was seen as 'the counter-threat to the vast armies and tactical air forces of our potential enemy . . . it gives us some degree of initiative in the cold war, instead of dancing to the enemy's tune'.[57] The Western advantage in air power was to be exploited to the maximum and formed a major part of Dulles's 'New Look' strategy.

In spite of the importance of the 'Great Deterrent', there was an overall tendency towards a reduction in the number of American bases. The United Kingdom was not exempt from this trend and saw a drop in the number of bases and personnel from the peak in 1953. The number of overseas bases (in the sense of permanent operational bases) declined, from 1953 until the present, in actual numbers from 150 to 30.[58] The Soviet Union, in the same period, increased its facility arrangements abroad 'to a point where they are roughly equal to the United States in terms of access to foreign facilities and their requirement for bases and facilities will grow as they continue to project themselves on a global scale'.[59] The Decline in American bases was due in part to Dulles's emphasis on cutting back on expensive conventional overseas commitments in favour of select SAC bases capable of deep penetration into the Soviet Union. The decline may also be accounted for by the gradual development of bombers with longer ranges that could be deployed from the United States alongside the development of missile technology.[60]

The strong SAC presence in the United Kingdom led to fears amongst some, like the former Secretary of State for Air, that Britain must beware of 'putting all [Britain's] bombing eggs into the copious basket'.[61] The Labour opposition gave Churchill's government support for the creation of an independent strategic nuclear force. Although the first squadron of Victor bombers was not operational until 1958 the decision to build such a force signalled an awareness of the dangers of total reliance upon the US strategic force. Although the force was not anti-American the need for an independent force was demonstrated in 1954, when strong American pressure was applied to Churchill's government to join a coalition with the French, who were facing a humiliating defeat at Dien Bien Phu in Laos. In Washington, DC, the Chief of the Imperial General Staff joined Allied military men in planning a response to China's likely intervention on the side of the Vietnamese insurgents led by Ho Chi Minh. They recommended that an air attack should be launched, aimed at military targets, and that to achieve 'a maximum and lasting effect nuclear as well as conventional weapons should be used *from the outset*'. The ageing Churchill confided in his private papers, 'The British people would not easily be influenced by what happened in the distant jungles of South-East Asia; but they did know that there was a *powerful American base in East Anglia* and that war with China, who would invoke the Sino-Russian Pact, might mean an assault by hydrogen bombs on these islands.' Churchill perceived the risk of total war as extreme, and 'of all the nations involved, the United States would suffer least'.[62]

Great emphasis had been put on Soviet Union's greatest and cheapest military asset, manpower, from the immediate postwar years until the 1950s. With the explosion of the first Russian atomic bomb, the implications of her hegemony in East Europe became more serious and American bases became vulnerable to the threat of Soviet atomic attack for the first time. The Soviet Union, for her part, had long been a vociferous critic of the American military presence in Europe and particularly in the United Kingdom. The criticism increased in the late 1950s and at the start of the next decade, which heralded the so-called 'missile gap', when missile technology gradually displaced the need for bomber bases. Nikita Khrushchev was careful to warn the United States in the 1960s that 'bases on foreign territory will not spare the United States from nuclear rocket blows'.[63]

Marshal Yeremenko, a leading Soviet strategist, was more charitable about the American need for overseas bases in the years where the short range of bombers made them a necessity:

> Of course, for that stage of development of armed forces when both sides based their strategic striking power on bomber aviation, the existence of bases on foreign territory was in any case explainable from a military point of view.[64]

Yeremenko also maintained, with the United Kingdom in mind, that the retention of air bases on foreign soil past the mid 1950s was a profitable means of getting rid of an obsolete armed service, such as bomber aviation was becoming by this time. However, far from being 'obsolete' the extensive system of overseas bases made it difficult for any aggressor to contemplate a simultaneous strike against SAC bases.

Ironically, in the year Sputnik was launched Henry Kissinger commented that the bases geographical location 'makes a simultaneous attack on all US bases virtually impossible'.[65] Since the United States SAC bases were located at a much greater distance in flying time from the Soviet Union's territory than overseas bases, the Soviet Long-Range Air Force had two options. Either it could launch attacks simultaneously against bases in the United States and overseas with the result that the Russian planes would be detected overseas before the plans destined to attack the American domestic bases reached the DEW line, or it could alternatively choose to strike two sets of targets simultaneously, giving overseas bases the same warning time as bases in the United States. An effort to attack both sets of targets simultaneously could, as Kissinger points out, 'expose the Soviet Union to a counterblow launched from our overseas bases while Soviet planes were still crossing Canada'.[66] It should be pointed out that because NATO doctrine concedes the first blow to the other side, the dispersal of the Strategic Air Force was not just of importance but a necessity.

Until the advent of widespread missile arsenals, the Soviet Union had many defence disadvantages and had to be prepared to repel retaliatory raids from many directions where American bases ringed the periphery. The advantage in geographical proximity enjoyed by American forces also made aerial refuelling a more useful NATO tool since even if a surprise attack on overseas bases forced the Americans to retaliate from bases in the United States the bombers could still refuel over friendly territory and out of range of Soviet detection. Later thinking in the missile era was to challenge the value of overseas bases when intercontinental missiles posed cheaper and effective alternatives to costly overseas bases that were often subject to political disturbances or disruption. The development of missiles also saw air bases becoming increasingly vulnerable to a strike before they could make their forces airborne. The launching of Sputnik and fears that NATO was vulnerable in the face of a Soviet intercontinental missile capability led to fears of a 'missile gap'. It was in response to this, alongside fears of growing vulnerability of the air bases, that it was decided to deploy intermediate-range ballistic missiles (IRBMs) to Europe. The introduction of IRBMs was to stress once again the importance of overseas bases and Britain was to take the greater share of the deployment:

> The introduction of IRBM's into NATO must be recognized as an addition to the base picture, for it will not immediately result in our being able to reduce our bases already in existence in view of the need for maximum dispersion and the fact that our bases in the European NATO area are, with the exception of the United Kingdom, intended more for the support of tactical than strategic forces.[67]

The proximity of Britain to Europe, just as it had been ideal in 1948 to locate a strategic air strike capability, was to make it ideal as a base from which to use IRBM's in Western Europe and the North Atlantic area. Far from heralding the end of the bomber era and thus overseas bases, the arrival of Thor missiles also saw a demand for 'an IRBM launch complex, a major Army communications facility, four LORAN stations, naval air facilities at Machrihanish and fleet facilities in the Clyde area, POL and ammunition facilities, and a communication link facility'.[68] This new stage of expansion was to bring the total US defence personnel in the United Kingdom to 42 739 in March 1957, and the bases covered some 28 000 acres of UK territory.[69] This force constituted a 'political and sociological experiment of the greatest interest',[69] for never before had a foreign force on this scale been stationed in Britain during peace time.

6 A Political and Sociological Experiment

This chapter will address some of the less obvious problems that beset the US basing in the United Kingdom. The sociological and potential political hazards of contact between visiting forces and residents are not always realised, but constitute a central concern. Whilst this chapter is not a full sociological account of the impact of US bases upon the British public, it does, by examining the legal basis of these relations and some main events in this area, seek to throw some light on this little explored area.

One of the most prominent problems that has beset relations between the visiting forces and the local populace has been in questions of law. The law regarding visiting forces is a limited guide, or more often than not, no guide at all. Aside from the immediate legal issues, the US bases have also had a considerable economic (and thus sociological) impact upon adjacent towns and villages. Much care and attention is paid by the visiting US forces to keep local community relations healthy by means of open days, bazaars, visits and public relations officers. Although the economic benefits that have grown out of the US presence are valuable, they do not, in themselves, form a rationale for the future retention of US bases in the United Kingdom. The question of the general desirability of US bases, therefore, becomes an essentially legal and political one.

A SOCIOLOGICAL EXPERIMENT

At the start of 1951, Eisenhower became Supreme Commander of the Allied Forces in Europe, and on 5 March 1951 he wrote:

> God knows, I'd personally like to get out of Europe and I'd like to see the United States able to sit at home and ignore the rest of the world. What a pleasing prospect, until you look at the ultimate consequences, destruction.[1]

In spite of such a statement, which must have expressed the feelings of many American servicemen overseas, there were nearly thirty air-fields, supply depots and other installations in Britain at the end of

Churchill's term of office. For many servicemen and their dependents, it was not so much a question of transferring to a new culture but of importing as much of their own culture and tradition as they could. Although the RAF ensign flew over the American bases and bases were still called RAF bases the culture inside the perimeter fences is unmistakably American. Each base has developed as a 'little America' and, as far as possible, a home away from home for off-duty servicemen and dependents.

When American 'GIs' first reappeared in peacetime Britain as members of the Third Air Division (Provisional), it was suggested by Lord Tedder's Deputy Chief of Staff, Sir William Dickson, that the American bases should remain designated as RAF stations. This was in large part an effort to avoid confrontation and alleviate local hostilities, and remains the system to this day. The bases also have a RAF 'commander', who is often of inferior rank to the US commanding officer, and in reality acts as little more than a liaison officer. Before leaving the United States for Britain servicemen were issued with a small booklet or 'conduct code' which warned against criticism of the British, the Royal Family, and not to 'flash your money around', since the American serviceman's living was high by British standards – an image that had stuck from the Hershey-bar and nylons-dispensing wartime GIs. Inevitably the wealthy American servicemen sought and were the objects of varied types of female attention causing resentment amongst local populaces, which in turn gave rise to the reappearance of the popular wartime adage that American servicemen were 'overpaid, oversexed and over here'.

If the disparity in income was a cause of resentment to some, it was, to others, a source of valuable business. *The New York Times* hinted at the profits to be made from the ever-growing stream of servicemen when it observed that 'a captain in the Third Air Force earns almost as much as the nominal salary of the Dean of Cantebury'.[2] With the establishment of the Third Air Force, and the rapid growth of American service personnel, the 'GI Problem' (as the popular press dubbed it) reached serious proportions. The year 1952 saw a whole series of assaults on US servicemen in major cities (in particular, Manchester), and similar patterns were observed in Bordeaux. The unrest was apparently caused by 'disparity in income levels and charges of "immorality"'.[3] The problem was serious enough to cause Major–General Francis Griswold to schedule a series of flying visits to US bases all around England to lecture on 'the importance of good behaviour and the desirability of maintaining friendly relations with the British allies'. The tour resulted in the creation of a number of Public Affairs Officers whose job was to act as spokesmen in base issues concerning community relations, and generally to try to sort out any social or adjustment problems American servicemen might have. The social unrest, fomented by inflammatory headlines in the staunchest opponent of the American presence, the Communist newspaper *The Daily Worker* – which regularly proclaimed 'Yanks go Home' or 'GI Joe, you gotta go' – led the British government to examine the problems of community relations with the bases. This did, by today's standards, lead to some rather stifling requirements, for instance, 'for local dances the WVS (Women's Volunteer Service) issued 'guest cards' to suitable girls living in the neighbourhood who had sent in their names – no girl was allowed to attend a dance unless she was sponsored in writing by a local person or respectable citizen'.[4]

Whilst there was value in stimulating local ties between servicemen and populace, there was still concern about the 'danger of immorality' that arose when 'undesirable female elements, often coming in from large cities, mix with the type of enlisted men who tend to fall ready victims'.[5] The concern about undesirable female elements was felt by American base commanders who were worried by the number of hours being lost due to the extraordinarily high VD rate which had caused severe problems in the early long-term duties. It was believed by the British government that a senior serviceman in Britain nearing retirement would be needed to co-ordinate welfare activities and be available to deal with problems caused by the American presence, or alternatively, listen to American representations. At the end of December the Home Secretary approved a recommendation[6] to appoint a person to co-ordinate welfare activities for the United States forces in this country, who would work closely with the WVS and ESU on the one hand, and with USAF on the other. The man chosen for the job was Air Marshal Sir George Pirie.

Until the creation of the Third Air Force in 1951, most units were on rotational duty and dependents were thus not permitted on the 90-day tours. The problems of hooliganism, rape, venereal disease and brushes with the civil law were more frequent as a result, compared to later years when tours were longer. The advent of longer-term stays saw an improvement in local relations with the visiting US servicemen, and local base newspapers like the *Heyford Gazette* were published to keep local populace and servicemen alike informed about base activities. 'Open days' also proved popular attractions and smoothed relations, providing a chance for social integration. The long-term tours of duty (normally three years) introduced into the Third Air Force meant that servicemen were permitted, unlike their '90-day wonder' Seventh Air Division counterparts, to bring wives and families. The complement of wives and children posed considerable logistical problems, since they had to be housed and fed; the children had to attend school and older family members even took American degree courses at British branches of their university. Yet in spite of the problems incurred by the presence of dependents, it has undoubtedly proved, over time, to be an important factor in the relative harmony between the base personnel and the surrounding indigenous population.

The yearly figures for American servicemen stationed in the United Kingdom grew so that at its height in 1957 there were over 40 000 American service personnel, many with dependents, assigned to twenty-eight bases of various kinds. The presence of such a sizeable contingent first caused problems because of a lack of accommodation in the vicinities of the bases. This is still a problem, but the bases provide a familiar atmosphere for visiting servicemen. If a US serviceman so wished he or she could virtually live an American way of life although servicemen in the United Kingdom, unlike their counterparts in Germany, do not have access to US forces transmissions. The bases use regular US dollars, although at one time there was an American base currency called 'scrip' which was apparently phased out because of currency speculation. Shopping is mainly done at a Post-Exchange or PX at preferential rates. Petrol, or 'gas', is sold at American prices for official duties. When the Americans first arrived, price differentials and scarcity of certain commodities in ration-bound Britain led to repeated black-market scandals, as good were smuggled out of PXs.

The expansion of the major bomber base network under the SCP at Brize Norton, Fairford, Greenham Common and Upper Heyford were the objects of much local grievance. With the construction of new runways or the extension of old ones, houses and pubs were bulldozed, roads redirected, and agricultural land compulsorily purchased from farmers. At Greenham Common common land was taken over to make way for a longer runway. In addition there was the problem of noise from aircraft constantly flying overhead. These factors caused considerable ill-feeling towards the US servicemen, often serious enough to threaten their safety outside the bases.

While the presence of the airmen and their families created problems on an already crowded island, it also brought benefits and provided opportunities in the economic sphere. The British economy has over the years profited from the expenditure of hundreds of millions of dollars by US forces. During 1953 the American military forces stationed in the United Kingdom meant a significant contribution to the economy, with the presence of over 35 000 personnel, mostly airmen, and 9000 of these officers and men accompanied by dependents. The monthly expenditure figures for that year, according to Third Air Force figures, were substantial:

> monthly expenditure of US service contracts to the British amount to 2 700 000 dollars and services in connection with the base exchange stores account for a further 1 370 000 dollars a month, of which 1 225 000 dollars is spent on British made items sold in exchange for stores and on the cost fixtures . . . 150 000 dollars are spent on civilian employees of military units and 5 800 000 dollars represents the monthly conversion of dollar instruments into sterling by US military personnel and dependents.[7]

This expenditure amounted to some $10 145 000 per month, and outstripped tourists as a dollar source for the United Kingdom. It was estimated that 'dollar earnings made available by the presence of American airmen and their dependents represent more than ten per cent of the total value of British exports, both visible and invisible, to the United States'.[8] To put the figure into perspective it represented £6 million more than the total carried by the tourist trade in 1952 and £12 million higher than the dollar profits on Scotch whisky. Apart from the local benefit to trade, the early years of the American bases created some side benefits for employment. It was decided, as part of a cost-cutting exercise by the Third Air Force, that almost four thousand American personnel would be replaced by British civilians. *The Herald Tribune* in 1953 estimated that the cost of 'sending a single US airman to Britain, maintaining and paying him there averages about £1750 pounds per annum. The average salaries for the Air Ministry replacements will be about £535 per annum'.[10] This, obviously, meant a slight boost in local employment levels.

The figures for 1985 show that the US forces still have a significant impact on Britain's economy. The financial impact[11] of the US Air Force, Army and Navy totalled £504 million (exchange rate calculated at $1.45 = £1.0). In addition 4000 British civilians are employed to help meet US needs (this contrasts with 2500 US civilians employed by the Third Air Force in Britain). These figures have to be balanced by the cost of the bases to the British government where all land used by US forces is provided rent-free and, where expansion has taken place, the British government has had to pay for the land required. Between 1973 and 1982 the British government spent £45 million[12] on new land for US bases. While the financial impact of US forces might still be significant for the British economy it should not be considered as a rationale for the continued presence or expansion of the US base network.

Alongside the economic effects of the American bases, there has been significant long-term social integration. During the first half of the 1950s records of the Third Air Force show that American airmen had married British women at the rate of 3000 annually. Such a procedure meant repeated visits of both prospective parties to the American base chaplain, who would explain the obligations and requirements of marrying a US serviceman. For American sevicemen, whether married or single, there is an impressive array of facilities available although accommodation still remains a problem. The early base facilities were spartan, but current facilities boast 'a rod and gun club, a skeet range, an eighteen lane bowling center' at RAF Bentwaters; Alconbury has schools for dependent children 'on base for all grades'; all have some form of social centre and some form of medical care, as well as larger wartime support hospitals like that at Little Rissington[13] or Upper Heyford. Perhaps the most curious importation to make US base life more like home can be seen upon arrival at RAF Lakenheath: there stands a bronze replica of the Statue of Liberty, dedicated on 25 November 1981 to commemorate the fortieth anniversary of RAF Lakenheath.[14]

However, as the American base network grew, both in the United Kingdom and elsewhere, the question of the legal status of the forces became increasingly pressing. By 1952 about 10 per cent of American military power deployed on the European side of the Atlantic was in the United Kingdom.[15] The legal position of American servicemen and British civilians employed by the United States Air Force was ambiguous under the 1942 United States (Visiting Forces) Act and demands to clarify it became more frequent as the numbers of the American forces reached a peak in 1954.

THE LEGAL STATUS OF AMERICAN FORCES IN THE UNITED KINGDOM

When American forces made their reappearance in peace-time Britain during the 'first real crisis of the Cold War', it was understood that since the stay was of an intermediate length the 1942 United States (Visiting Forces) Act was applicable. An earlier agreement recognised the right of 'sending states' to exercise jurisdiction over members of their forces, but granted no exemption from the jurisdiction of local courts in cases of offences against local law. This principle was recognised in the 1940 Allied Forces Act and applied to American forces by the United States (Visiting Forces) Act. The arrival of American forces in the United Kingdom during the Berlin crisis saw the United States government trying, according to its traditional policy, to gain exclusive rights of jurisdiction over its members. The 1942 Act provided that 'Subject as hereinafter provided, no criminal proceedings shall be prosecuted in the UK before any court of the United Kingdom against a member of the military or naval forces of the United States of America'.[16]

The United States has tried consistently to obtain exclusive jurisdiction of its forces abroad, whereas the United Kingdom has been firmly in favour of the principle of territorial sovereignty.

With the adoption of the United States (Visiting Forces) Act it was agreed that American servicemen who have committed offences in Britain were to be tried by American military courts. The American government could, however, ask for a particular case to be tried in a British court. This happened in one notable case, the 'Cleft Chin' murder of 1945, in which an American serviceman and a British civilian were jointly accused. Although as a general rule the United Kingdom and Canada 'do not recognise any principle of international law exempting visiting forces from local jurisdiction'[17] it was decided to enact this legislation because of the extraordinary wartime circumstances:

> It is a proposal unique in the constitutional history of this country, but the Government of the United States have been so ungrudging in the aid given to this country that if they expressed a desire for such legislation no one would hesitate to grant it.[18]

The 1942 United States (Visiting Forces) Act was a considerable departure from the traditional system and practice of the United Kingdom. The Act became operative on 27 July after an exchange of notes between the respective governments. The notes exchanged made it clear that the arrangements in respect of criminal jurisdiction should operate 'during the conduct of conflict against our common enemies and until 6 months (or such period as may be mutually agreed upon) after the final termination of such conflict'.[19] In fact the Act was still operative when the B-29s arrive in East Anglia during 1948. It was not until the American government – through Ambassador Douglas – suggested that USAF might want to increase their numbers that it became clear that the 'visit' was not so temporary and that it was infringing British sovereignty to allow such an Act still to exist. A further impetus towards revising the 1942 Act was the 17 March 1948 Treaty of Brussels. As part of the Treaty, an Agreement on the Status of the members of the Armed Forces of the signatory powers of the Treaty of Brussels was reached in December 1949. Although never put into force, it did inspire the NATO Status of Forces Agreement when in Article 7, paragraph 1, it declared that it was the 'duty of members of a foreign force to respect the laws in force in the receiving state and to abstain from any activity inconsistent with the spirit of the present agreement and, in particular, from any political activity.' The receiving state was to enjoy exclusive jurisdiction only when the offence against international law was not at the same time punishable under the law of the sending state.

The Brussels Treaty was an excellent excuse for the British government to apply pressure on the American government to change the 1942 Act. A memorandum to the State Department from the British Embassy made the government's position clear:

> Since it appears probable that United States forces will be stationed in this country for some time to come, and since the introduction of permanent legislation dealing with the position of visiting forces from the Brussels Treaty Powers would certainly result in attention being drawn to the existing temporary provisions with regard to US visiting forces. His Majesty's government feels that it has no alternative but to propose permanent legislation.[20]

The American reaction was swift and unequivocal. In a letter from Thomas Finletter to the Secretary of Defense, opposition to the revision of the 1942 Act, in part or whole, was made clear. The British remained adamant that revision was necessary on the grounds that the Commonwealth and Brussels Treaty countries with forces in Britain only had concurrent jurisdiction, whereas the United States had exclusive jurisdiction over her overseas forces under the 1942 Act. Finletter's letter to Secretary Johnson concluded that a 'repeal of the 1942 Act at this time might be viewed in the United States and elsewhere as an indication of a weakening of the past solidarity of the two countries'.[21]

The American opposition to a repeal of the United States (Visiting Forces) Act was seen as wholly indefensible from the British perspective. Although the United States government maintained pressure for a continuation of their exclusive jurisdiction it was pointed out that there exists 'no generally recognized rule of international law which extends the principle of immunity from jurisdiction, in the case of a sojourn of foreign troops by consent, in respect of offences against ordinary law'.[22] During 1948–50 there were reminders from the British that the 1942 Act seemed to cover the war period only. Lee Rankin, the Assistant Attorney-General, Office of Legal Counsel at the Department of Justice, reported that he had been 'advised that with the British, it [the 1942 agreement] was limited to the war period. The agreement gave us exclusive jurisdiction'.[23]

Britain indicated that it would terminate the 1942 Act and send notes to the relevant personnel on 30 April 1948 and again on 16 June 1950. The Department of State was said to have terminated the Act before the outbreak of Korean hostilities. During the year the United States (Visiting Forces) Act came to an end, the United States entered into public agreement including provisions with regard to jurisdiction over American forces in the United Kingdom. The discussions resulted in the new Visiting Forces Act of 1952, replacing the earlier United States (Visiting Forces) Act; but this did not become law until 12 June 1954. The 1952 Act was implemented in accord with the NATO Status of Forces Agreement, which has the effect of an international multilateral treaty. The SOFA was a purely NATO document and the Visiting Forces Act of 1952 was legislation enacted by the British parliament to implement SOFA. Under the SOFA, agreed between parties to the North Atlantic Treaty in London on 19 June 1951 and effective from 23 August 1953, the primacy of the territorial sovereign was recognised as a general principle, but it authorised the exercise of extraterritorial jurisdiction by the sending state in the receiving state's territory in certain cases. Whilst recognising jurisdiction over the sending state's forces by the host state, it was still a departure from the principle that a nation 'possesses and exercises within its own territory an absolute jurisdiction'.[24] The phrase 'absolute and exclusive jurisdiction' was defined by Lauterpacht to mean that 'all individuals and property within the territory of a state are under its dominion' and that a state must not 'perform acts of sovereignty in the territory of another state'.[25] However, the VFA of 1952 did recognise the *general* jurisdiction of the receiving state, and therefore marked a partial withdrawal from the unlimited powers of 1942.

The agreement between parties to the North Atlantic Treaty,

regarding the status of their forces, states in Article 2 that 'it is the duty of a force and its civilian components and members thereof as well as their dependents to respect the law of the receiving state, and to abstain from any activity inconsistent with the spirit of the present Agreement.' Article 7 went on to explain that 'the authorities of the receiving state shall have the right to exclusive jurisdiction over members of a force or civilian component and their dependents with respect to offences including offences relating to the security of that state, punishable by its law but not by the law of the sending state'.[26] The NATO Status of Forces Agreement outlined an exception to the principle of exclusive jurisdiction of the receiving state; names, when an act or commission was done in the performance of 'official duty'.[27]

Article 4 of the new Visiting Forces order dealt with the matter of jurisdiction.[28] Under the new agreement the United States government was given the right to exercise jurisdiction over offences committed in the territory of another sovereign state, where the accused is a member of the US forces. If a state of war exists, there is 'exclusive jurisdiction *wherever* the offence is committed,' if a state of war does *not* exist there is exclusive American jurisdiction over all offences committed and 'US interest offences' committed inside the leased areas. The US government was also given the right to exercise jurisdiction where the accused is a British subject or a local alien, and a civil court of the United States is sitting in the territory. Lastly, there is exclusive American jurisdiction where the accused is not a member of US armed forces, a British subject or local alien, but is a person subject to US military or naval law.

Under the Visiting Forces Act the receiving state has no jurisdiction over offences arising out of or during the execution of 'official duty'. The precise interpretation of this term has proved vague and difficult as the Girard Case revealed.[29] Although it is difficult to define precisely what is 'on duty', it is a generally recognised principle in international law that: 'No person carrying out an act as an agent of a State should be held personally responsible before the courts of another State for the criminal or civil consequences of that act, unless the Act itself should be a crime under international law'.[30] As far as legal precedents are concerned, the SOFA marked a radical departure from the laws governing forces abroad. The NATO bases are not considered 'foreign' bases because 'they do not depend on a foreign country but on a federal organization in which the receiving country participates, therefore they do not constitute "military bases" installed in a foreign country, but federal bases on which troops may stay'.[31]

The Visiting Forces Act of 1952 gave concurrent jurisdiction to the military and local courts in all classes of offence except those of a security breach, those committed in a leased area, or those of a military nature in which the United States had absolute right in the first instance to assume and exercise jurisdiction. Nothing was to restrict the jurisdiction of the United States in matters of discipline and internal administration. The Visiting Forces Act was necessary in order to apply the SOFA to the United Kingdom, because the Third Air Force was not assigned to NATO command.[32] (The Commanding-General of the Third Air Force, Major-General Griswold in this case, was directly responsible to the Commander-in-Chief, USAFE.)

A constant American fear of loss of constitutional rights under the SOFA led to a Senate resolution that no person under United States military jurisdiction can be deprived of, or denied in any way, the legal rights afforded by the US constitution. In accordance with this resolution, American military representatives are required to attend such courts to see that the legal rights of the accused are safeguarded. For the Third Air Force the most significant part of the Visiting Forces Act was Article 7, by which United States armed forces could surrender criminal jurisdiction and Article 8, by which claims against the USAF are processed, settled and paid by a British Claims Commission. The United States has jurisdiction over all offences committed in the line of duty, official duty cases and cases prejudicial to the security of the United States. The United States can, if it so wishes, waive its jurisdiction in these cases in favour of a British court. In other cases, one Third Air Force historian pointed out that 'generally speaking if a member of the United States military force commits an offence against British law, the British can try him and will try him'.[33]

The most significant effect of the 1952 Act was to correct the general impression that American military personnel were not amenable to the jurisdiction of British courts. Implementation of the agreement has been cumbersome and long-winded due to extra paperwork because it must report, witness, and monitor all cases tried before British courts. In addition to being difficult to implement, the Visiting Forces Act was by no means clear and left many ambiguities. Under Section 11(4), whether or not the offence is committed on duty is resolved by the issue of a certificate by the visiting force to be given to the 'appropriate authority of the sending country.' The position of the Coroners Court is also unclear under the Visiting Forces Act. The death of a Ramsgate cyclist who was in collision with a car driven by an on-duty American serviceman[34] illustrated this. In any case (like this) where an American serviceman is involved and an inquest is ordered, the coroner, upon hearing that a United States serviceman is involved, must adjourn the hearing and may only re-open the inquest with permission from the Home Secretary, thus causing long delays, unnecessary suffering and sometimes, for the sake of wider Anglo–American relations, trivial sentences.

Civilians hold the same status as the military under both SOFA and the Visiting Forces Act. These specify that civilian components of a foreign military force are regarded for jurisdictional purposes as members of the force. The basis of the jurisdictional rules of the NATO agreement is that civilian components are subject to the military rule and jurisdiction of the sending state, but to local law if the offence is committed 'off duty'. However the Supreme Court ruled in the culmination of six cases in 1960 that 'a civilian entitled as he is by the Sixth Amendment to trial by jury, cannot legally be made liable to the military law and jurisdiction in time of peace'.[35] As a consequence of this ruling the civilian component can only be tried by the courts of the receiving state. The Supreme Court decision, by conferring jurisdiction on the courts of the receiving state, was to render ineffective the safeguards of the NATO agreement whereby civilian components would in cases most closely affecting the force be subject to American military law and procedures.

In the case of families of members of the US forces the tendency has been for the receiving states to allow the sending state the same rights over dependents as the Agreement grants with respect to civilian components. Under Article 6 of the SOFA it was stipulated that the authorities of the force were the sole components to exercise jurisdiction over their members, including dependents. A later judgement by the US Supreme Court confused the situation and it is generally accepted that they are now tried by courts of the receiving state or, if a criminal offence, the case may be tried by civilian or military courts as agreed upon between civilian judicial authorities and military authorities.

The SOFA was ratified by Britain in 1954 and implemented by the Visiting Forces Act, and all NATO states had ratified SOFA by 1955 except Iceland. Although each NATO country had jurisdiction over crimes committed against the local population by members of a visiting force while off duty, it was clear that the United States still had a more general jurisdiction. The JCS recommended confidentially to the Secretary of Defense that 'we continue to seek exclusive jurisdiction over all US forces outside of NATO' and that 'when negotiating bilateral agreements with NATO countries for military rights, we seek a general government-level waiver of criminal jurisdiction which those countries will have by virtue of the Status of Forces agreement'.[36] The exercise of criminal jurisdiction by foreign tribunals over US citizens subject to military law in the case of 'serious offences' covers murder, rape, manslaughter, arson, robbery, larceny and related offences, burglary and related offences, forgery and aggravated assault.[37] (For a full breakdown of the exericise of criminal jurisdiction by foreign tribunals over US citizens subject to military law see Appendix 4, Table A4.2.)

The 1952 Visiting Forces Act helped to correct many of the difficulties of the exclusive jurisdiction that the United States had under the United States (Visiting Forces) Act of 1942. There is still little public awareness of the vast legal powers and immunities available to United States forces in Britain, whilst the open definition of what is 'on duty' remains. Presumably, stretched to an extreme, if a Cruise missile or other nuclear weapon in transit caused a devastating accident 'no one would have the right to sue the United States government for a pennyworth of damages'.[38] There have been several instances of magistrates and judges encountering difficulties or sometimes obstruction in dealing with US servicemen, and they have 'been dismayed to find that the Visiting Forces Act can make them powerless'.[39] There was the case of a 24-year-old man in 1958, who was struck and killed by a US serviceman's car near Northolt air base; although driving outside the base, the serviceman was tried by American courts because he was deemed to be engaged on 'official duty'. The parents of the deceased man tried to sue for damages, only to discover that the serviceman was back in the United States and no one appeared to answer the charge – not even a USAF or US government official. The judge presiding over this case commented that it did seem 'rather unfortunate if visiting soldiers or airmen could leave the country and leave an action of this kind to proceed in their absence . . . one would have thought that . . . the responsible authorities [would attend] to the material results of the judgement'.[40]

In short the Visiting Forces Act allows 'visiting' forces to carry arms and to police their own camps, as well as being immune from prosecution or civil proceedings in a 'receiving state' if they are carrying out 'official duties'. Immunity from prosecution in local courts also applies if the offence involved only US property or if only American servicemen were victims of the crimes against the person. In spite of the generous interpretation of official duties, some servicemen obviously feel that the Visiting Forces Act deprives them of their constitutional rights. One irate USAF captain wrote to his Congressman; 'This is to inform you that I, along with thousands of other servicemen serving overseas, am opposed to this so called Status of Forces Agreement which deprives us of our basic constitutional rights as American citizens.'[41]

During a crisis or war the United States intends to obtain more extensive powers under an emergency Status of Forces Agreement which, once signed, would give 'local US commanders the right to deploy nuclear weapons and military forces as they pleased and the right to quell local disorders by any 'unilateral' means necessary.'[42] However, Britain, unique amongst her NATO partners, was exempted from the emergency SOF agreement. This was in part due to the fact that the United States already enjoys considerable powers under the Visiting Forces Act and it is generally assumed that in time of emergency United States commanders would have complete jurisdiction.

Despite some well-documented problems with the Visiting Forces Act, there is a general tendency towards co-operation between our civil legal process and US military law. There is also considerable sensitivity to potential legal problems, highlighted by the fact that it has been British, not American, military forces and police who have dealt with imposters at Greenham Common. The risk of an American serviceman injuring or perhaps even killing a demonstrator is too great for US forces to take in front of the British press, although under the Visiting Forces Act they could be acting on 'official duty' in so doing. Much still revolves around the problem of defining what is 'on duty', which must be balanced against the political sensitivity of host and sending nations to one another's interests.

7 Consolidation: Part 2 1954–63

The years 1954–63 marked a thaw in international relations followed by a crisis. In terms of Anglo–American relations, it was a crisis followed by a thaw. The crisis were occasioned by Cuba and Suez respectively. With the exception of the Suez debacle, bilateral relations were good, but the bases in the United Kingdom became increasingly expensive, with the built-in problem of bomber vulnerability. The period was marked by a general intensification of US overseas basing; in the United Kingdom's case this was particularly noticeable with the introduction of Thor missiles. By 1963, the high point of British integration with US forces had been reached in tactical, strategic and intelligence collaboration.

In the wider international arena, the Soviet Union demonstrated arms reduction of a unilateral nature that the United States showed no signs of reciprocating. For example, the return of Porkkala naval base by the Soviet Union to Finland in January 1956 was a major political coup for Soviet diplomacy. Khrushchev expressed the political and strategic significance of this move when he observed that 'it was high time to demonstrate that we had no territorial claims on Finland and no intention of forcing Socialism on the Finns at bayonet point'.[1] The return of Porkkala was related to the conclusion of the Austrian State Treaty and the removal of Soviet troops from Austria; the Soviet Union had already returned Port Arthur to the People's Republic of China[2] long before the issue of Porkkala arose. The Soviet Prime Minister Bulganin argued that:

> It was incontestable that the removal of military bases situated on foreign territory by other states also would significantly assist the further relief of international tension and would assist the creation of the conditions for ending of the arms race.[3]

In the case of Porkkala, technological developments since the end of the Second World War had made it possible for the Soviet Union to close off the Gulf of Finland from its southern coast, thus making the need for a military base on both sides of the Gulf Otiose. Nevertheless, the unilateral reduction taken together marked significant political concessions: but these were not seen as gestures worth emulating in

Washington. The crisis in superpower relations that culminated in Cuba in 1962 was to illustrate once again the importance of military bases in the global military balance and international diplomacy.

THE THOR ERA

In response to a question in the House of Commons at the beginning of 1954, the Prime Minister stated categorically that 'the arrangements for United States Air Force use of bases in this country will continue so long as it is needed in the general interests of world peace and security'.[4] Churchill recognised that the United Kingdom was still in the 'front line', but a general policy of rearming in conjunction with the United States and making strong defence arrangements had played a significant role in the diminution of international tension. Would this be true in the years that followed? Would advancing missile technology make the bases obsolete? Were American bases protecting the United Kingdom or making it more of a target for the Soviet Union? Were the bases serving the general interests of Western peace and security, or those of the United States? These and many other questions were prevalent in the minds of policy makers from Churchill downwards.

In the second part of this study, the focus will be upon the changing role of the US defence bases when, at the end of 1954, the NATO Council adopted a tactical nuclear doctrine placing greater stress on the role of nuclear weapons in deterring any likely Soviet aggression. During the same year the first signs of renewed American willingness to share atomic information appeared in the new Atomic Energy Act amending (at Eisenhower's request) the McMahon Act,[5] empowering the President to transfer to 'friendly powers of regional defense organizations' data on the tactical use of atomic weapons, as well as information on training for atomic warfare and an evaluation of the atomic capabilities of potential enemies. The veto on exchange of information concerning the construction and design of atomic weapons remained until the amendment of the McMahon Act in July 1958. Churchill had also welcomed the President's 'Atoms for Peace' proposal and subsequently published the text of the Quebec Agreement of 1943.[6] The decision to publish the agreement was made apparently with the idea that the Labour attack on British inability to influence American policy on atomic tests ought to be turned against those who had effectively waived British rights in 1948. Congress was furious when details of the Quebec Agreement came to light. In Britain the lack of any real control over the American use of the bomb was not generally realised by Parliament, since the government successfully blocked attempts to make the *modus vivendi* public. The only thing the government could depend upon was a pledge given by Eisenhower to Churchill reconfirming the earlier agreement made with Truman, promising consultation on the circumstances in which the bomb might be used, and also suggesting consultation about the targets against which it should be deployed. In spite of the apparent closeness between Eisenhower and Churchill Anglo–American relations were felt to be strained partly because of open difficulties between the respective Foreign Ministers, Anthony Eden and John Foster Dulles, and differences of opinion over the French struggle in Laos.

The explosion by the Soviet Union of a hydrogen bomb in August 1953, less than two years after America's, alongside evidence of Soviet success in building ballistic missiles and of continuing Soviet superiority in conventional forces in Europe (in part due to the failure of NATO countries to meet the Lisbon goals),[7] led the United States to search for new ways of strengthening the North Atlantic Alliance. In December 1954 the North Atlantic Council, by authorising military commanders to plan for the use of nuclear weapons, was in effect giving a 'green light' to the shipment of tactical nuclear weapons to Western Europe. The first tactical US missiles appeared in Europe the same year stationed in Germany with the warheads under strict US custody.[8] The fears of growing Soviet military might led to the beginning of moves to place intermediate range nuclear weapons in Europe, culminating in the deployment of Thor and Jupiter missiles.

The deployment of IRBM's has often led to an underestimation of the effectiveness and size of the American Air forces in Europe; but by the end of 1957, when Thor was deployed in Britain, the Third Air Force, under the command of Major-General Ernest Moore, comprised four tactical wings, three offensive and one defensive. The atomic offensive wings were at Wethersfield (the 20th Fighter Bomber Wing equipped with F-100D Super Sabres), Bentwaters (81st Fighter Bomber Wing utilising F-84s) and Sculthorpe (the 47th Bombardment Wing (Tactical) using B-45 type aircraft). All of these aircraft could carry nuclear weapons and were NATO-committed under SACEUR's Atomic Strike Plan. The defensive wing, the 406th Fighter Interceptor Wing, was located at Manston, Kent, and used F-86 Sabres. In addition to the Third Air Force there were also the Twelfth Air Force and Seventeenth Air Forces under jurisdiction of USAFE commanded by General Frank F. Everest. The Seventh Air Division under SAC control was commanded by Major-General William H. Blanchard, who administered the 'Reflex' programme – under which combat-ready wings were rotated from their bases in the United States to overseas training stations. Both the Third Air Force and Seventh Air Division were supported by the Northern Air Material Area at Burtonwood and a sub-depot at Brize Norton. There were at this stage 43 000 American military personnel in the UK, 35 000 dependents and about 1000 US civilians. Thor was to mark a significant but, in terms of the overall American force levels in the United Kingdom, small development.

Apart from internecine British party quarrelling, the critical year for the future of United States defence bases in the United Kingdom was 1957. It was in this year that strenuous efforts were made on both sides to pick up Anglo–American relations from the all-time low they had reached during the Suez crisis. After the Suez crisis, Winston Churchill, no longer Prime Minister, wrote a long letter to President Eisenhower.[9] The letter, unknown to the Foreign Office or Secretariat at 10 Downing Street, appealed for the restoration of close ties between the two countries. The United States desperately needed UK bases which was the incentive to restore relations. The new Prime Minister, Harold Macmillan, who came to office in January 1957, made the restoration of relations a cornerstone of his foreign policy. The proposal to deploy IRBM's on British soil was put forward by Eisenhower in January and agreed to, initially as a bilateral arrangement outside NATO, at the Bermuda meeting between the two heads of state on 21–24 March 1957.

In the wake of the Soviet launching of Sputnik on 4 October 1957 and the threat of a 'missile gap' that American observers believed to exist between the superpower nuclear arsenals, the US presented a plan to the NATO Council in December to disperse IRBMs in Europe. Italy and Turkey were the only other allies to respond positively. The 'missile gap' theory, later determined to be, if not false, based on overemphasis of the Soviet arsenal, was nonetheless influential. IRBMs in Europe and the Pacific would give the United States the capability to mount pre-emptive strikes on Russian bases from close quarters, with a reduction in warning time compared to intercontinental strikes. It was agreed bilaterally at the Bermuda meeting that Britain was to be given sixty Thor missiles, and, as a new sign of trust and restored relations, the weapon was to be deployed under a 'dual-key' system. The missiles were to be based on US bases in East Anglia, with the warheads provided by the United States and the supporting facilities by Britain. Further signs of co-operation were evident when in October two technical committees were established under Sir Richard Powell[11] and Admiral Lewis Strauss[12] to consider collaboration on weapons systems and the nuclear field respectively. The growing evidence of co-operation resulted in the amendment of the Atomic Energy Act of 1954 in 1958, thus opening the way to shared nuclear information and strategic planning.

To explain away the strategic necessity of the IRBMs in Europe, as merely a temporary measure before America's successful development of ICBMs sufficient to fill the 'missile gap', would be inadequate. While it is true that the US programme did provide a hedge against difficulties in the ICBM programme, implicit in the logic was the idea that the sooner ICBMs could cover all the targets of interest, the sooner the need for IRBMs would fade. The reaction of the Soviet Union to IRBM deployments in Europe 'suggested that IRBMs were not for them just a temporary stop-gap until a sufficient arsenal of ICBM had been built-up'.[13] The Soviet Union had always had an interest in targeting both the United States and Western Europe and the introduction of Matador and Thor missiles into Europe provided not only a target but implied the need for two different kinds of weapons, ICBMs and IRBMs.

The American executive branch at this stage had a very different view of nuclear weapons to that held by subsequent governments. A senior defence analyst observed that, 'nuclear weapons were viewed as simply another piece of conventional artillery . . . from the perspective of the 1950s, the decision to send nuclear weapons to Europe was a natural one'.[14] It was only with the advent of the H-bomb that serious moral and political fears were voiced since the weapon implied a different threat. It was in this context that the United States has approached the British government to request permission to store nuclear weapons, and was now seeking permission to station medium range ballistic missiles in order to compensate for the 'missile gap' and for the deficit in NATO's European-bases missile arsenal. After considerable resistance on the part of some European allies permission was granted to station a total of 150 IRBMs in Europe. Sixty Thor missiles were to go to Britain and forty-five Jupiter missiles each to Italy and Turkey. Accompanying the fear of the 'missile gap' was the urge to regain (or retain) the advantages that the United States had enjoyed in the use of advanced bases overseas, during the era when

strategic bombing depended wholly on manned bombers. The installation of IRBMs on the Soviet periphery seemed to herald a return by
the United States, at least to equality, if not superiority. Deployment
of the IRBMs was, however, far slower than anticipated and at the
start of 1959, the only American IRBMs actually sited in Europe were
those in the United Kingdom. The arrangements for use of the missiles
were seen as a renewed sign of Anglo–American trust, since they were
deployed under a 'two-key' system.

The deployment of Thor was to coincide with a formative stage in
British defence planning, which in turn cast light upon the Anglo–
American relationship. In 1957 the Minister of Defence, Duncan
Sandys, presented a White Paper to the House of Commons. During
the course of its presentation, he remarked:

> So long as American forces remain in Europe, and American
> bombers are based in Britain, it might conceivably be thought safe –
> I am not saying that it would – to leave to the United States the sole
> responsibility for providing the nuclear deterrent. But, when they
> have developed the 5000 mile intercontinental ballistic rocket, can
> we really be sure that every American administration will go on
> looking at things in the same way?[15]

The decision outlined in this notable White Paper[16] was one to give
the H-bomb the main role in British defence policy, cutting many
things to make that possible including national service by 1960. In spite
of the plans put forward in the White Paper regarding the need for a
central role for the H-bomb[17] (which Denis Healey dismissed later as 'a
virility symbol to compensate for the exposure of its military impo-
tence at Suez'), the Thor missiles were seen as advantageous for
defence because Britain had no rocket deterrent, and was thus given a
deterrent long before she could hope to produce one herself. Such a
move would also provide full training for future British missile
regiments. Thor also illustrated a paradox in British military planning;
on the one hand, Britain recognised her interdependence with the
United States but, on the other, the 1957 White Paper marked a British
desire for independence from the United States.

A fortnight after the launching of Sputnik on 4 October 1957, which
had demonstrated Soviet scientific and potential military might,
Macmillan saw Eisenhower in Washington and issued a 'Declaration
of Common Purpose'. In spite of the prompt and easy acceptance of
Thor missiles in Britain, all allies, with the exception of Italy and
Turkey, refused the IRBMs. On 19 February 1958, the Anglo–

American Agreement on the stationing of IRBMs in Britain was published and, according to the Prime Minister, 'caused little hostile comment'.[18] Under the agreement, it was specified in Clause 2 that the United Kingdom 'shall provide the sites and supporting facilities required for the deployment of the missiles.' In Clause 4 it specified that the missiles would be manned and operated by United Kingdom personnel, trained by the US government 'for the purpose of this project at the earliest feasible date.' But under Clause 8 it specified that 'all nuclear warheads so provided shall remain in full US ownership, custody and control in accordance with US law.' Most important of all was Clause 7:

> The decision to launch these missiles will be a matter of joint decision by the two governments. Any such decision will be made in the light of the circumstances at the time and having regard to the undertaking the two governments have assumed in Article 5 of the North Atlantic Treaty.[19]

In terms of Anglo–American strategic relations, this agreement represented a growth of British influence – at least when compared with the Amercian SAC bases, where Britain had no practical veto. It was to this extent 'a triumph for British diplomacy and an outward proof of our restored relations.'[20] Time has mellowed this judgement to a degree. Britain had in effect agreed to buy,[21] man and deploy a missile to which it could not fit its own warhead. Given the British veto over the use of the Thor missiles, their role as a deterrent was restricted to general NATO purposes approved by both the United Kingdom and America. The joint Thor headquarters and missile bases at Feltwell, North Luffenham, Hemswell and Great Driffield, along with their charge of four missiles bases each (three missiles were to be stationed at each base including the four joint Thor headquarters, making a total of sixty missiles), could not be adapted for use by any other missiles and cost the British government roughly £10 million.[22] It must also be borne in mind that US bombers were still to form the basis of the Western deterrent for some years to come.

Britain had agreed to help the United States bridge the 'missile gap' at a certain financial cost to itself, and more seriously, owing to the vulnerability of Thor which invited a pre-emptive blow, at considerable danger. The first squadron of Thor missiles in Britain became operational in June 1959, by which time the Soviet Union had deployed IRBMs which made these liquid-fuelled, fixed 'soft' missiles very vulnerable:

They were more clearly a Russian first-strike target than even the SAC bases, because of the greater probability that they could be knocked out completely on the ground and the negligible probability that anything could be done about the missiles once they were fired.[23]

In spite of the fact that the opposition urged the postponement of Thor's deployment, the Government took the line that they were no more provocative than the United States bomber bases in Britain. Unlike the case with current deployment of GLCMs, the American administration never claimed that the deployment of IRBMs were in European interests. The prime purpose was to reduce the likelihood of a Soviet ICBM strike against American targets for a three-year period, before the United States herself possessed ICBMs in significant numbers.

If Britain's agreement to deploy Thor American IRBMs was seen as a 'triumph for British diplomacy', she was less enthusiastic about Thor's effectiveness as a missile. General LeMay, in his testimony before a Congressional session, confided that 'the British never were very enthusiastic about Thor as a weapons system'.[24] The last Thors were installed in 1960, when the sixtieth operational missile was airlifted to Britain. Even before the full complement had been installed, doubts about the technical reliability of the weapon were well known. The *New Statesman* talked of Thor developing an 'uncomfortable wobble' in flight, along with the fact that before their deployment only five of the ten tests were successful. IRBMs had been deployed in this state partly because of the panic engendered by the 'missile gap', and partly because the development of ICBMs assumed higher priority in American military circles. Early in 1958 Neil McElroy, Secretary of Defense, was inclined to give emphasis to the quick deployment of IRBMs, in order to allow more time to make crucial decisions on ICBMs. Secretary McElroy testified before the House of Representatives that, in his opinion, the Department of Defense should take a 'calculated risk and move faster than the testing results could in themselves justify'[25] in preparing for the deployment of Thor and Jupiter. On 20 February 1958 the 705th Strategic Missile Wing (IRBM–Thor) was activated at RAF Lakenheath and assigned to the 7th Air Division. A few months later the 705th merged with the 7th Air Division headquarters at South Ruislip.

Shortly after the initial deployments in Italy of two squadrons (30 missiles) of Jupiter missiles, Turkey agreed to take a squadron of

Jupiter IRBMs.[26] The Sub-Committee of the Congressional Joint Committee on Atomic Energy recommended, on 11 February 1961, that the Italian Jupiters be replaced by mobile IRBMs and that the Turkish deployment be halted, largely because of security fears that the thick skinned liquid-fuelled missiles were vulnerable to sabotage and first-strike missile attacks. A subsequent recommendation stated that the Polaris submarine operated by US personnel should be assigned to NATO, in lieu of the fifteen obsolete Jupiter missiles due for Turkish deployment – but this met with a firm refusal from the Turkish government. There were similar, less well publicised reasons for fear about the vulnerability of Thor missiles in Britain.

Much confusion seemed to surround the technical aspect of the Thor missile. Firstly, tha actual deployment time was claimed to be anything from fifteen minutes to several hours. The Deputy Secretary of Defense, James Douglas, testifying before the Senate Appropriations Committee, claimed 'When I say the sites could be brought up to a quick reaction time, missiles could be fired. The goal would be 15 minutes. I would state with certainty that they could be fired within 20 minutes to half an hour if not 15 minutes. I am being conservative'.[27] Even allowing for some unfamiliarity with the missiles on the part of RAF personnel, Secretary Douglas did admit that in reality the launch time was vastly different; 'with the decision of the Air Ministry and ourselves the whole squadron could be brought to a quick reaction capability in a reasonable length of time. You cannot do it in an hour . . . I said in a hearing that it was a matter of quite a number of hours, and this is the case'.[28]

Senator Stuart Symington visited the first Thor squadron in Britain on a fact-finding mission, and found the missiles stored in sheds with 'no protection of any kind' connected to 'little trailers'. Each shed was designed to slide off the launcher in a horizontal fashion to expose the missile. It was agreed that the Senator would have a demonstration countdown: however this failed, even after Senator Symington had left and came back an hour or so later.[29] Senator Symington's testimony thus made the vulnerability and unreliability of the Thor missiles obvious.[30] Scarcely two years previously, the Secretary of Defense, then Neil McElroy, had extolled the benefits of advanced bases with an IRBM capability giving 'less probability of error compared to the ICBM projects and much greater control because of the shorter distance'.[31] It would appear that if anybody was being duped into a false sense of security, it was the British public, although some in the American administration including the new Secretary of Defense,

Thomas Gates, had doubts about Thor's reliability.

The agreement to station Thors in Britain, signed by Christian Herter and Sir Harold Caccia, launched a tirade of publicity and outspoken opinions. One of the Washington papers on 25 February 1958 published a headline declaring, 'US to set up four bases in Britain for firing 1500 mile Thor missiles.' Dulles, the Secretary of State, was quick to observe that it was 'a little unfortunate to have headlines that give the impression that these are American bases . . . they are really joint bases in the sense that they are to be used in accordance with the principles of the North Atlantic Treaty'.[32] In Britain on 1 March, nearly 10 000 people poured onto the streets in a nationwide demonstration against the rocket bases; and a march, led by the Communist Party General Secretary, John Gollan, of some 4000 people paraded through South Ruislip. The *Daily Worker* chose to celebrate the occasion with the headline 'GI Joe, You Gotta Go!'[33] Much of the uneasiness about the missile bases was wide of the mark since, in principle, they were no different from the American bomber bases that far outnumbered the missile bases in numbers and destructive potential.

In retrospect the British government could be criticised for accepting Thor missiles on grounds of cost, reliability, preparation time and vulnerability. In the Western haste to keep pace with the Soviet arms build-up, Britain had allowed the United States to persuade her to take a weapon which America technology had developed but which, owing to its short range, would have been quite useless to America alone. The drawbacks to the system were further revealed when it was realised that, aside from pre-emptive use, there was scarcely enough time to use Thor in retaliation before a Soviet second strike. The following actions had to be completed in order to launch the missiles: (1) a decision made that Russian aggression had started; (2) a launch order sent to the Thor bases; (3) the American-guarded warheads then turned over to British firing crews; (4) jointly the warhead fitted to the missile; and (5) the missile then fired for launching – which in fact required a whole convoy of trucks and personnel ranging from fuel tenders (and hence, fire units, since the fuel was volatile liquid oxygen which was super-cooled so that the missiles had to be used immediately or stood down) to compressors, launch vehicles and command posts. It was, in short, difficult to imagine all the steps being successfully carried out.[34]

The presence of Thor also led to a wider debate about the future of American bases in Britain. In a forthright manner, Richard Crossman put the Thor deployments into perspective:

Whether or not we have these weapons makes very little difference to our military dependence on the USA. The government's attitude to Thor proves that up to the hilt. There is no question of getting rid of the Americans. On the Contrary they are here 'for keeps' and we are to become a rocket base instead of being a bomber base as now . . . can we be militarily independent of America? On the contrary. The Suez fiasco revealed that.[35]

Although the obsolenscence of the Thor missiles was recognised in 1963 and the last missile withdrawn by August of that year, the value of having intermediate range missiles in Europe *as well* as intercontinental range missiles in the United States had long been accepted contrary to the admonitions that the IRBMs were a stop-gap measure until the successful development of ICBMs. In a debate on the Mutual Security Act of 1958, it was pointed out that even if the United States had predominantly ICBMs, the 'value of bases with shorter range missiles on them is that it makes it more impossible for the Russians to knock everything out simultaneously and, therefore, adds to the retaliatory capacity which in itself, is the deterrent to their starting a war'.[36]

The deployment of Thor missiles in Britain followed incidents that heightened anxiety over American basing in the United Kingdom, and reawakened questions concerning the status and control of United States bases in Britain. The first incident involved an American colonel by the name of Zinc; the second concerned reconnaissance missions from the United Kingdom.

On 27 February 1958, the American and British governments were embarrassed and surprised by a statement made by an American Air Force officer, Colonel Zinc.[37] He was to command the first Thor IRBM ballistic missile squadron (the 705th Strategic Missile Wing) in Britain, and therefore he claimed to have in his hands 'full operational control of rockets and rocket bases in Britain.' This statement, obviously, was directly at odds with the earlier Anglo–American agreement consenting to the installation of Thor missiles on British soil, providing that 'missiles shall not be launched except by a joint positive decision by both governments'.[38] Duncan Sandys had gone to considerable lengths to stress 'governments', not military commanders, would be the decision-makers. The Prime Minister, Macmillan, described the strange affair in his memoirs:

There was a great flap this morning over an extraordinary statement by a Colonel Zinc – an American 'Eagle Colonel' of the Air Force who claims to be about to take over command of the rockets/rocket bases in Britain. As this was in direct contradiction (a) to the terms of the agreement published last Monday and (b) what we told Parliament on Monday and in the debate yesterday, Colonel Zinc has put his foot in it on a grand scale.[39]

Although Colonel Zinc was quickly corrected by a Pentagon statement, explaining he was responsible only for training activities, it caused enough alarm for Macmillan to bring up the question of control over the missiles at a meeting with the President on 7 June. The meeting resulted in American assurances that the agreements arising out of the Bermuda discussions[40] were adequate and clear.

The Zinc case echoed an earlier political debate in Parliament about the carriage of nuclear weapons by USAF from British bases on security flights around the coast of Britain (the aircraft also carried the apparatus for arming them). The Prime Minister replied that the 'carriage of weapons is a normal feature of training and patrol, and I should expect to be kept informed by the United States Air Force of developments in its programme as new weapons come into service'.[41] The bombs on board the aircraft would not be armed, unless an order was given after agreement by both governments. The Prime Minister argued that there was indeed a case to be made in favour of a rapidly armed H-bomber in the air around our shores because 'if we are in favour of the deterrent and are to reply on the policy of the deterrent, the greater its efficiency the more likely it is to achieve its purpose, which is the prevention of war'.[42]

Doubts were also raised in Parliament about whether the agreements governing American forces stationed in the United Kingdom applied to units of the Seventh Air Division used for long-distance operations refuelling, but not actually based in the United Kingdom. Macmillan was quick to assuage doubts when he assured Parliament that 'all types, including aircraft not permanently stationed in this country' are covered by the 1952 agreements. These and many other questions, although not new, typified the unease felt with the stationing of nuclear missiles in Britain whilst pressure for a 'more formal' agreement continued. The political apprehensiveness felt with such a situation was further exacerbated by the notorious RB-47 incident.

On 1 July 1960, an American RB-47 aircraft[43] set out from Brize Norton airfield in Oxfordshire. It was never to return. The aircraft, as stated in the official explanation, disappeared while on an 'electromagnetic' survey over the Arctic Ocean. Ten days later the Soviet authorities announced that the aeroplane had been shot down over

Soviet territorial waters. This was soon followed by a strong warning to the British government of the dangerous consequences that might follow this 'provocative act of the American Air Force operating from British territory.'

The official United States reply on 13 July to the Soviet Union's allegation insisted that the RB-47 was not flying over Russian territory when it was chased and shot down by Russian fighters. During the period between the Soviet accusation of spying activities and the American reply there was a dispute in the House of Commons, and the question of American aircraft flying from British bases was once again a political issue. The RB-47 incident was a particularly sensitive issue, following the ill-fated espionage mission across the Urals flown by CIA pilot Gary Powers from Peshawar in Pakistan in May 1960. The question of defining the phrase 'in an emergency' laid down in the January 1952 communiqué arose, as did doubts of whether the Truman–Attlee agreement on 'joint decisions' covered such activities as the reconnaissance flight of the RB-47 or U-2 types.

Parliament was deeply split over the RB-47 incident. Philip Noel-Baker asked the Prime Minister whether reconnaissance flights were covered by the Truman–Attlee agreements. Macmillan claimed that there were 'occasionally mistakes . . . but broadly we have consultations and agreements for operations which we regard as essential, if there is to be a deterrent and if its value and strength is to be maintained'.[44] Emrys Hughes reminded the House about Churchill's warning of the dangers to this country caused by creating American bomber bases in Britain.[45] He also added that the latest incident had 'burned into the minds' of the English people the dangers of the bases agreement, and that 'they expected the Prime Minister to speak for the people of this country and not to be a mere puppet of the Pentagon'.[46] The Prime Minister was quick to retort and defend the Attlee and Churchill agreements with President Truman:

> I am bound to say there are those of us who feel that the presence of United States bases in this country is . . . a threat to national security. There are many more of us who feel that their absence would be an even greater threat.[47]

Denis Healey questioned the purpose of the RB-47 flights and in particular NASA's explanation of 'routine weather flights'. In the face of concerted attack that was joined by Hugh Gaitskell, who spoke of US bases in the United Kingdom as being used for 'various expeditions' of one kind or another, it became clear that the circumstances surrounding the original agreements were different from those of 1960. Macmillan was content to answer Gaitskell by observing that it was not 'a question of a written formal agreement. There was not one before. *All kinds of activities* went on from 1948 onwards under all governments'.[48] Exactly what 'all kinds of activities' meant became clearer as time passed by, but it was obvious that reconnaissance flights of the RB-47 type had been occurring regularly, with both American and British aircraft involved. The Prime Minister refused under pressure either to reveal the decision-making procedure to be followed before any operational use of nuclear forces stationed in the United Kingdom, ot to sanction reconnaissance flights from US bases. Publication of such issues was deemed 'not in the public interests'.

From an international perspective, the issue was closed by a formal reply to the Soviet note on 19 July. The British reply concluded:

> Her Majesty's Government cannot agree that the use of United Kingdom territory by the United States Air Force for legitimate operations in international air space can in any way be regarded as an aggressive action, and accordingly cannot accept the allegations contained in the Ministry's note.

Information now available shows that the scope of US reconnaissance activities from United Kingdom bases was far greater than Macmillan was prepared to reveal for fear of endangering national security.[49] During a US Senate enquiry into the Gary Powers affair, it was discovered that Lakenheath had been used for U-2 operations.

The U-2 reconnaissance flights were initiated after the Killan Committee report entitled *The Threat of Surprise Attack*. A sub-committee under Edwin Land of Polaroid stressed the need for greater intelligence and reconnaissance facilities. The CIA duly agreed to finance the construction, out of 'reserve funds', of a high altitude reconnaissance aircraft that could overfly the Soviet Union on photographic missions to record Soviet military preparations on the ground. During the summer of 1955, the first U-2s and a squadron of pilots (former USAF pilots, but now on the CIA payroll) were moved to Lakenheath. As soon as they arrived, the Prime Minister, then Anthony Eden, refused permission for them to use Lakenheath. Britain herself had muddied Soviet relations by sending a frogman, Lionel Crabbe, to spy on a Russian war vessel which was on a goodwill visit to Britain. He was later found drowned. Eden was thus in no mood to be further embarrassed by becoming involved in American espionage activities. Chancellor Adenauer had no such qualms, and allowed them to use Wiesbaden airbase. This apparently was not the end of the story:

> What the Soviet Union never discovered was that, despite Eden's ban on British involvement, the RAF and SIS soon became mixed up in the U-2 operation . . . The Americans decided that a convenient way to maximize their chances of permission for overflights was to convert the exercise into a joint Anglo–American operation, but to do it on such terms that *either* the Prime Minister *or* the President could authorize a flight by either British or US personnel . . . The idea was accepted by the British government, and a number of RAF pilots were brought to the United States, trained on U-2s in Nevada, and then became part of the U-2 operation in Turkey. Like their fellow fliers among the Americans, they 'resigned' their commissions and became 'civilians'.[50]

In spite of President Eisenhower's assurance to the Soviet Union that such flights would be discontinued in future, this did not satisfy Sir Harry Legge-Bourke, who said that 'one of the greatest anxieties which people in this country have is lest the military machine should become the dictator of political policy'.[51] Norman Dodds argued in the House of Commons that 'many people doubt that any American politicians will be able to control successfully the American military machine and as a consequence there will now be more doubt than ever as to the value of the bases here'.[52] In spite of the apparent confidence in the 1952 agreement by Macmillan's government, there was enough underlying anxiety to merit a delegation, led by the Foreign Office Deputy Under-Secretary, Sir Patrick Deane, to visit Washington in order to discuss the Churchill–Truman understandings. Although the documents have yet to be released, it is apparent that the understanding were not modified.

The debate sparked off by the RB-47 incident was to rumble on, and statements made by each successive government did little to clarify the argument. In spite of pressures for change in the Truman–Churchill agreement, new understandings reached with the Kennedy administration merely reconfirmed earlier ones. The Prime Minister made it clear, after discussions with the new American administration, that the British government's only real freedom over US bases was that of terminating the entire arrangement. Macmillan observed that the British government was free because the forces were located in Britain, but the American government was not free with respect to her forces located here; and 'as a matter of practice, there is an understanding which I had with President Eisenhower and now have with President Kennedy that neither of us would think of using power of this kind without consultation with each other; but that does not take away the independent right of both the American and British governments'.[53] The scepticism surrounding the reliability of Thor, alongside the RB-47 incident, served as cautionary notes against excessive dependence on the United States, which could lead to policies or actions which were not in Britain's national interest. Without her own nuclear deterrent, Britain would be in a weak position to argue. The RB-47 incident also stressed Britain's growing importance as a major reconnaissance base, and there are to this day regular flights from Mildenhall, where the 6954th Electronic Security Squadron is stationed, using, amongst other aircraft, the sophisticated 'Black Widow' spy plane.

THE CHANGING ROLE OF UNITED KINGDOM BASES

The Thor missiles, whose obsolescence had long been recognised, were eventually withdrawn in 1963; their disappearance overlapped with some important changes in US basing policy in the United Kingdom. Contrary to the anticipated pattern, whereby a diminishing reliance on manned bombers from expensive overseas bases would be replaced by ICBMs and long-range jet bombers, the force levels in the United Kingdom remained much the same. This was largely because the role of the defence bases was subtly changing, a change that actually stressed the importance and value of overseas bases to the United States. A report prepared within the US Department of Defense confidently concluded:

> Overseas bases will continue to play an essential role in the national defense for the next decade and the advent of the ICBM and the SLBM will not eliminate or reduce substantially the requirements for overseas bases . . . there is a continuing need for the forward deployment of other ground, sea and air forces in being close to potential trouble spots to deter or deal swiftly with any military action against areas of the free world.[54]

The bulk of the American strategic deterrent overseas in the 1960s comprised 'reflex' forces with a quick reaction time, but the arsenal was increasingly being supplemented by battlefield nuclear weapons. The bases in the UK, apart from hosting a major part of America's

European 'reflex' forces, were also in demand for peacetime storage, communications, tracking and intelligence facilities. However, despite the continuing need for such bases, there was also a sombre warning in a report prepared for the President that America should 'seek to limit dependence on a single base, or group of bases. . . . Given the increasing diplomatic and political cost of maintaining base and facility rights overseas, we should make every effort to dispose in whole or part of outmoded or unnecessary facilities'.[55] Thus, in response to political considerations, the bases in Morocco were scheduled for release in 1963, and a few years later, under constant attack from General de Gaulle and the French military withdrawal from NATO, the United States saw her greatest base loss. Many of the American units in France were relocated in Germany and in the United Kingdom under operation FRELOC, a move that further emphasised the importance of the United Kingdom as an American military base complex. The growing Polaris fleet also meant a major naval base development programme to which the Holy Loch base was to be central. The growth of SLBM technology alongside the development of land-based missile technology that in turn required 'flight maps', meant the growing requirement for a world-wide communication network which, in the words of the 1960 report, is mandatory in order to insure adequate control of modern military forces with atomic weapons, to facilitate the transmission of intelligence to the United States and to administer the deployed forces'.[53]

From the mid-1950s onwards, the role of the SAC bases in the United Kingdom was to maintain 'Reflex' forces of medium bombers (mainly B-47s). Reflex operations began at Upper Heyford, Greenham Common and Fairford in January 1958 and at Brize Norton in April after the 100th Bomb Wing finished the last of its 90-day rotational assignments. 'Reflex' operations were based on the premise that a few crews and aircraft on ground alert at overseas bases would be more effective than maintaining complete wings at these bases on 90-day rotational training duty. Between 1960 and 1963 the medium bomber inventory in the USAF was reduced by forty squadrons, while missile forces (mainly ICBMs) increased by twenty-five squadrons. Up until the mid-1950s most medium bombers had been stationed in the United States (known as ZI or Zone of the Interior), but the expense of one and sometimes two refuellings required during their rotational tours made the operation cumbersome and expensive. All medium bombers were in due course to be transferred to overseas bases for 'Reflex' operations. In addition to the mission assigned to overseas units, namely the initial deployment of bomber strike and tanker forces, the overseas bases were also required for recovery or post-strike operations. The increased Russian capability in long-range missiles dictated the need for the maximum degree of dispersal and for the quickest reaction possible on the part of American strategic striking forces. This was to be accomplished in large part by the 'Reflex' forces stationed overseas, alongside the tanker refuelling facilities available to SAC. The B-47 Reflex Action programme replaced the 90-day deployments of entire wings with shorter over-lapping rotations of small elements of aircraft from various wings with extra crews to support a high alert rate.

The 'Reflex' programme marked a change of the Seventh Air Division's mission from forward deployment to post-strike support; in fact it marked the start of a gradual winding-down of SAC operations in the United Kingdom. At about this time, the Seventh Air Division released ten bases from its twenty-seven base deployment plan, for use by RAF or USAFE as satellites of main operating bases. By 1960, the Seventh Air Division had reduced Mildenhall, Chelveston and Bruntingthorpe to stand-by status, retaining only Brize Norton, Fairford, Greenham Common and Upper Heyford as main 'Reflex' bases. The gradual decrease in SAC facilities in the United Kingdom was not due solely to the end of rotational tours and the introduction of Reflex operations. It had long been felt by senior US military personnel that some of the UK bases were too close together in the event of an attack. However, the main reason could be seen as the expansion of the RAF Strike Command V-bomber force alongside the joint installation of Thor IRBMs which, in the words of an official USAFE history, 'served to make the Seventh Air Division air bases a less important factor in the strategic equation'.[57]

The Third Air Force remained instrumental in assisting RAF air defence, as well as providing NATO's initial tactical nuclear strike force, but even they were to suffer a reduction in numbers. In September 1962, the Third Air Force returned Bruntingthorpe and the B-66 wing at Sculthorpe was deactivated. Project 'Clear Water' (see Chapter 8) saw a major cut-back of US air operations in the United Kingdom. This gradual paring down should not be thought of as a reduction of forces *per se*, but rather as a concentration of forces into the functions and base deployment patterns that exist today. The diminishing USAF presence was compensated for by an important growth in the United States naval presence in the United Kingdom. The USN found itself in a similar position to that of USAF ten years earlier – namely that of needing to be in close proximity to the Soviet Union for mounting an attack, due to the limited range of the first new Polaris missiles.[58] Since neither Norway nor Japan would accept the presence of nuclear weapons it was to the United Kingdom that the United States once again looked.

POLARIS NEEDS A HOME

The realisation that land-based deployment of missiles was increasingly vulnerable to accurate enemy strikes had led to active consideration of alternative modes of deployment for NATO's nuclear deterrent. Sea-based modes of deployment provided the obvious answer. and they presented several advantages over their land-based cousins, as a letter to *The Times* point out. 'The solution to this problem is to launch the rockets from ships, preferably submarines. This would be far easier to accept politically with the added strategic advantage of giving greater launch-site mobility and hence greater security from bombardment'.[59]

Although affording strategic advantages, the decision of the British government to allow US Polaris submarines to use a base on the west coast of Scotland was to prove one of the most controversial deployments, attracting considerable public attention. The proposed phase-out of the American IRBMs from Europe in 1963, and the collapse of the proposed substitute – a multilateral force (MLF) of some twenty-five surface ships, equipped with 2500 mile range Polaris missiles – made the search for an alternative urgent. Neither Britain nor France would give up its own independent deterrents, and critics pointed out that the MLF placed no restrictions whatever on the US deterrent, yet gave Washington the freedom to veto MLF operations. The obvious alternative was for the US to base her Polaris force overseas. The choice of the west coast of Scotland for a potential submarine base was ideal, since the submarines needed a base close to their 'patrol' areas but at the same time not at too much risk of detection. The first approach made by US officials early in 1960 was to discuss not only possible sites[60] for Polaris submarines, but also for the full range of navigation and communication facilities this implied. In the records of the Director of Naval Operations at this time, a small entry reads:

> The CNO (Chief of Naval Operations) has stated a requirement to base Fleet Ballistic Missile Submarines in the Northern UK. Certain

UK Naval and Governmental authorities have been informally contacted to discuss this requirement . . . when this program is implemented, the provision of support will become a major logistic task.[61]

The background to the Holy Loch base was a deal worked out between Prime Minister Macmillan and President Eisenhower. It was agreed between the two heads of state at Camp David, from 21–27 March 1960, that in return for the sale of Skybolt ballistic missiles to Britain (for use by the V-bomber force), the United States would have the use of Holy Loch for its Polaris submarines. The Skybolt discussions were accompanied by the reassurance that 'if by some mischance the development of Skybolt proved unsatisfactory we would be able to maintain in substitution the essential elements of Polaris to be fitted to submarines of our own construction'.[62] It was however made clear that the United States policy was in favour of a multilateral NATO force, and did not want Britain to have control of her own Polaris missiles. After the Skybolt deal, Macmillan cancelled the problematic British development of a long-range missile, Blue Streak. The formal agreement on Skybolt was finalised when Harold Watkinson, the British Defence Minister, visited the United States in May. The arrangement whereby Britain would provide a submarine base on the west coast of Scotland was seen by the Prime Minister as 'more or less in return for Skybolt'.[63] The two agreements were kept separate and upon Watkinson's return the Cabinet was determined to tie the two deals together. Macmillan persuaded Cabinet to accept the broad assurances that Eisenhower had given at Camp David as a kind of 'gentleman's agreement'.

It became apparent by the end of the Eisenhower administration that the Skybolt project was in trouble. The new Secretary of Defense under Kennedy, Robert McNamara, applied new management techniques to conclude that Skybolt was not cost-effective, particularly compared to the nearly completed Minuteman project and the good reports about Polaris from defence planners. In November 1962, the Skybolt project was scrapped upon the grounds that it was 'unsuitable' and unnecessary for American defence strategy'.[64]

Even before the Skybolt deal, senior US navy personnel had their sights on 'going into somewhere in Scotland'.[65] Admiral Ramage, who was working in 'Op-31' – responsible for obtaining base rights overseas – saw clear advantages in the Holy Loch area for submarine deployment mainly because of 'location and easy access of getting from there to the prospective launch sites'.[66] The anxiety of the USN to deploy Polaris in Europe was displayed when Admiral Ramage criticised the British for a lack of speed during the negotiations; 'The British, of course, were holding out trying to get the best deal they could and they wanted to get in the Polaris program as much *quid pro quo* as they could. This became rather sticky. They were dragging their feet. Naturally we were anxious to get on with it'.[67]

To speed up negotiations, Admiral Ramage's deputy in 'Op-31', Admiral Fritz Harlfinger, was instructed to approach the Germans and discuss with them the possibility, if the British would not let American submarines into a Scottish port, of basing submarines in Bremerhaven. This had the desired effect when the British got hold of the possibility of the USN putting Polaris into Bremerhaven:

> their Secretary of Defense came over here to discuss this problem and the price for his agreement to any such base rights over there was for us to give them at least one or two Polaris submarines . . . we weren't about to give them outright a Polaris submarine. [Mountbatten originally wanted six submarines.] But we did cooperate in every respect in their building one.[68]

However, not all top USN personnel were as enthusiastic about basing Polaris overseas. Admiral Arleigh B. Burke, who retired in 1961, saw that there was no absolute need for Holy Loch or for another similar base at Rota, in Spain. The Polaris programme was in fact based on the premise that there would eventually be no need to use any foreign bases whatever. What Rota and Holy Loch would permit was more time on station and less time in transit to the station.

The British government's decision to agree to a Polaris submarine base on the Clyde, hitherto secret, was made public on 1 November 1960 when it was announced to parliament – although the Prime Minister refused to publish a White Paper setting forth the agreement. Somewhat surprisingly Hugh Gaitskell, the leader of the Opposition, and his front bench were silent and there was no vote of censure in spite of backbench pressure. The Campaign for Nuclear Disarmament, now considerably expanded since its early days, was a major force in British politics and was to make its opposition clear. Meanwhile, in the United States, Admiral Burke indicated that the agreement was that the United States Navy would use tenders instead of a big group ashore (perhaps in the mistaken hope that this would divert attention and protest) and that the USN would keep its submarines on the surface until they were 'a certain distance' from Holy Loch,[69] thus preventing the use of Holy Loch as a launching area. The 'certain distance' was probably three miles, or in other words, the limit of our territorial waters. Admiral Burke also maintained that 'in essence the British government themselves picked the location at Holy Loch', and it was then accepted by the USN after very careful inspection. Britain was not required to provide any support facilities, merely a harbour and a space to overhaul ships. Those opposed to the basing of Polaris submarines at Holy Loch did not go unnoticed, as Admiral Lawson Ramage remembers:

> we did have some opposition you know. Kooks came up and demonstrated and we had quite a few demonstrations there at one time . . . I don't think there was any reluctance or hesitation on the part of the British for us operating submarines out of there because they were most anxious to get them themselves.[70]

The most serious criticism, not surprisingly, came from the Soviet Union. The Vice-Chairman of the USSR Council of Ministers addressed a gathering in Moscow on 6 November and was highly critical of the American naval presence in the United Kingdom, pointing out that the base was near Glasgow, 'Britain's second biggest city . . . the base is being created to serve as a point of departure for American atomic submarines equipped with nuclear missiles. Who will fail to see that this is a case of a most dangerous adventure on the part of the American military – an adventure designed to worsen the international situation sharply and fraught with dangerous consequences to its American sponsors and their British allies?'[71] Such opinions were taken up enthusiastically in the United Kingdom. The *Sunday Express* denounced the deal as 'humiliating' and claimed Britain's leaders had 'ceded the base to America. They have surrendered any right to ask what use it will be put to . . . it could involve Britain in the responsibility for war. Would any tenth-rate banana state under American tutelage allow itself to be put into such a position of humiliation and danger?'[72]

In the course of a Parliamentary debate on the Holy Loch base, announced during the Queen's speech on 1 November, the vague nature of the unpublished agreements became only too clear.[73] The steadfast refusal by Macmillan to publish the exchange of notes constituting the agreement was worrying in the light of conflicting claims concerning the agreement. To one American the Holy Loch negotiations, like the Truman–Churchill agreement, resulted in an agreement with 'not quite the formality of a treaty'.[74] Denis Healey on

4 November enquired whether there would be any power of veto over orders given by the American commander and to stop any action contrary to the British interests, and would the permanent British personnel involved fall under the control of the Admiralty? He also enquired about an 'absolute veto' over the firing of missiles from Holy Loch and territorial waters and the envisaged consultation procedure. Denis Healey was not satisfied with Macmillan's earlier statement when the Prime Minister told MPs:

> It is impossible to make an agreement on all fours with the bomber agreement. The deployment and use in periods of emergency of the submarine depot ship and associated facilities in the United Kingdom will be a matter for joint consultation . . . wherever the submarines may be, I am perfectly satisfied that no decision to use the missiles will ever be taken without the fullest possible previous consultation.[75]

A US State Department spokesman, Lincoln White, expressed surprise at the Prime Minister's statement pointing out that there might not be time for consultation. Harold Watkinson, who succeeded Duncan Sandys as Minister of Defence, insisted a day after the statement that it was clear that Polaris submarines would not fire their missiles from British territorial waters but were still only a few miles from the coast.

To patch up the concern felt over the arrangements surrounding Polaris and questions by critics like Denis Healey, the Prime Minister told the House of Commons:

> As regard facilities in the territory . . . we have exactly the same control in an emergency as exists over United States bomber or missile bases in this country. That is to say there will then be joint consultation regarding the use of these facilities.[76]

Although Macmillan had stressed that 'there should be fullest possible consultation in the case of Polaris' he admitted before the House of Commons that consultation 'might be impossible in circumstances of surprise attack on the West . . . we would not wish to insist on prior consultation'[77] which could compromise the effectiveness of the deterrent. Macmillan's statements on the Polaris agreement were confusing and his steadfast refusal to make public the full agreement merely added to the confusion.

Macmillan had stated that it was impossible to make an agreement 'on all fours' with the bomber agreement. Only a week later he insisted that Britain has 'exactly the same control' over the new base. The earlier agreements covering the bomber bases had agreed that the use of bases in an emergency was 'a matter for joint *decision*'. It was curious that the Prime Minister relegated the earlier agreement by insisting that it was the same as the Polaris agreement which was 'a matter for joint *consultation*'. The second indication of confusion in the Government's understanding of the earlier Truman–Attlee and Truman–Churchill agreements was the mention of 'missile bases'. This was obviously a reference to the Thor agreement (which was published) where Britain had the power of veto under the 'two-key' system, unlike the Polaris agreement which appeared to rest upon hazy 'consultation' – if there was time. If, as Macmillan insisted, the Holy Loch agreements are 'exactly the same' as the agreements covering bomber or missile bases, it puts a sinister meaning on the British government's understanding of the original airbase agreement since there might not be time for joint consultation or decision-making which would render the agreement useless in the case of an emergency.

Aside from the vagueness of the agreement, the timing of the Polaris base announcement could not have been made at a more unfavourable time, particularly in the aftermath of the RB-47 incident which naturally raised speculation that Polaris submarines might also be used for patrols close to (or in) Soviet waters. Anthony Greenwood was quick to connect these events in the House of Commons; 'I cannot believe that there is much security in having on our territory the nuclear bases of a power which was so appallingly irresponsible as to send the U-2 plane over Russian, to call a general alert on the eve of the Summit Conference and, even after that, to send the RB-47'.[78] Chapman Pincher was also quick to join these events together and draw unfavourable implications for the future of US bases in the United Kingdom; 'The Russians may sink a Polaris submarine as they destroyed the RB-47 reconnaissance bomber and claim that it was in territorial waters when it was not . . . my general conclusion is that far from being a defence, nuclear bases are a real source of danger, and perhaps Polaris is the most dangerous of the lot'.[79] The opposition in Parliament was critical of the Polaris arrangement not only because of the RB-47 incident that cast doubt upon the Government's ability to control the US Polaris forces in our territorial waters but also because of new dangers faced by the 'civil population of this country [which] has no adequate defence in the event of a nuclear war'.[80] The Government stressed, in an attempt to assuage fears, that 'given time' the depot ship would sail out of Holy Loch.[81] It is inconceivable that

Holy Loch itself would be omitted in the event of a nuclear attack on the United Kingdom, even if the depot ship had departed.

Since March 1961, Holy Loch has been the site of a Submarine Support Base for the USN's 14 Submarine Squadron (or 'SubRon 14') and is known as Submarine Refit Site One.[82] Holy Loch is not a NATO facility and exists solely through the bilateral agreement between President Eisenhower and Prime Minister Macmillan and is largely subject to American strategic needs. Late in March the USS 'Patrick Henry' surfaced at Holy Loch with its apt motto 'Liberty or Death'.[82] The initial strength grew from one to five, as submarines of the George Washington class were put into service, and this was later doubled to ten, comprising the whole of that class. The submarines can also be refitted at Holy Loch but this reportedly 'does not include dismantling to remove and replace the nuclear core'.[84] The submarines are serviced by an auxiliary floating dry dock that is moored in Holy Loch, called the USS 'Los Alamos', over 1000 feet long and with a lifting capacity of 40 000 tons. It has been moored in Holy Loch since 1961. There is also a 19 000 ton submarine tender that is used for arming the submarines and supporting the crews of Polaris (now Poseidon) submarines. The USN has five such tenders that rotate every two to three years. Alongside the tender and 'Los Alamos', three large tugs and a host of smaller support and supply vessels keep Holy Loch's SubRon 14 running.

The Polaris agreement did not cover just the Holy Loch base. It was made clear at the time of the negotiations that it was a 'package' that included important support and communication facilities. The agreement was the start of a major naval build-up in the United Kingdom.[85] On 12 November 1959, the State Department obtained 'approval in principle from Her Majesty's government for the United States Navy to establish a radio intercept station at the presently inactive RAF base at Edzell, Scotland'.[86] The station was officially occupied by one officer and eight enlisted men on 11 February 1960 and on 1 July 1960 the United States Naval Security Groups was established. The brief given to Edzell's commander was to 'furnish communication support to US Fleet Units operating in this area, provide radio navigational services related to air–sea rescue, conduct technical research in support of US Naval electronic research projects, and perform other such operations as may be directed by the Chief of Naval Operations'.[87] Edzell was one of three signals intelligence (SIGNIT) stations; the others were at Keflavik in Iceland and Bremerhaven (now closed). The idea behind Edzell was to detect any unknown radio signals in and around the

Polaris deployment area. The role of Edzell was updated in 1969 when the growing USN network in Scotland was linked together by a microwave radio network. The Edzell publication *Tartan Log* explained that the updated role of the US Naval Security Group Activity is to 'provide rapid and secure communications essential to the defence of the US and the Free World'. After 1969 Edzell became part of the UK Wideband Microwave system supporting the mission of US Naval Communications System (Londonderry).[88] Edzell's task was also the maintenance and repair of facilities at the following northern United Kingdom Wideband Microwave Systems: Browncarrick, Sergeant-law, Kirk O'Shotts, East Lomond, Craig Owl Hill, Kinnaber, Edzell, Inverbervie, Aberdeen and certain portions of the intelligence network of RAF Mormond Hill.

The development of Polaris and Poseidon submarines also necessitated some form of communications network from shore to submarine. Two stations, one at Londonderry and the other at Thurso near Wick in Scotland (opened in July 1962) were to provide this. Thurso and Londonderry (the latter closed in 1977) were equipped with low-frequency transmitters that could penetrate the sea to a depth of about five metres and thus enable communication without the submarine actually surfacing. Fear of the vulnerable bases being attacked also led the United States to deploy intermittently a squadron of TACAMO (Take-charge and move-out) aircraft. These were converted C-130 Hercules aircraft that would tow an aerial wire about three miles long and signals could be sent to the submarines in case of a breakdown in on-shore communications. Thurso's mission is defined as 'to manage, operate, and maintain those facilities, equipment and devices and systems necessary to provide requisite communications for the command, operational control and administration of the Naval establishment, and to perform such functions as may be directed by the Chief of Naval Operations'.[89]

Another important naval installation was commissioned on 7 March 1968 at Machrihanish near Campbeltown in Argyllshire. The mission of the base at Machrihanish was unlike the others, and was to 'receive, store, maintain, issue and transship classified weapons in support of the US Navy and NATO operations'.[90] Machrihanish was placed under the command of the Commander in Chief US Atlantic Fleet and significantly the first USN personnel to arrive there in mid-1967 were members of a Mobile Mine Assembly Unit who had previously been stationed at Mildenhall. Machrihanish also plays host to the USN's Special Forces unit in Europe (known as SEALS) which forms part of the Special Operations Task Force Europe designed to train partisans behind enemy lines and carry out acts of sabotage in the event of war. The Explosive Ordnance Disposal Group, US Atlantic Fleet, also has a detachment at the US Naval Aviation Weapons Facility, Machrihanish. This beautiful spot on the remote Mull of Kintyre was to become a major weapons storage depot mainly for Atomic Demolition Munitions (ADMs).

The Polaris Sales Agreement whereby the United States would make available to Britain Polaris missiles without warheads was signed in April 1963 and was seized as further evidence by those opposed to American bases that they were unnecessary and took security affairs out of the United Kingdom's hands. The availability of the Polaris, it was noted, was intended to restore some of this lost independence. The Polaris A3 missile by this time had a range of some 2500 miles and was soon to be succeeded by the more accurate Poseidon missile with a range in excess of 3000 miles and 14 MIRVed warheads. The phase out of Polaris missiles by 1977 and their replacement by the Poseidon missile meant that, because of the greater number of warheads on Poseidon, Holy Loch was supporting twice as many warheads accompanied by no public or government announcement. To the argument that the Holy Loch base posed a threat to Britain's national security could now be added another argument that the threat was even worse because of British acquisition of a sea-borne independent deterrent. Even those who supported a British independent deterrent cast doubts upon how independent it really was, since we were largely reliant on the United States for warheads.[91] Gordon-Walker, arguing for intimate participation with the United States, and against the Conservative independent nuclear deterrent, pointed out that if the United States were to be custodians of all, or most, of the nuclear power, the Western alliance and the foreign policy of West European states would need to be inextricably aligned to American policy. The arrival of US Polaris submarines at Holy Loch also marked the heyday of the CND Aldermaston marchers and the first of what we now term 'peace camps' was established at Kilmun in 1961 where opposition to US bases in the United Kingdom was no less outspoken than opposition to the 'anti-American' independent nuclear deterrent. As time went on the arguments for maintaining such a controversial base became thinner, particularly since the advent of the Trident missile with a far greater range. Holy Loch is now the only major USN European submarine base since the major Poseidon base at Rota in Spain closed.

8 1964-84: From MLF to INF

During the two decades covered in this chapter, the United States government began to think more in terms of European relations than in terms of Anglo–American relations. This reflected an American belief that the European defence effort within NATO needed to be highly co-ordinated. The Multilateral Force (MLF) which establishes the start of this period, and the Intermediate Nuclear Force (INF) which ends it, were both attempts by the United States to unify NATO's European defence effort. The common problem that both the MLF and INF were designed to address was West Germany, which occupied the unenviable position of non-nuclear status in the front line. Whilst the INF was a later attempt to solve this precarious position, by deploying land-bases missiles in Europe, the earlier MLF proposals did at least have the benefit of being sea-borne. The 1960s and 1970s were also important for arms-control negotiations, when many of the US forces in Europe were put onto the bargaining table.

Outside Europe, in the context of superpower relations, there was a gradual easing of tension between East and West due to a decline in Cold War rhetoric and the advent of the spirit of detente. This in turn was to challenge the long-accepted *status quo* of US military involvement around the world, which previously had been justified by the Cold War. Although the period covered in this chapter starts after the withdrawal of Thor and Jupiter missiles, the major issues concerning bases in the following decades were again related to the possible basing of nuclear systems in Europe.

FROM MLF TO INF

Relations between the United States and the United Kingdom had improved considerably in the 1960s from the low ebb of the Suez crisis. There were, however, general irritants in mutual relations that were always close to the surface. Difficulties in NATO, and in Germany in particular, had led the American Secretary of Defense, Robert McNamara, to propose a Multilateral Force. But the government of

150

Sir Alec Douglas-Home reacted to the MLF with little enthusiasm: it expressed severe reservations about the control of the MLF, not least because it would nominally be under the control of SACEUR who was by tradition an American and on economic grounds MLF could divert resources away from more necessary acquisitions. Douglas-Home was also anxious to keep the Independent Nuclear Deterrent, since it was widely seen as a 'ticket of admission' to top-table discussions as well as a factor enabling the United Kingdom to retain a certain amount of independence from the United States. The Labour opposition under Harold Wilson took the chance to appear as 'the party most closely aligned with the United States by arguing for the abandonment of nuclear weapons . . . and relying instead on closer relations with the Americans'.[1] Such a stance appealed greatly to McNamara, who was well known for his opposition to independent nuclear forces and advocated greater conventional forces to support the new 'flexible response' strategy. The Labour stance also meant that if the United States was to have custody of all the nuclear arsenals of the Western alliance, the foreign policies of West European countries would have to be more closely aligned with the United States at a time when Europe generally was demonstrating a decidedly independent spirit.

The election of Harold Wilson's Labour party in October 1964 saw the new government facing President Johnson, who was a fervent advocate of the MLF, much more so than Kennedy. The Labour Party's suspicion of the MLF, primarily on the grounds that they did not want a German finger on the trigger, resulted in alternative proposals being put forward by the Labour government. The proposed Atlantic Nuclear Force (ANF) would include the V-bomber force and the Polaris submarines, matched by an equal or greater number of American submarines and any forces that the French felt fit to subscribe. The control of the ANF was to be by a single authority linked to NATO and containing representatives of all participant countries, any one of which could veto the use of all elements of the ANF. The ANF proposals were put forward by Harold Wilson to President Johnson at a meeting in Washington from 7–9 December. Even before the meeting it became clear that the ANF had little support either from Congress or from Europe (opinion was divided in Bonn and unanimously against in France). Accordingly, the MLF/ANF issue died a quiet death. Whether the ANF proposals were a deliberate attempt to torpedo the MLF proposals is still open to debate. The British were faced with the possibility of an American–German agreement on MLF or perhaps a nuclear arrangement between France and Germany. The ANF proposals were put forward as a serious option to counter these fears, but also allowed Wilson to disinherit the British independent deterrent while claiming it would not be *his* fault if the ANF proved unacceptable to other countries.[2] The ANF proposal was designed to defuse the MLF debate whilst also allowing a British hand in fashioning the Atlantic nuclear defences.

Of more interest to this study, however, was the Prime Minister's insistence at the December meeting that less stress be put on the special relationship and more on a close relationship. This was in part a tacit recognition that relations were not as close as they had once been, but also it was a concession to backbench concerns that they might be seen to be toeing an American line. President Johnson, for his part, was very cautious to avoid the pitfalls of the Nassau experience of 'appearing to settle the problems of the Western Alliance on exclusively Anglo–American terms. He placed great stress on not offending the French or the Germans by appearing to make an agreement with the British without German support and at least acquienscence from the French. Subsequently, the notion emerged that a way must be found to give Germany a status of equality with Britain in nuclear matters'.[3] Talk of growing equality between the United States and other European allies was difficult for many in Britain to accept, when they had been used to assumptions about Britain's special place in the Alliance and Europe.[4]

The decade starting in the mid-1960s also saw a general erosion of the global military partnership that had existed between the two countries. Britain withdrew her forces from SEATO on 31 March 1969, and in 1975 a White Paper announced that British forces would no longer be designated for CENTO. These two organisations had helped symbolise the worldwide partnership in arms between Britain and the United States. The withdrawal of the British military contribution and subsequent winding-up of SEATO on 1 July 1977 highlighted the decline of the close defence relationship.

All these events were to prove significant in their effects upon US bases in the United Kingdom. The retention of the British Polaris force by the Labour government, in spite of electoral promises to seek its removal, marks a paradox which is still present: on the one hand it says, the United Kingdom is prepared to trust the United States substantial forces and investment for our protection, and on the other, it suggests the sneaking feeling that the bases are predominantly serving US interests and that the retention of the IND is (to use Macmillan's phrase) an 'insurance policy' in case of a clash of interests.

THE DEACTIVATION OF THE SEVENTH AIR DIVISION

The growing vulnerability of the Jupiter missiles in Turkey, and Italy and Thor in Britain, led to their removal in 1963 during the aftermath of the Cuban Missile Crisis. In spite of their removal the overall number of nuclear weapons in Europe continued to rise, and the issue of allied control over the weapons became acute. With the failure of the MLF plan to gain widespread support in Europe, thoughts turned once again to the United States' bases. The expense (in both economic and political senses) led to a favourable consideration within the American government of an increasing reliance on SLBMs and TNWs in Europe. The already large arsenal of nuclear weapons in Europe ranging from Atomic Demolition Munitions (ADMs) to Polaris submarines made the 'Reflex' operations look undesirable. The manned bomber had limited usefulness in contemporary strategy as Robert McNamara recognised in 1961:

> The introduction of ballistic missiles is already exerting a major impact on the size, composition and deployment of the manned bomber force, and this impact will become greater in the years ahead. As the number of ballistic missiles increases, requirements for strategic aircraft will be gradually reduced. Simultaneously, the growing enemy missile capability will make grounded aircraft more vulnerable to sudden attack, and further readiness measures will have to be taken to increase the survivability of the strategic bomber force.[5]

Missiles did however bring new dangers of their own, particularly to the country hosting them. Manned bombers could at least be recalled, whereas missiles could not. The dangers of placing missiles on bases near a potential adversary were adequately shown during the Cuban missile crisis.[6] The shock of the near success of the Soviet Union in constructing missile launching sites at San Cristobal was interesting, when the United States already had missiles on Russia's doorstep in Turkey. While there is nothing to suggest that Thor missiles were withdrawn in response to the crisis as a conciliatory measure, the situation underlined the importance of improved reconnaissance and surveillance to stop a repetition of such an incident. On 24 July 1964 President Johnson discreetly announced the development of the SR-71 'Blackbird' spy plane capable of flying at about 80 000 feet, and although its speed is classified, it was to set a New York–London time of 1 hour 54 minutes in test flights. RAF Mildenhall was later to be an important 'host' for this most unusual visitor.

Of more importance that the spin-offs from the Cuban missile crisis was Secretary of Defense Robert McNamara's announcement of 'Project Clear Water', which was aimed at disposing of all B-47s and KC-97's by the end of the FY 1966. This also signified the gradual winding down of 'Reflex' operations. In April and May, B-47s stopped Reflex operations at Fairford, Greenham Common, and Zaragosa in Spain. Fairford and Greenham Common were returned to the RAF on 26 June and 30 June respectively. By the end of 1964 only five overseas bases continued to support Reflex forces, two being the bases at Brize Norton and Upper Heyford.

The advent of Project Clear Water signified a change in the composition of US arsenal; from 21 April 1964 onwards the number of ICBMs on alert outnumbered the manned bomber alert force. The USAF saw the key to its future bomber needs as either a supersonic, high-altitude capability (like the XB-70 or SR-71 being developed) or a bomber capable of low-level penetration, a role at which the F-111 excelled. The fears about the slowness and vulnerability of overseas manned bomber alert forces close to 'the enemy' led to the gradual phasing out of the Seventh Air Division. With the return of Brize Norton to the Air Ministry and Upper Heyford to the Third Air Force, SAC's United Kingdom role effectively ended. The Seventh Air Division was deactivated on 30 June 1965.

Although the official SAC presence ended in 1965, it did continue to retain a toehold at Upper Heyford, using it as a stop-off point for reconnaissance and refueling aircraft. SAC also retained the right to use some bases in the United Kingdom as 'Forward Operating Bases' in time of emergency. By 1966 the USAF presence in the United Kingdom had diminished appreciably from its peak in the early 1950s. Three bomber wings and one reconnaissance wing remained, comprising about 300 aircraft. Against the apparent run-down in force levels must be considered the presence of the American Polaris submarines at Holy Loch and the growing importance of the United Kingdom as an intelligence and reconnaissance centre and, in time of war, as part of an early warning system.[7]

THE NUCLEAR PLANNING GROUP

The failure of the MLF and ANF proposals was due in large part to the question of control over nuclear weapons. The MLF would still have left non-nuclear allies dependent on the nuclear commitment of the United States, while her 'nuclear allies' would continue to be very sensitive to American strategic whims. Similarly, the successful attempt to apply a doctrine of flexible response to NATO planning was seen in European circles as a unilateral US move. Mounting European resistance to such unilateral moves as well as a feeling that America's allies had little say in the determination of alliance nuclear policy led Robert McNamara to suggest, at a meeting of Defence Ministers in Paris in 1965, the idea that a Nuclear Planning Group should be established (NPG). The design behind the proposal was to increase allied participation in nuclear planning whilst also implementing the Athens Guidelines which were, in effect, an agreement to consult with allies in the event that the use of nuclear weapons were contemplated if time and circumstances permitted.

Two bodies were eventually established to deal with nuclear planning and consultation: the Nuclear Defence Affairs Committee (NDAC) and the seven-member NPG. The NDAC was open to all of America's allies and would receive reports from the NPG, which was the discussion chamber for nuclear matters. On the one hand this meant that a large number of countries had access to nuclear information, but also it meant that the discussion group (and hence the likelihood of paralysis through disagreement) was small. France, Iceland and Luxembourg chose not to participate in the new bodies. The NPG has four permanent members (the defence minister of Germany, Italy, Britain, and the United States) and the remaining three members are from the NDAC, serving in rotation for eighteen month periods. The NPG represented 'an attempt to redefine the relationship of the US to the non-nuclear weapon allies in such a way as to avoid the search for a formula by which the allies could share with the US control over the decision as to whether or not nuclear weapons would be used'.[8] It was also a way to mitigate the impact of US veto power 'on the confidence of her allies in the nuclear commitment of the US by involving the allies more closely in the process by which a decision to use nuclear weapons might be reached'.[9]

Although the NPG was designed to assuage European anxieties over NATO's dependence on the American nuclear commitment, by establishing a right to be consulted, this right has not always been observed. The NPG also proved to be an American platform for building confidence amongst the allies in order to persuade them that a credible nuclear posture existed, while at the same time it gave non-nuclear allies some hope that they could influence the actions of both the United States and Britain in support of their nuclear commitment to NATO. In practice the NPG has not had the desired impact upon US planning and action that was initially hoped for. A sizeable proportion of the theatre nuclear weapons are stockpiled for the use of US forces and are therefore not subject to such constraints or consultation. Virtually the entire US strategic force remains outside the system of alliance control. Thus, far from clarifying the vagaries of the Athens Guidelines, the NPG merely gave America's European allies the illusion of being involved in the consultation procedure. The US nuclear alert during the 1973 Middle East War[10] illustrated that where there was a direct clash of interests, far from consultation taking place, there was no question of anything other than the wishes of the US administration prevailing.

It is hard to see why the President would consult with the allies if there was any likelihood of such consultations being adverse to American interests; and, as was claimed in the 1973 alert, time could be too short for consultation. Furthermore, an American study has argued that the President does not have to consult with his allies if in his 'consideration of the attendant circumstances it is deemed necessary to order the use of nuclear weapons without such consultation'.[11] In spite of pressure within the NPG for some kind of dual or two-key device, one that would constitute a physical veto to ensure prior consultation before the proposed use of nuclear weapons, it had been a general US policy (with the exception of Thor, Jupiter, Lance and Pershing I missiles) 'never to allow its allies a physical veto over the release of nuclear warheads to its own and allied nuclear-capable forces deployed in the European theatre'.[12]

The creation of the NPG coincided with the official adoption of NATOs new flexible response strategy and, perhaps significantly, there has been no major change in NATO strategy or arrangements for the use of nuclear weapons since 1965. Shortly after the NPG came into existence the alliance was thrown into disarray by General de Gaulle's decision to withdraw France from NATOs integrated command structure. French doubts about America's nuclear guarantee, as well as dissatisfaction with the consultation procedure, eventually led to an independent French *force de frappe*. There is no evidence to suggest that the French example offered a serious alternative for the United Kingdom, but de Gaulle's decision was to have profound effects on US basing in Europe: as a massive operation began to relocate US forces from France, many came to the United Kingdom. Since much of the strategic debate within NATO had been between

France and the United States the French withdrawal opened the way for the rather unenthusiastic adoption by NATO of flexible response strategy in 1967.

OPERATION FRELOC: US FORCES LEAVE FRANCE

The deactivation of the Seventh Air Division and the fall in US force levels in the United Kingdom went largely unnoticed by contemporary observers. The increasing reliance upon ICBMs, which challenged the role of the vulnerable manned bomber, was disguised because scarcely a year after the apparent wind-down of the US military presence in the United Kingdom, the air force build-up was to start again. This increase was due to General de Gaulle's announcement about France's withdrawal from the unified military command structure of NATO, and his ordering of US bases and NATO headquarters out of Paris. The storm that finally broke with de Gaulle's decision had been long in the making. American nuclear-capable aircraft had in fact left France as long ago as 1960, and de Gaulle, in his frequent attacks upon the credibility of the American 'guarantee', often claimed that 'no one could expect the United States to risk its cities for the defence of Europe'.[13] Such utterances undoubtedly lost some of their impact through constant repetition. An American Embassy official in Paris commented on a speech made by de Gaulle that he 'offered a variation on his standard theme about American reluctance to use nuclear weapons in defense of Europe', and the Gaullist arguments like that above were seen as 'normal procedure'.[14] But in spite of what would appear to be adequate warnings of the imminent expulsion of US bases, the decision caused embarrassment and confusion. The response was the hasty relocation of United States forces from France to West Germany and Britain, dubbed Operation Freloc.

There is little to indicate that the French withdrawal from the integrated military command of NATO and the expulsion of US bases prompted similar sentiments in the United Kingdom. French differences on defence policy with the United States had always been more extreme than Anglo–American divergencies. De Gaulle openly doubted the credibility of the US guarantee to Europe and, since US involvement in Vietnam, France had made a deliberate attempt to distance herself from US policy. The degree to which the United Kingdom could have been independent, if a decision like the French had been made, is open to doubt. Even the British nuclear deterrent that was supposedly *independent* was in fact *interdependent* with US facilities. The targeting plans of SAC and Bomber Command were integrated, and the deterrent role of the V-bombers was made dependent upon US reconnaissance information, as is presumably the case with Polaris.

The loss of its French bases was a severe blow to the United States. France had occupied the central role for the supply of ammunition reinforcements, fuel and other supplies to front-line forces. Effectively this meant France was the key logistic support between the United States and the central front, considered most likely to be Germany. Some of the French-based American forces were to be relocated in Germany (mainly headquarters and military depots), some units were disbanded and sent back to the United States, and most of the aircraft were transferred to Britain. Operation FRELOC marked the addition of some 8000 airmen to the Third Air Force by 1 April 1967, the day on which all American forces had to have left France. Upon the completion of Operation FRELOC, the total number of United States Air Force personnel in the United Kingdom would rise to about 25 000. This was still only about half the number of a decade earlier. Thus, overall there had been a significant reduction in United States Air Force personnel in the United Kingdom.

Operation FRELOC was to shape the future role of many United Kingdom bases. For instance, transport aircraft at Evreux in Normandy and Toul-Rosières in Lorraine were transferred to Mildenhall – which soon became known as, and still is, the 513th Tactical Airlift Wing. From Laon airbase three squadrons of RF-101 and RB-66 and a few R-4 reconnaissance aircraft were moved to Alconbury and Upper Heyford. The 66th Tactical Reconnaissance Wing at Upper Heyford was disbanded in 1969 to make way for the Tactical Fighter Wing, which was transferred from Wethersfield in April 1970 with 72 of the new General Dynamics F-111E 'all-weather' strike aircraft. The headquarters of the 322nd Division Military Airlift Command was transferred from Châteauroux to High Wycombe in September and Burtonwood was reopened as a US Army storage site late in 1966. Three storage sites in Britain were reopened as bases for USAF supplies and equipment moved out of France. The bases – Greenham Common, Chelveston and Sculthorpe – were to have no aircraft based there, but 'certain equipment was to be transported by air to Greenham Common and Sculthorpe'.[15] The logistical problems were also huge since an estimated 820 000 tons[16] of supplies, equipment and reserve ammunition had to be found a new home.

The US Army, which before 1967 had no significant military

presence in the United Kingdom, now transferred weapons, ammunition and other stocks from France. This transfer meant that the old USAF depot at Burtonwood was once again opened along with four new sites at Ditton Priors (also a storage site) and weapons and ammunition storage sites at Bramshall, Caerwent, and Fauld. The storage site at Caerwent was eventually enlarged to incorporate all the stocks sent to Bramshall, Ditton Priors and Fauld. Burtonwood continues to be the major US Army storage depot in the United Kingdom, holding 'permanent stocks sufficient to equip US Army divisions which would be sent to Europe for emergency reinforcement'.[17] Burtonwood, along with eight West German depots, are together known as POMCUS (Prepositioned Military Core Unit Stocks) which, in the event of war, would provide everything needed in case of war. The units using the material stored at Burtonwood would presumably be shipped to Liverpool, collect their equipment and set off for the European battle-ground as happens in a regular series of exercises called 'REFORGER'. However, a US Senate investigating team cast doubts upon the efficiency of POMCUS stocks in 1975. They found that 'some ammunition was useable only in an emergency, and that hundreds of vehicles were rendered unusuable by rust, broken parts and faulty or non-existent maintenance. Radios and radar sets had gone missing; some equipment had been supplied to the Middle East during the Yom Kippur War. Fifteen million dollar's worth had been "lost"'.[18]

Operation FRELOC saw a resurgence of the American military presence in the United Kingdom, and the diminishing air role was strengthened. Nevertheless, the advent of ICBMs meant that the traditional role of the United Kingdom as the 'unsinkable aircraft carrier' had changed. More emphasis was now put on deploying US forces to Britain only in time of emergency. Meanwhile the importance of Britain as a base for reconnaissance and intelligence activities grew. It would, nonetheless, be wrong to underestimate the still important role that USAF played in the United Kingdom. *The Times* commented that the Third Air Force is 'by far the largest single command in Americanized Britain claiming 16 000 of the 20 000 airmen over here, and with 31 000 dependents[19] . . . the Third Air Force operates 27 schools at 17 different locations and supplies 12 500 schoolchildren and students, flies out of 6 main operating bases with some 320 tactical aircraft and shares British skies for 10 000 flying hours every month . . . one out of every 7 single airmen marries an English girl . . . good for the special relationship'.[20]

The decision made in 1967 to redeploy certain United States forces from Western Europe to the United States, so that they would have main bases in the United States, but were redeployed to Europe occasionally for exercises, was known as REFORGER for the Army units and CRESTED CAP for the Air Force. It involved approximately four squadrons of tactical/fighter aircraft (about 96 aircraft) and roughly 5000 Army and USAF personnel. Although the concept known as 'dual basing' was never expanded after 1967, it did focus the attention of the American administration on the issue of forces overseas and specifically the questions of how many and how much. This, alongside the French expulsion of US forces from France and the failure of Britain to support the United States in an increasingly expensive and domestically unpopular struggle in Vietnam, brought about a major reconsideration of overseas basing. A report published by the US Air Staff late in 1966, entitled 'European Air Base Study',[21] indicated the changing way of thinking and the development of new basing concepts.

As a result of the study the Department of Defense and services took significant action to streamline military organization in Europe, particularly Project REDCOSTE (Reduction of Forces and Costs in Europe) implemented by Secretary of Defense, Clark Clifford, in June 1968 and follow on programmes directed by Melvin Laird. Unfortunately the loss of French air bases posed serious operational weaknesses for USAFE in fighting a conventional war under the newly adopted flexible response strategy as well as denying access to well developed lines of communication across France and the Forward Area.

The overall picture by the end of the 1960s was one of a greatly reduced American presence in the United Kingdom due to SACs ceasing operations. This did not mean any diminution in United Kingdom defences. By the time SAC left, the RAF had been supplied with sufficient British made A- and H-bombs for her V-bomber force. The overt reliance upon the airborne nuclear deterrent had, moreover, been rectified by the growing Polaris and, later, Poseidon forces. Of the 300 or so US aircraft left in the United Kingdom, the majority were intended for nuclear missions. In Spring 1970, the Third Air Force received its first F-111, which was deployed from Upper Heyford with deep-interdiction missions in mind. SAC reserved rights to use Forward Operating bases at Brize Norton, Fairford, Marham and Upper Heyford – these factors taken together signified a refinement in the United Kingdom's role as not only America's 'airstrip one' but also as a listening post, intelligence post, and surveillance centre.

Anglo–American relations, which had seen a general decline in the late 1960s, were to see little improvement in the 1970s despite attempts by the Conservative government under Edward Heath to revive a close relationship. The erosion of the global military partnership (signified by the British withdrawal from SEATO in 1969 and CENTO in 1975), the entry of Britain into the EEC, and a clear move in a European direction in defence policy, active European pursuit of detente and differences over the Yom Kippur War in 1973 – all strained relations and prompted questions about the future of US bases in the United Kingdom.

Disenchantment with expensive and controversial overseas basing reached a height in the United States in the early 1970s, particularly since the Vietnam war was draining her economy, and met with much European criticism. The issue was brought to a critical point between 1971–74, when Senator Mike Mansfield (Democrat, Montana) intro- duced several amendments to legislation designed to reduce the United States burden for the defence of Western Europe. The resolution called for a 'substantial reduction' of United States forces permanently stationed in Europe and was sponsored by 33 Senators (three were Republicans). The first such resolution had actually been introduced in 1966[22] and twice during the next few years. These resolutions were not brought to a vote, although the issues were debated extensively in Congress and across the country. Subsequent attempts to introduce the resolution in 1971, 1973 and 1974 took the form of amendments to legislation that would force votes decisively up or down.

The official adoption by NATO ministers, meeting in Iceland in June 1968, of the Mutual Balanced Force Reductions (MBFR) stance was severely set back by the Soviet invasion of Czechoslovakia in August. The setback allowed for the introduction of a new Mansfield resolution in 1969.[23] The resolution was, however, introduced too late for serious consideration in that Congressional session. The Senate Foreign Relations Committee conducted an extensive study during 1970 on security agreements and commitments abroad. The House Foreign Affairs Committee also held hearings on US relations with Europe during February–April 1970. Thus by 1971 the political debate surrounding force reductions was at its hottest and this was the time that Senator Mansfield chose to introduce a proposal on troop reductions. The proposal, introduced in the form of a Senate resolution, aimed at halving the total US forces in Europe. Senator Mansfield maintained that the remaining 150 000 US troops in Europe would be sufficient for the defence of that area.

The Soviet Union, following NATO's proposal, did not warm up to the idea of MBFR negotiations. Moscow wanted to go ahead with their proposal for a general conference on security and co-operation in Europe (CSCE). This had a cool reception and coincided with the reintroduction of Mansfield's amendment. The Mansfield Amendment prompted strong opposition from the Executive branch under Richard Nixon. Nixon's campaign against the amendement gained support from an unexpected quarter, when Secretary Brezhnev intimated an interest in negotiations on reducing forces. Kissinger described this unexpected intervention as 'manna from heaven'.[24] The Soviet move was designed to bring the Western powers towards the idea of a European security conference. The outcome of the haggling was an agreement in 1972 between the US and USSR to go ahead with CSCE *and* MBFR negotiations.[25] The commencement of these negotiations was the effective end of Mansfield's campaign to reduce US forces in Europe, Secretary Kissinger, in a letter to Senator John Stennis, Chairman of the Senate Armed Services Committee, had warned that 'as unreciprocated reduction of US forces would remove Soviet incentives to negotiate seriously since they will hardly pay a price for something that is about to be handed them by us'.[26]

By the end of the Mansfield debates it became evident that the US forces in Europe had become a powerful bargaining tool which, to a large extent, reinforced a feeling of European alienation when their interests were negotiated only as a sub-section of overall superpower considerations. It is questionable whether Brezhnev forwarded the Tbilisi proposal to stop the Mansfield amendment, since it is arguable that the American presence in Europe *ipso facto* legitiminsed the Soviet presence. The CSCE talks held in Helsinki were significant for one major reason: rather surprisingly the Soviet Union accepted the US presence at the Helsinki negotiations on *European* security issues. This above all was a sign and a tacit recognition by all parties involved of the permanence of America's European defence involvement.

The second lesson that can be drawn from the Mansfield debates is that although Senator Mansfield and his supporters failed to get majority support (very narrowly in 1973 by a 44–51 vote), they did 'serve notice on the Europeans that the present levels of American military support could not be taken for granted in the future'.[27] Soon after the defeat of the amendment, the Jackson–Nunn Amendment to the 1974 American Defense Appropriation Authorization Act required the US government to 'reduce forces in NATO Europe to the extent that their foreign exchange costs were not met by the European allies'.[28] This did little to improve Anglo–American relations, which were already at a low point following disagreements over the Yom Kippur War.

CONSULTATION AND THE MIDDLE EAST WAR, 1973

If the Mansfield Amendment prompted a general questioning of America's overseas military commitments amongst American politicians and public alike, the 1973 Middle East War was to prompt similar questioning amongst British politicians and public conerning the US bases. The Middle East War was to provide an example of the 'matter for joint decision', as mentioned in the Truman–Churchill agreement, in operation. The interpretation of the communiqué had always been vague (as shown in Chapter 4); the American understanding is that the communiqué is in no sense a formal or binding agreement. Successive British governments confirmed as satisfactory the 1952 agreement in the belief that Britain *would have to give positive agreement* before a nuclear weapon was fired or launched from British territory.

The alert of US forces worldwide actually took place after the main fighting in the Middle East. The UN had passed ceasefire resolutions on 22 and 23 October. The Soviet Union was particularly concerned that Egypt and Syria should suffer no defeat. But after persistent ceasefire violations, which Israel used as an excuse to advance and put pressure on President Sadat, Soviet concern reached panic levels as the Egyptian Third Army faced imminent defeat. The US support for Israel was on a massive scale. In the midst of the Middle East War there were more than 550 American missions to Israel sending in over 1000 tons of military aid per day, an operation bigger than the Berlin Airlift. On 24 October the US President received intelligence reports stating that seven Soviet airborne divisions totalling some 50 000 men had been put on alert and 85 ships (including landing craft and ships carrying troop helicopters) were in the Mediterranean.[29]

Responding to fears that the Soviet Union might unilaterally put forces into Egypt to support the Third Army, Kissinger, Haig, Schlesinger, Scowcroft, Moorer and Colby (Director of CIA) met in the White House situation room at 11 pm. It has never satisfactorily been resolved whether or not the Soviet alert was *actual* preparation for military intervention in Egypt against Israel – as had happened in

January 1970 when, at Nasser's request, surface-to-air missiles with Russian crews and Soviet pilots were supplied. Alternatively, the Russian alert centred could be seen as a warning, or display, of Soviet anxiety. The substance of the European critique following the US alert centred upon the question of whether the Soviet Union actually intended to send vast forces into the Middle East. There was also some nervousness that Europe could become embroiled in a cause that was not specifically a European concern.

At the end of the metting in the White House situation room, a recommendation, approved by the President, suggested that in the light of a diplomatic note from Brezhnev threatening military intervention, along with intelligence reports indicating such moves were already afoot,

> We put all American conventional and nuclear forces on military alert. In the early morning hours we flashed the word to American bases, installations, and naval units at home and around the world . . . it had been a severe shock to the American people to wake up and find that during the night our armed forces had been placed on world-wide military alert.[30]

It was quite a shock to most European countries hosting US forces as well. Britain, it appears from the records, was actually informed through Lord Cromer, the British Ambassador in Washington, at 1.03 am (East Coast, USA time) on 25 October, of Brezhnev's threatening letter of military intervention and consequent US 'readiness' measures. Lord Cromer was informed barely an hour after the preliminary decison to place all military forces inside and outside the US onto Def Con III. The Ambassador later confirmed the American assessment of Brezhnev's threat.

It would appear in this particular case that 'joint decision' actually meant 'inform' – after the fact. There was no previous consultation with any of the United States' European allies. American documentation from the National Archives makes it plain that the administration believed that their only obligation towards their allies in time of emergency was to 'notify' them of developments.

The British government had never been given any specific promises to be actually consulted in a binding sense, and on two occasions it was made clear that 'a matter for joint decision' meant that the United Kingdom would be 'notified' in the event of an alert. The first assurance was made in July 1960 in a letter from the Secretary of Defense to the Minister for Defense, Harold Watkinson. The letter assured the Minister for Defence that since the American Secretary of Defense is 'intimately involved in any such decision [for an alert] taken here, and am notified immediately should one of the [above] commanders be compelled to direct an alert of his forces. I should be happy to ensure that you are *notified* of any decision to alert US forces in the UK'.[31] A year later in a memorandum to the Secretary of Defense, dated 6 January 1961, the JCS referred to the commitment whereby 'the Minister of Defense of the United Kingdom would be *notified* of any decision to alert US forces based in the United Kingdom and its territories' and stated that 'the procedures established to accomplish this notification have been reviewed and are considered adequate and appropriate'.[32]

James Schlesinger, then Secretary of Defense, when asked about the US administration's handling of the 1973 incident, said that 'Lord Cromer was informed – it was not handled well by the United States Government. There was time for consultation and discussion that could have been utilized'.[33] The British government were at least informed, whereas other European allies hosting US forces were not even notified of the alert. Kissinger, in his memoirs, justifies this position by admitting that whilst 'abstractly' America's allies were justified in this complaint, the US government had to go ahead with the alert: 'we had little time and we had to balance serious considerations. Our eye was on the imminent Soviet military move; our plan was to increase readiness and permit the Soviet Union to detect our preparations . . .there was no middle position between alert and no alert . . . *to be frank, we could not have accepted a judgement different from our own'.[34]*

This offers little comfort to America's European allies for the future and is of particular relevance to the present deployment of Cruise missiles in Europe. Kissinger foresaw the same type of problem arising in the future; 'emergencies are sure to rise again; and it will not be in anyone's interest if the chief protector of the free world's security is hamstrung by bureaucratic procedure in the face of imminent Soviet intervention'.[35]

Similar agreements to those negotiated between the United States and the United Kingdom concerning the use of bases had been negotiated elsewhere in Europe. The reaction in other European countries to the lack of American consultation during the Middle East crisis was severe. The West German government declared on 25 October that weapons deliveries, use of West German territory or installations from America depots to one of the warring parties, would not be permitted. Spain, on the same day, refused to acknowledge that the US forces alert applied to Spain because 'consent' of both countries was required for such an action. France, a day later, suspended work on NATO draft declarations as a sign of displeasure over American high-handed actions. Italy, on 27 October, made it known that membership of the Alliance did not oblige her to assist America's Middle East policy.

Comment from Britain was practically non-existent, apart from a report in the *New York Times*[36] that the Prime Minister Edward Heath, had pointedly refused to endorse the nuclear alert, which caused much displeasure in Washington circles. There was a general feeling in the American press that Britain was not supporting her erstwhile ally. Kissinger, somewhat acidly, took the British government to task when he wrote that 'unwilling to draw attention to the fact that they still enjoyed preferential status in Wasington, British officials did nothing to stem the tide of criticism from other allies – and fell in with the prevailing brouhaha over inadequate consultation'.[37] It gradually dawned on the American administration that the European objections were not just formalistic or institutional:

> Europe, it emerged increasingly, wanted the option to conduct a policy separate from the United States and in the case of the Middle East objectively in conflict with us . . . our allies were content to saddle us with the responsibility for the diplomacy, but they were not prepared to share its risks.[38]

This, it seems, could be a fitting epitaph for what Kissinger himself had dubbed 'The Year of Europe'. In this particular case, the real difficulties were over political stances which consultation alone could not remove. As for Britain, she had been at variance with American Middle East policy since 1967. Although she had been *informed* of the American alert, it is a worrying omen for the future if 'joint decision' is interpreted in its most restrictive sense which evades the spirit, if not the essence, of the base agreement. Yet because Britain is host to the American forces, she would share the responsibility and repercussions for any military action emanating from her shores.

The Middle East crisis and the US forces alert illustrates the need for at least a clarification of the Truman–Churchill agreement which, in practice, has proved open to question and potentially dangerous for British security. The 1962 Athens Guidelines did little to clarify the consultation procedure and merely provided that special weight would be accorded to the views of the NATO countries on, or from, whose territory nuclear weapons would be deployed, countries providing the nuclear warheads, or the countries providing or manning nuclear delivery systems. It was stressed that 'overly elaborate procedures' which might inhibit action or endanger the credibility of the deterrent should be avoided and that the agreed consultation procedure would be exercised, 'time and circumstances permitting'. The guidelines also stressed that 'nuclear powers have the responsibility for making the decision on whether or not nuclear weapons will be used'.[39] Above all the importance of the October 1973 Yom Kippur War was not so much the consultation procedure, but 'the clear and sober realization that identity of interests in the Atlantic Alliance is not something natural'.[40]

The year after the Middle East War nuclear alert, the UN General Assembly passed a resolution defining 'aggression'. Amongst the acts that, regardless of a declaration of war, qualified as an act of aggression were two of particular relevance to any future nuclear alert of US bases in the United Kingdom in the absence of a prior joint decision:

> The use of armed forces of one State which are within the territory of another state with the agreement of the receiving State, in contra-vention of the conditions provided for in the agreement or any extension of their presence in such territory beyond the termination of the agreement.[41]

But, in Section (F) of the resolution aggression could also mean:

> The action of a State in allowing its territory, which it has placed at the disposal of another State, to be used by that other State for perpetuating an act of aggression against a third State.[42]

While it could be argued that the United Nations 1974 definition of aggression might guard against future violations of the 1952 bases agreement between Truman and Churchill. the Chinese represen-tative expressed doubt in the General Assembly about the usefulness of such a definition[43] since the superpowers could prevent the Security Council adopting any decision condemning the aggressor and support-ing the violated.

BRITAIN LOOKS TO EUROPE, 1970–9

The successful negotiations that saw Britain joining the EEC in 1972 marked a growing commitment to European defence interests and weapons procurement, as projects like the Jaguar or Tornado multi-role combat aircraft (MRCA) showed. The British Defence Secretary, Roy Mason, as Chairman of the Eurogroup in 1975, was particularly active in encouraging such European co-operation. In 1978 the Klepsch Report to the European assembly advocated defence and other collaboration independent of the United States. David Green-wood has been a strong advocate of such a policy, arguing that the core countries of NATO in Europe should quicken the pace towards defining a distinctly European theory of defence and providing the equipment for it – falling short of a wholly independent West European defence effort, yet providing greater independence from the United States.[44]

The growing feeling that Europe should have a greater voice in her own defence matters was also expressed by the creation of the Independent European Programme Group (IEPG) in February 1976. The IEPG was independent of the Eurogroup and integrated military structure of NATO, thus enabling France to join, but acting within the North Atlantic Treaty's terms of reference. The IEPG was aimed at alliance standardisation and preserving European defence industries. Britain's membership of the IEPG was significant for two reasons. On the one hand it signified the extent to which the United States was now dealing with the United Kingdom as part of a wider European set-up rather than on the limited 'special relationship' or bilateral basis. However, Britain's membership also signified the extent to which Britain was identifying herself with a wider set of European interests in negotiations with the United States. In spite of a move by Britain towards a greater European identity, the US bases still remained as an open reminder of the United Kingdom's dependence on the United States.

The 1970s were remarkable for the detente process with SALT negotiations between the superpowers and Brandt's *Ostpolitik* in Europe. Due in part to the detente process questions were being asked on both sides of the Atlantic about the continued necessity of the large US military presence in Europe. Compared to earlier decades the *military* justification for such a presence was thin. In the mid-1950s the declining requirement for bomber bases overseas was briefly balanced by the need for overseas launching sites for Thor and Jupiter IRBMs. These in turn were given way to ICBM's and long-range B-52 bombers based in the United States. The development of Polaris in the 1960s with its limited range had again necessitated overseas bases, but the development of the fleet ballistic missile (and, in particular, Trident) made this necessity look doubtful. In recognition of this, the Rota SSBN support facility in Spain was closed. Apart from strategic considerations, the real future of overseas bases for the United States was a political question, a fact made clear in a research paper intended for Department of Defense consumption:

> Simply put, our ability to continue to use facilities in a foreign nation to support our far flung military forces rests fundamentally on the degree to which we and that nation have shared interests . . . even our best and closest allies cannot fail to be aware that their interests and ours simply do not – or seem not to – coincide as completely, as frequently, and as easily as they once did. All of this comes at a time when, by virtue of its own massive defence expenditures and its nurturing of potential basing sites abroad, the Soviet Union is becoming a global superpower with no part of the world outside the range of its military forces.[45]

Anglo–American relations were continually troubled during the 1970s by the presence of a strong peace movement, who chose as a focus of attack the US 'nuclear' bases. Nevertheless, one vitally important area of the US presence in the United Kingdom had continued its quiet but steady growth; this was in the field of intelligence co-operation. The history of Anglo–American intelligence co-operation went as far back as the wartime 'Ultra' system. The reliance upon the UK for many American intelligence operations was emphasised during the Iranian revolution of 1978–9, when the United States lost a valuable source of intelligence that was particularly important for verifying the SALT 2 agreements. This loss stressed the importance of U-2 flights from Akrotiri (Cyprus) and Wethersfield in Essex. President Carter went out of his way to reassure SALT sceptics that 'other forms of surveillance still exist, including the use of British facilities'.[46] Information in the media during the Official Secrets trial in 1978[47] indicated the importance attached to co-operation in military communication and the sizeable NSA contingency at GCHQ in Cheltenham suggests that this facility is still largely regarded as an Anglo–American trust.

The United States has branches of its four most secret services bases in Britain, the CIA, National Security Agency, the National Reconnaissance Office, and the Defense Intelligence Agency. The NSA in particular works closely with GCHQ; their 'prime joint purpose is the long range electronics surveillance of Russia's clandestine activities'.[48] The British Defence Staff, Washington, DC (BDSW), illustrates the importance that Britain continues to attach to co-operation in intelligence and military fields. The CIA reciprocates by mounting operations from the US Embassy in Grosvenor Square. The BDSW totals approximately 170 personnel with 75 front line British staff in Washington, compared to seven in Bonn and ten in Paris, and with it rests primary responsibility for defence co-operation work in America. The BDSW representation and the range of defence contracts that they help secure suggests that 'although the United Kingdom's defence effort has increasingly centred on Europe it has retained a "special relationship" with the United States in defence matters which is of vital importance'.[49]

Apart from the considerable intelligence community there were, by the late 1970s, about 25 000 American airmen, soldiers and sailors based on 20 primary military establishments in the United Kingdom. The ranks of the US servicemen in the United Kingdom were further swelled when SAC forces returned to Britain in September 1979, with over 1000 personnel and 2000 dependents. They occupy a large base at Fairford used by the 11th Strategic Group to provide tanker support for tactical fighter forces or perhaps the Rapid Deployment Force in the Middle East.

By the end of the seventies the United Kingdom was host to roughly 40 per cent of the United States air commitment to NATO as well as a major submarine base. Aside from the notable exception of the 1973 US forces alert, the US bases in Britain were seldom in the headlines or in the forefront of political discussion. This was to change dramatically in 1979 with the NATO Council decision to deploy GLCMs in Britain.

THE ADVENT OF CRUISE MISSILES

The decision by the NATO Council in December 1979 to deploy GLCMs in the European theatre raised fresh questions about whether or not the US and the United Kingdom still had a common set of interests and values. Since the information of the Nuclear Planning Group (NPG) and NATO's adoption of flexible response in 1967, attention generally concentrated on short-range or battle-field systems. By the late 1970s growing asymmetries in US and Soviet theatre nuclear forces (TNF) led to more attention being paid to long- and medium-range components. The worry was that superpower parity in the central strategic systems could lead the Soviet Union to threaten use of its long-range theatre nuclear force (LRTNF), upon the premise that the United States would be deterred from striking back with its intercontinental force. After the removal of Thor and Jupiter missiles from Europe in 1963, NATO's LRTN force consisted almost exclusively of ageing British Vulcans and the US F-111s. During this period the Soviet arsenal had changed rapidly. The SS-4 and SS-5 IRBMs (roughly comparable to the liquid fuelled Thor missile) were gradually being complemented by the more advanced SS-20 IRBM. The Soviet Air Force was also carrying out some significant changes, replacing the TU-22 Blinder and TU-16 Badger with the Backfire bomber.

There was uneasiness in Europe over the possibility that the Strategic Arms Limitation Treaty (SALT 1) had in fact bargained away European defence interests and security. Whilst SALT 1 had codified 'strategic parity', it also accentuated existing imbalance at lower levels. Critics of the SALT process were quick to point to the emergence of Soviet systems, like the SS-20 and Backfire bomber, that were outside SALTs provisions but highly relevant to Europe (the so-called 'grey area' systems). The new Soviet weapons strengthened the feeling in Western defence circles that modernisation of NATO's LRTNF was urgent. The United States was quick to recognise the possibilities of putting their own 'grey area' system in Europe to counter the Soviet threat. The first signs of active consideration to deploy GLCMs in the United Kingdom were mentioned in 1976, in *Strategic Survey*, which noted that USAF had begun studies on the possibility of replacing the F-111s in Europe with cruise missiles.[50] In fact it turned out that they were considering an addition to the F-111 force in Britain.

The British reaction to the varied rumours was less enthusiastic than the American faith in the new cruise missile. In January 1977, a report prepared by Malcolm Currie (Director of Research and Engineering on the GLCM) commented that 'the advent of long range, highly accurate cruise missiles is perhaps the most significant weapon development of the decade'.[51] European suspicion of the US attitude towards cruise were not without basis since, although the Vladivostok agreement excluded Backfire and cruise, the Soviet Union had been pressing hard for permanent constraints on cruise and in particular for a no-transfer clause. The suspicion held in some European defence circles was that over time the United States, in order to reach an agreement, would mortgage systems more likely to serve West European interests rather than American interests. As a result of European pressure, the NPG ministers created a High Level Group (HLG) to study NATO's long-term requirements for TNF and the technical, military and political implications of alternative TNF postures (i.e. whether TNF should be sea-based or land-based).

The HLG started work in December 1977. Their deliberations are well-documented elsewhere;[52] but briefly it was decided that LRTNF modernisation should be an 'evolution', rather than a radical change, in NATO's defence posture. A direct matching of the SS-20 capability was considered unnecessary and an 'offsetting' capability was all that was required. Lastly it was decided that a 'highly visible' deployment mode was preferable: this decision was largely prompted by political rather than military considerations. This package was put before the NATO Council in December 1979. A 'dual-key' system for the proposed missile deployments by the US in Europe was apparently offered. West Germany declined the offer on economic grounds (acceptance would have meant accepting some of the research and deployment costs) and it was also felt that deployment of the missiles under American control would demonstrate alliance cohesion. No other country *at the time* indicated any interest in purchasing the launch vehicles and sharing control. The new system was thus to be deployed with American forces only, and under US command and control. Although vague noises were made about the possibility of reaching bilateral understandings with host goverments, concerning the appropriate consultation procedure in the event of a requirement to fire (in Britain's case the 1952 Churchill–Truman agreement applied), it was made clear that '. . . such consultation procedure *does not imply* any actual inhibition on the capability of the United States to operate the systems'.[53]

The pragmatic case for LRTNF modernisation lay in the deficiencies of the current LRTNF forces. SLBMs have limits in yield and accuracy, and were considered too close to the central strategic systems. The long-range strike aircraft based in England, the F-111, is old and vulnerable to pre-emptive attack, and would have difficulty penetrating Russian air defences. These factors were seen by the HLG as creating a gap in the deterrence spectrum which the Soviet Union could exploit during a crisis. Largely due to German pressure, first mentioned by Helmut Schmidt in his Alastair Buchan memorial lecture before the International Institute for Strategic Studies (IISS) in 1977, it was also decided to link the deployments with an arms-control posture.[54] Helmut Schmidt was concerned about the implications of SALT 2 for European security and about the increasing significance of the European nuclear balance; it was on the basis of these two points the NATO's December 1979 decision established the duality of arms control and modernisation. The decision was dubbed the 'Dual-Track' (or 'Twin-Track') decision. Many suggested that the NATO LRTNF modernisation and Dual-Track posture, aimed mainly at countering the Soviet SS-20 missiles, was inadequate, because Moscow's modernisation was not just centred upon the SS-20 but consisted of several new weapons – including the SS-21, SS-22, and SS-23 battlefield nuclear support missiles, the Backfire medium-range bomber, and the SU-19 Fencer attack aircraft.

The apparent Soviet threat that appeared to have been 'discovered' in the form of growing numbers of SS-20 missiles in close proximity to Europe was not in fact new. A glance at *Military Balance* for the years 1969–70 shows that there were 700 Soviet MRBMs within reach of Europe at that time. To some, the introduction of 572 warheads into Europe was only, to quote General Haig, 'political expediency and tokenism'. There was also doubt that the SS-20 was a significant enough jump in capability to justify NATO's LRTNF modernisation. Critics also pointed out that it would not be long before a Russian 'cruise' missile appeared which would again upset any hopes for balance.[55] It is unlikely that any amount of juggling with the geographical location of American nuclear capabilities could satisfy the permanent doubters of the American military guarantee, in part because 'this problem is inherent in the geostrategic structure of the alliance and the physical detachment of the chief guarantor from its allies'.[56] Perhaps the biggest concern of all was not just the presence of such missiles on European soil (they had, after all, predecessors in Matador and Mace), but what they now symbolised. The point was succinctly put by Laurence Martin in the 1981 Reith Lectures:

> By far the most important potential arena for [nuclear] conflicts is Europe, where the interests of the superpowers are most clearly defined and where the most powerful military forces in history have been concentrated. If nuclear deterrence is the doctrinal centrepiece of contemporary strategy, Europe is its geopolitical focus.[57]

Of little comfort for many in the United Kingdom was the fact that for the first time in sixteen years NATO's LRTNF was no longer exclusively based in the United Kingdom. The British government fully supported the modernisation at the NPG meetings and at the NATO Council's final decision. The Defence Minister, Francis Pym, argued forcefully for a unanimous decision, pointing out that NATO's entire LRTNF (US F-111s and British Vulcans) was based in the United Kingdom. The NATO plan would spread the weapons more widely through Europe, which would give enhanced strength to the United Kingdom and the Alliance. It was only after the December 1979 decision that some Labour opposition members voiced complaints about the plan. To them, the proposed stationing of GLCMs illustrated the psychological dangers inherent in the presence of US defence bases on our shores, namely those of over-reliance and misunderstanding. The GLCM debate also detracted from the real weakness in NATO – the conventional forces. Michael Howard, at a conference held by the IISS in London, warned that NATO countries must seek 'a far greater emphasis on conventional defence of Europe as opposed to nuclear deterrence by American systems which so many people misunderstand and mistrust . . . it no longer appears plausible to defend Western Europe by threatening the use of nuclear weapons which would be utterly counter-productive if used.'[58] Moreover, the stationing of American cruise missiles on UK territory had created popular opposition because 'the European peoples have ceased to feel that the defence of their territory is in their own hands . . . mistrust of the United States, anti-Americanism, is a sort of by-product of this'.[59]

The NATO modernisation debate was carefully followed by the Soviet Union. Early attempts to block deployment were made, in particular, by President Brezhnev during a speech in East Berlin on 6 October 1979, when he announced the withdrawal of approximately 20 000 troops and 1000 tanks from the GDR. He also hinted at 'possible reductions' in the number of Soviet MRBMs in the western part of the USSR if the US did not deploy new TNF forces on the continent. The decision to deploy the new TNF systems by the NATO Council was taken seriously by the Soviet leadership. To Brezhnev it would 'change the strategic situation on the continent' and 'break down the balance of forces'.[60] It was also seen as a move by the Pentagon to put more emphasis on the role of forward-based systems in Europe. The Soviet Union also claimed that deployment of GLCMs and Pershing 2s would violate SALT 2 since they were strategic, a belief that the Soviet Union still holds.[61]

THE BASES INTO THE EIGHTIES – THE CRUISE DEBATE

The cruise missile deployment has proved to date the most controversial development in the history of US bases in the United Kingdom, from the standpoint both of the control of these weapons, and of the unwillingness of US and British authorities to use them. Whereas the

B-29s that arrived in 1948 were more of an American than a European initiative, there is a sense in which the GLCM proved to be a product of European inadequacy. The decision to deploy cruise and Pershing 2 missiles in Europe coincided with a general lack of confidence in NATO's 'flexible response' strategy. The weakness of European conventional forces again put pressure upon NATO to adopt a first use stance that would invite crushing retaliation.

The Thatcher government announced soon after the December NATO Council meeting a series of diplomatic and military measures, the most important of which was that the government had agreed to allow forty launch vehicles with 160 GLCMs, owned and operated by the United States, to be based in Britain. The Prime Minister was asked whether she had a right to veto the use of US nuclear weapons based in Great Britain in all circumstances. Mrs Thatcher's reply, echoing that of previous Prime Ministers, was that 'The understanding which continues to apply today provides that the use of these bases in an emergency would be a matter for joint decision by Her Majesty's Government and the United States Government in the light of circumstances prevailing at the time'.[62] Less confidently Francis Pym indicated that the United Kingdom 'will have *a degree of say* in the authorization for the use of the new systems'.[63] However the precise implications of his statement are far from clear.

The mission of US overseas forces commitments, from the 1970s into the 1980s, continued to be based upon the premise that the best place to begin the defence of the United States is as far forward as possible. America's European Command (EUCOM) protects American national interests and, through NATO, supports the mission of deterrence against all forms of aggression. Should aggression occur in Europe, the mission of US forces will be to:

> Conduct an initial conventional defense as far forward as possible; preserve or restore the integrity and security of the NATO area; conduct deliberate escalation of the conflict if aggression cannot be contained and provide an appropriate nuclear response if the aggression is in the form of a major nuclear attack.[64]

The supreme national interest for the United States would obviously be to keep the United States outside the area of direct nuclear warfare. However, to launch an attack from Western Europe on the assumption that the Soviet Union would then conveniently retaliate against Western Europe (and the US forces stationed therein), rather than against American territory, is wishful thinking. The strategy of 'flexible response', NATO's official strategy, is seen as increasingly outmoded and dangerous by many Europeans. Hopes of controlling the process of escalation from the British perspective must be limited. The phrase 'matter for joint decision' now appears to be particularly anachronistic. The increasing speed of missiles and the possibility of a first strike use puts an additional burden on the 1951 agreement made in the age of propellor-driven bombers.

The twin problems of the troubled NATO 'flexible response' doctrine, coupled in the United Kingdom with vague agreements on the use of American bases, have been exacerbated by the arrival of GLCMs. The cruise missiles to be stationed in Britain, Sicily, Belgium, Holland and Pershing 2s in Germany have given birth not only to bitter strategic debates but to anti-Americanism. In Britain the 'peace camps' are constantly in the news and have focused attention on the US military presence. The crux of the present debate surrounding these European deployments was well put by SIPRI:

> For the European countries new missiles make a difficult situation worse. More effective war fighting weapons, introduced into a major power competition which is not of European making but in which Europeans – East and West – may become the main losers, are clearly detrimental to their security. The host countries would, moreover, be burdened with a number of high-priority nuclear weapon targets which would make it virtually certain that West Europe would be drawn into almost any strategic war between the two great powers.[65]

The argument that there have been nuclear weapons bases in Western Europe since the 1950s and that the GLCMs therefore represent a qualitative improvement, but no drastic improvement in the West European deterrent, is not convincing. The premise that GLCMs presented no new threat, but were merely an updating of forces, was based upon the much publicised withdrawal of 1000 nuclear weapons from the European theatre, mainly in the form of Atomic Demolition Munitions (ADMs) and battlefield weapons. There are two faults with this argument. Firstly ADMs, designed to cause landslides and general havoc to attacking tank or troop formations, made a complete absurdity of flexible response doctrine and committed NATO to an early use of nuclear weapons on European soil. They had been militarily and politically unpopular for a number of years and it is likely that, cruise or not, they would have been retired anyway. Similarly, the much publicised withdrawal of some battlefield weapons neglected to point out that they were already due for retirement or replacement to make way for the new SMART weapons. Secondly, the need for a 'vivid political symbol'[66] of America's commitment to Europe led to the choice of a land-based mode of deployment. The visibility of the missiles was designed to boost confidence amongst Europeans in the US nuclear guarantee. Instead the missiles became the centre of European political debate and the focus of anti-American sentiment, while at the same time sabotaging any real hopes of long-term detente with the Soviet Union.

Even if one accepts the need for LRTNF modernisation, based upon Helmut Schmidt's warning to the Alliance[67] of the implications of parity in intercontinental systems and disparities in the European region, it is not necessarily a corollary that the modernisation has to be land-based. The deployment of the missiles on land served to make public opinion in many European countries more intense than would their deployment in a less conspicuous way, at sea, for example.[68] The choice of the HLG in opting for deployment of the missiles on land was to 'couple' the United States strategic deterrent to European defences. The presence of the missiles on soil was also supposed to reassure America's allies where other forms of deployment could give rise to suspicions of withdrawal or decoupling. Another less well known reason behind the land-based deployment was that originally it was suggested that the GLCMs might be sited at RAF Lakenheath or Upper Heyford and gradually replace the F-111 bombers. It is now quite apparent that the missiles have in fact augmented, not replaced, the manned dual-capable bombers. There was also fear that the cruise missiles would be the first of increasingly effective weapons that could be introduced into superpower rivalry, which is not necessarily of European making, and could make Europeans the losers.

The issue of dual-key control of the cruise missiles came to the forefront with the imminent arrival of the first cruise missile at Greenham Common. Dual-key was purportedly offered to the European 'host' countries, which would have meant purchasing the launch vehicles and perhaps covering some developmental costs. No country showed any interest at the time of the December 1979 decision. In a MORI poll conducted for the *Sunday Times*[69] at the end of October 1983, just over a month before the arrival of the first cruise missile and shortly after the US unvasion of the Commonwealth Island of Grenada, a representative sample of voters was asked, 'If the American government wanted to fire the missiles and the British government objected, do you think America would fire them anyway, or not?' The result was uneqivocal: 'would', 73 per cent; 'would not', 20 per cent; 'no opinion', 7 per cent. Opposition to cruise being allowed in Britain stood at 51 per cent, with 41 per cent in favour. Reassurances that the arrangements made in 1951 would safeguard Britain's interests were dismissed by Labour's re-appointed spokesman, John Silkin:

> Anybody who knows anything about defence has always known that the American President has sole control over the firing of cruise missiles. The common sense of the British people has come to the same conclusion at a time when the British government itself appears to be totally unaware of the fact.[70]

The fears expressed by many European protest groups, opposed to the new missiles, over the control and use of the weapons, were borne out in the war game codenamed WINTEX. This exercise consists of American and European officials meeting every two years to simulate exactly what their nations would do if a request to fire nuclear artillery shells or warheads came from an endangered European battle-field. In almost all cases, the decision ended up on the desk of the President of the United States. The *Washington Post*, observing one WINTEX exercise, witnessed the senior military official playing the President decide quickly to go nuclear and range deftly up and down the ladder of escalation. Low-yield atomic shells and medium-range missiles were mixed together in a three-day barrage. It was only afterwards that an official noted that 'not once had "the President" moved toward that button that would have launched Titan or Minuteman rockets from their US bases into the Soviet Union'.[71] Although too much can be made of such examples, they are, after all, exercises to overcome problems and shortcomings; and they did renew doubts about the mutuality of Anglo–American interests.

The decision to retain the F-111 Quick Reaction Alert (QRA)[72] force in addition to the GLCMs meant additional attention was paid to the survivability of both aircraft and runways. A hardened aircraft shelter (HAS) network was constructed for F-111s at Lakenheath and Upper Heyford, at Alconbury for Phantoms, and at Bentwaters and Woodbridge for A-10s. Shelters for the TR-1 at Alconbury have proven difficult so far on account of the wingspan of over one hundred feet. A HAS network has also been constructed at Boscombe Down which, in the event of an emergency, would receive F-111s from New Mexico. The F-111 force is further protected by the 42nd Electronic Combat Squadron which began operations out of Upper Heyford in

1984 using EF-111As. The EF-111As mission is to provide electronic counter measure support for tactical air forces. This mission is accomplished mainly through the ALQ99 jammer on the aircraft's tail fin which would effectively blind long-range air defence radar systems – the jammer has proven successful in tests on the West coast of America but cannot be tested in the United Kingdom air space because it would disrupt BBC services amongst other things. A major USAFE runway repair programme has also been undertaken so that runways may be repaired in a number of hours instead of days. The programme includes the stationing of a mobile runway repair unit called Red Horse in Britain and pre-positioning of stocks which include crushed aggregate to fill craters, the AM-2 aluminium mat to cover the aggregate and a glass-fibre-reinforced polyester cover. A pre-positioned concrete block method is also being considered.[73]

Doubts have also been raised about the vulnerability of cruise missiles which, being land based, will have to be deployed early in a time of tension or risk damage. However the manner in which the GLCMs will be deployed in time of emergency is far from clear. When the 501st Tactical Missile Wing was established at Greenham Common in 1983, the construction of six hardened GLCM shelters had just been completed. Each shelter houses the vehicles for one 16-missile flight – four Transport-erector-launchers (TELs), each carrying four GLCMs – and these are accompanied by two Launch Control Centres (LCCs).[74] The shelters are divided into three cells with two launchers each. At Greenham Common (and at Molesworth, when operative) a flight will always be maintained at immediate readiness, ready to 'leave the base on alarm and reach a nearby dispersed launch position. The theory is that mobility will ensure a high survival capacity.[75] In the event of a convoy leaving, carrying live warheads (thus far only dummy warheads have been used on exercise around Greenham Common), it will be described as 'All Round Up'. The dispersal to the secret launch sites will be between five and ninety miles[76] from the main operating base. When outside the base, a massive and unwieldy column of twenty-two vehicles forms the convoy (4 TELs, 2 LCCs, 16 'support' vehicles). The much publicised exercise deployments of cruise convoys with dummy warheads are protected by RAF regiment personnel from Catterick and security personnel from USAF. Furthermore, each 'normal flight of missiles will be expected to mingle with ordinary traffic'.[77] The convoys have proved not only slow but highly conspicuous. The dispersal of missiles in time of tension before war could be seen as both provocative and unlikely. There would be little need for the elaborate and expensive shelters if the GLCMs were to be dispersed. If, as the MoD insist, the cruise missiles will be moved from their bases to secret locations in time of tension, this could only be construed from a Soviet perspective as the signal that starts a full-scale nuclear exchange.

Of equal concern to the mode of deployment have been various claims of unreliability of the BGM–109G GLCM, particularly in its guidance system, which relies upon a pre-mapped route with 'visual' checkpoints (konwn as a terrain-matching system or TERCOM).[78] The fact is that vast areas of the Soviet Union are virtually featureless and cruise is no good at finding its way across flat snow-bound wastes. In-flight testing was conducted with Pierre Trudeau's agreement in a remote area of Canada thought to approximate closely much of the Soviet Union's terrain. Although difficult to detect because of its small radar cross-section and low flight altitude, once detected it is highly vulnerable, flying as it does at a preprogrammed speed and altitude. In spite of acknowledged doubts about TERCOM's reliability political motives led to cruise and Pershing 2s being deployed by IOC (Initial Operational Capability) in December 1983. Like the deployment of Thor missiles in Britain, any technical deficiencies were to be made up by the political and strategic significance of the missiles.

The Russian reaction to the deployment of cruise and Pershing 2 missiles in Europe was, as expected, highly critical. The proposal to link these new deployments with arms control proposals, such as President Reagan's 'zero option', met with little real enthusiasm. The Soviet Union has long insisted that the US nuclear systems on forward bases in Europe constitute a fourth arm of the American strategic force. The new deployments, and in particular the Pershing 2, were seen as presenting a new threat.[79]

Marshal Ustinov argued that implementation of the NATO plan would be considered as supplementing existing US forward based systems, as well as French and British independent nuclear forces, and thereby altering the strategic equation in Europe to NATO's advantage. 'This', Ustinov warned, 'would force the Soviet Union to adopt the appropriate retaliatory measures'.[80]

If, as seems most likely, cruise is to remain in Britain, there are two questions that should be answered. The first is, what is the purpose of the new modernised LRTNF? In an interim report on nuclear weapons in Europe, in which two British MPs participated – John Cartwright (SDP) and Julian Critchley (Conservative) – it was made clear that the views of some American officials indicated a more demanding role for the LRTNF than that required by European counterparts. The report argued that American officials 'believe that LRTNF constitutes warfighting capabilities rather than political signalling assets as many Europeans tend to perceive them'.[81] The second question, that follows on from the belief that the LRTNF is a warfighting force, asks, how effective are the tattered remnants of NATO's strategy of flexible response adopted in 1967? There is little or no agreement on guidelines for the follow-up use of nuclear weapons if a first attempt to communicate NATO's intentions through a 'controlled demonstrative use' did not succeed in 'persuading the adversary to halt hostilities'.[82] If the United Kingdom has little or no guideline concerning the use of cruise missiles, and given the possibility that the government might not be consulted in the event of their use, it would seem that now as never before there is a pressing need to re-examine the United Kingdom's base agreements with the United States.

9 Conclusion

SOME GENERAL ISSUES

Measurement of the value of United States bases in the United Kingdom, in terms of whether the UK faces a greater danger or enhanced protection as a result of the American forces stationed there, is necessarily subjective. However, two general trends can be discerned. The first is a growing feeling in the United States that Europeans generally should be prepared to play a greater role in their own defence, and this includes financial contributions. Britain herself has far too long relied upon American and her own nuclear weapons for the bulk of the defence effort, at the cost of running down conventional forces. Duncan Sandys, as Minister of Defence in 1957, presided over a massive cut-back in conventional forces, thereby increasing reliance upon nuclear deterrence. In outlining Britain's new look defence policy, Sandys said that 'it must be well understood that, if Russia were to launch a major attack on them [Western nations], even with conventional forces only, they would have to hit back with strategic nuclear weapons'.[1] As Field Marshal Lord Carver has observed,[2] the idea that NATO could avert defeat by initiating nuclear war is dangerous and irresponsible; it can only end in 'greater defeat'. It is therefore up to the United Kingdom and Europeans generally to reassess the need for the plethora of NATO – particularly American – nuclear weapons. Europe must also heed American calls for a greater European role in its own defence by building up its conventional forces, thus reversing a general decline. Nor, by the same token, must American fighters, submarines and missiles based in Europe be considered as a manpower substitute.

The second trend that can be discerned since the late 1950s is an increasing ruthlessness in United States attitudes towards European defence concerns. The general assumption concerning United States defence bases overseas has been that 'what is good for America, is good for Europe'. The continued support of the United States is likely to remain the keystone of NATO's future cohesion and the United Kingdom is central to the US military presence in Europe, as she remains America's closest European ally. But it should not be forgotten that, in the words of a Congressional report, 'the United States maintains forces in Western Europe not out of an act of charity, but for its *own* security interests',[3] a feeling also expressed recently by General Charles Gabriel, USAFE Commander-in-Chief.[4] The report also observed that the attitude of some countries within NATO towards American defence policy had taken a turn for the worse in recent years, and military personnel are the most direct recipients of these feelings. Although in the United Kingdom this is not as noticeable as say, in Greece, there is a growing feeling – particularly amongst the postwar generation who never witnessed the war-time special relationship – that British and American security interest are no longer synonymous. The cruise debate in particular has served to revive the question of whose interests are being served by the bases.

The United Kingdom is host to a relatively small but significant part of the United States overseas forces. It is doubtful that the United Kingdom could have afforded such cover as that provided by US bases and facilities in the United Kingdom. The United Kingdom's defence posture has developed with the US presence in mind. The early presence of B-29 bombers left the RAF free to concentrate on building up her own bomber forces, as well as giving Britain access to the benefits of America's nuclear arsenal before Britain had developed her own independent nuclear force. However, to some, the most serious detrimental effect of US basing in the United Kingdom was the added threat of nuclear devastation which the link with the United States had enhanced from the 1950s. Such fears were regularly expressed – when the B-29s were given an atomic capability in the summer of 1949, when Thor missiles were deployed in Britain, or when the Polaris base at Holy Loch opened in 1960 and more recently with the advent of cruise missiles in Europe – these events were supposed to have enhanced Russian motives for launching a strike against the United Kingdom.

The United States has over the years grown accustomed to having bases overseas as a matter of operational convenience, with little consideration of the absolute necessity of such facilities. The United Kingdom's military dependence upon the United States has meant a certain compliance with American requirements and needs. The American basing posture is 'too frequently one of indifferent status quoism. And for want of the capability or willingness ourselves to prioritize amongst various activities and facilities, we frequently find ourselves unable bureaucratically to set our own priorities. This can lead to inflexibility in bargaining; it can also lead to reluctant acceptance of the host countries priorities and agenda'.[5]

Historically the massive American military investment in Europe has been justified by the fact that Europe is central to United States strategic thinking 'because of the realities of power'.[6] Senator Church, in a speech before the National War College in Washington, argued that there was a growing consensus that it was time to bring to an end to American hegemony in Europe. The crux of the question seems to have been that of economics: the United States 'having turned on the tap, seemed unable to turn it off, despite the fact that these rich countries are making half the effort in proportion to ours'.[7] John Newhouse[8] argued that a reduced commitment would perforce stimulate European co-operation, unity and a greater European commitment to joint defence. Critics also argued that NATO could not withstand for long the anomaly of a fourteen to one configuration, the one supporting the fourteen. Senator George Aiken of Vermont in May 1971, during a debate on the Mansfield Amendment, said 'more than enough American troops are in Europe to serve our objectives, unless of course, our allies wish to pay for their continued presence'.[9]

The popular conception that the United States is paying for Europe's defence while the allies are not is simply false. Many European countries still have conscription and are acutely aware of their vulnerable location between two superpowers. Many of the United States' forces in Europe are subsidised. For instance Germany pays USAF landing fees at civilian airfields, provides free land, facilities and security for each forward operating base with A-10s. The Netherlands provides all security, civil engineering, fire fighting and recovery services at Soesterberg (F-15) airfield. The United Kingdom, perhaps the most generous of all, provides rent-free land at eleven air bases and over thirty other US facilities in addition to Rapier missiles and personnel for fighter bases. In addition the United Kingdom spends (1985) 5 per cent of the GDP on defence which compares favourably with the 5.8 per cent of the United States, the 4.3 per cent of Germany, 1.8 per cent of Canada and 3.2 per cent for the Netherlands.

Europe *does* pay for most of her own defence with approximately 3.3 million military personnel on active duty compared to 320 000 US military personnel in Europe, or about 10 per cent of the total. Whether Europe could provide an effective defence without a substantial US contribution is open to debate largely because Europe has yet to demonstrate the necessary political leadership and unity.

Would the redeployment of US forces back to the United States result in a saving to the American taxpayer? Robert Pfaltzgraff argues that it would not; short of the demobilization of US forces returned from Europe, the cost of redeploying them in the United States, including the initial capiatl investment and recurring expenses for equipment and airlift capability, would exceed the present cost of keeping them in Europe'.[11] Pfaltzgraff estimated that the cost of all United States military forces, wherever located in the world, committed to Europe for deployment there in the event of hostilities, totalled $17 billion in the financial year 1974. All but $4 billion of this figure represented defence expenditures that could not be reduced by the withdrawal of US forces in Europe, unless such forces were demobilised after they returned to the United States. In addition to the cost of transporting forces to the United States would be the cost of transporting the forces back to Europe to defend against aggression. The cost of providing this kind of mobility for one division and one tactical fighter wing would cost $4.3 billion dollars from FY 1983–7.[12] Mobility of all US forces in Europe would obviously be economically prohibitive, aside from the logistical problems which would involve massive movements of material, for example, 800 000 tons of Army tank ammunition alone.

The argument often put forward by defenders of the *status quo*, that the United States should maintain its present force levels because any force reductions could engender political or military threats to Europe (and hence the United States), is also exaggerated. To balance the argument, it should be observed, and the US bases in the United Kingdom are a case in point, that once established a base tends to assume a justification of its own in spite of the fact that its mission is outdated. Overseas bases were originally required at America's behest because of the short range of bombers, missiles and submarines that did not permit deployment from the United States. They were also a sign of political solidarity and support for a shattered European economy after the Second World War. Both these reasons no longer apply directly to the 1980s. This point arose in a Senate committee report which concluded:

> arguments can always be raised to justify keeping almost any facility open. To the military, a contingency use can always be found. To the diplomat, a base closing or reduction can always be at the wrong time in terms or relations with the host country and other nations.[13]

However, reliance upon the continued US military involvement in Europe should not be taken for granted and certainly should not prevent European countries planning and taking a greater role in their own defence.[14]

THE NUCLEAR QUESTION

The future of US nuclear weapons in the United Kingdom, and more generally Europe, is unclear. In Britain and the second Thatcher government allied its defence posture very closely with that of the United States. The Labour opposition made its commitment to NATO clear, cruise missiles would be 'sent back to the United States on the election of a Labour government'.[15] There seemed to be little logical reason for the level of nuclear weapons in Europe in the mid-1980s, apart from the assumption made in the 1950s that any war with the Warsaw Pact would be nuclear. Little thought was given to the role of non-nuclear forces. The United States built a large production base for fissionable materials and the JCS regularly projected requirements that would use them all up. This was done 'without any coherent plan or doctrine for the conduct of a theatre nuclear war'.[16] Under Secretary of Defense, Robert McNamara, the number of tactical nuclear armaments in Europe levelled off at about 7000 (excluding the British and French independent nuclear deterrents). The presence of such a large number of nuclear weapons in Europe has been criticised for two reasons. First, tactical nuclear weapons cannot defend Europe, only ensure its destruction. Second, there is no believable doctrine of how to fight a tactical nuclear war. Conversely there are some who see tactical nuclear weapons as a guarantor of NATO's safety, because they act as a deterrent, backed up as they are by the implicit threat of a large American strategic arsenal.

There exists within NATO some confusion between conventional and nuclear roles. The F-111s based in Britain are an example of the confusion that reigns in this area, since their 'dual-capable' role is more likely, in the actual event, to be nuclear. The result is not dual-capable aircraft but 'extremely expensive and inferior nuclear forces'.[17] The reduction of American nuclear forces in Europe would free a sizeable number of military personnel for non-nuclear missions and thus enhance NATO's conventional capability and proficiency.

For the immediate future and particularly after the advent of GLCMs, substantial reductions in manpower or nuclear armaments are unlikely, although great show was made of the scrapping of a number of obsolete and strategically volatile nuclear weapons in 1979. Force levels will be maintained at a level commensurate with American interests. Kenneth Rush criticised talk of United States forces being in Europe for the defence of Europe alone. He impressed upon a Senate hearing that 'the contribution to NATO must be understood for what it is: a matter of United States self interest'.[18] Nowehere else is the element of United States self-interest better epitomised than in the shakiness of NATO's consultation procedures on the use of nuclear weapons.[19] Not only can the US warheads be released solely by the President, but the central strategic forces are also under the President's control. The President can also act to release nuclear weapons unilaterally to SACEUR as NATO commander; any decision to use nuclear weapons by the Supreme Commander would technically be taken on behalf of NATO. SACEUR, who is by tradition American, is also overall commander of the United States forces in Europe and could thus be ordered by the President to employ the nuclear forces under his command. Consultation with America's NATO allies will only take place where time and circumstances permit. The shakiness of the consultation procedure combined with open doubts about NATO's 'flexible response' strategy produces a nightmarish vision of the future painted by Morton Halperin:

> The NATO doctrine is we will fight with conventional forces until we are losing, then we will fight with tactical nuclear weapons until we are losing and then we will blow up the world.[20]

The tight US control over the bulk of NATO's nuclear deterrent also extends to information concerning the composition of the deterrent. The official figures for the fluctuation in the number of US nuclear weapons in Europe over the past decade, the number of European countries in which nuclear and chemical (binary) weapons are stored, the number of forward based aircraft in NATO, the precise number of US allied aircraft in Europe on quick reaction alert: all are classified. The reason for keeping these facts secret was put forward by Stanley Hoffman as 'fear of political repercussions in Europe, or what would happen if the Europeans should suddenly wake up and discover through an American report that here are nuclear weapons stored on their soil and they didn't know about it'.[21]

The use of nuclear weapons, in spite of the Attlee–Churchill understanding and the Athens Guidelines on consultation, seems likely to remain an American trust. In a revealing question-answer session Senator Stuart Symington asked General Goodpaster (the SACEUR) what would happen if a decision was made to use nuclear weapons by the United States, but other NATO nations did not concur. How many of the 7000 nuclear weapons in Europe would *not* be available for use?

Now, in the circumstances that you describe, once the decision of the nuclear power was given to me in response to my request and if the situation still required the use of these weapons, I would direct their use. *All 7000 would be available for such use.*[22]

Statements like this have led to demands in the United Kingdom and elsewhere that US actions from or at these facilities be in concordance with the terms of the original agreement and policy with which the host government is associated. Alongside this is the need for the host governments to be reassured that US actions supported or sustained through such installations will not involve the host government in situations or risks that are inconsistent with their national interest.

For the United Kingdom the US defence bases seem likely to remain a contentious issue. Opinions are still split about the overall contribution made by the US defence bases to the security of the United Kingdom. To some the relationship would seem to have proved eminently in Britain's favour in terms of financial savings, military technology and enhanced security – but not without some cost.[23] To those who take a less favourable view of America's contribution to the United Kingdom's security a case can be made for reducing (or streamlining, as suggested above) US forces in the United Kingdom, and more generally Europe, to a level at which 'the American role in Europe is politically durable and not constantly an issue in domestic politics'.[24] Britain's future role would thus also be that of a European power, while the special relationship and the original bases agreement fade into more general security concerns that beset Europe as a whole.

SOME ALTERNATIVES

The United States bases in the United Kingdom remain significant as a form of military commitment and as a continuing symbol of a political identity of interest – although this notion has been challenged in recent years, in response to a growing awareness that other types of military liaison with the United States are available and present alternatives to the British model.

Short of a total review by the United States government of their basing needs in Europe, and the renegotiation of fresh base rights, there are politically less controversial ways of maintaining forward base systems while also saving on expensive deployment costs. The extended use of co-located bases and prepositioned stocks and equipment is one way in which the 'peacetime' US presence could be reduced to a lower and less politically controversial level. Several co-located bases, as pointed out earlier, already exist in the United Kingdom. Prepositioned munitions (POMCUS) have proved, thus far, largely unpopular and seem unlikely to command future support if the heated Congressional debate over $33 million for POMCUS at Diego Garcia is instructive.

The last decade has seen major changes in the European posture towards the American military presence, with the exception of the United Kingdom. The policy that each NATO member has pursued in relation to basing on its territory is essentially the result of regional perceptions of the balance of power, that in turn provides alternative basing patterns from those in the United Kingdom. The Nordic balance, by way of contrast, depends partly on consideration of natural phenomena like the geographical position of the area, superpower confrontation, repercussions of Central European problems and Finland's special position regarding the Soviet Union. There are also self-imposed restrictions, as where Sweden has opted for a position of neutrality. Denmark and Norway have followed a policy of no foreign 'bases' or nuclear weapons on their soil, although they do contribute to NATO's infrastructure. In spite of US pressure, 'Norway has consistently refused to accept any attempts to reduce its sole right to interpret the conditions under which it might feel inclined to change this policy'.[25] Denmark has pursued a parallel policy which was formalised in 1963 by her Prime Minister, when suggestions were forwarded for the stationing of allied forces in Denmark. The hardening attitude of some of Britain's European colleagues towards US basing has accentuated the importance of US defence bases in the United Kingdom which, apart from strategic considerations, have assumed extra significance because of the government's traditional political compliance with American values.

If the US force posture in the United Kingdom is modified in any way priority must go to the conditions of use for the bases which, in spite of successive Government endorsements, have proven imprecise in practice – the vagueness of the communiqué of 9 January 1952 has again been cast into the public consciousness through cruise deployments in Britain.[26] The world in the 1980s is a very different place to that which existed over thirty years ago when the base agreements were reached. Both Spain and Turkey, who are hosts to major US bases, have shown that it is possible to renegotiate base agreements. The earlier Spanish–US bases agreement negotiated with the Franco government in 1952, known as the Treaty of Madrid, was riddled with secret clauses and obscurity. In its dealings with the Franco government it was made clear by the United States government that 'the conditioning factor of even a minimal economic support was precisely the granting of military facilities by the regime'.[27] After the fall of the Franco regime a new 'Treaty of Friendship and Cooperation' was negotiated with Henry Kissinger in 1976, replacing the earlier Treaty. The new treaty allowed the United States the continued use of three airbases and other minor facilities, but this was subject to two conditions: first, the withdrawal of all American nuclear weapons, and second, the closure of the large Poseidon submarine base at Rota by the end of 1979. Turkey, likewise, negotiated a new agreement with the United States, when in March 1980 the 'Agreement for Cooperation of Defence and Economy' was signed, restricting the use of the bases specifically to obligations arising out of the North Atlantic Treaty. All US bases were officially called Turkish Armed Force Installations where American military forces were authorised to participate in 'joint defense' activities, and all information gathered from intelligence installations would be shared by the two governments. A further example could also be cited of the new agreement with Greece on 15 July 1983, which similarly restricted the American use of bases until the start of 1989. The precedents exist for a new agreement that puts US bases and facilities firmly under British control, and restricts activities from those bases solely to NATO operations – instead of the current vague agreement and the cosmetic RAF designation of US bases that was originally designed to make the presence of US forces in Britain more palatable.

The United Kingdom, because of its strategic location, will remain critical to the deployment of many far-flung parts of the US military apparatus as well as for intelligence and communication operations. The communications network that runs through the United Kingdom is intrinsic to the global options of US strategy. The communications network covers facilities like AUTOVON, a worldwide automatic phone network for the US military, or Croughton's Automated Digital Weather Centre coordinating meteorological information from Europe, Africa and the Soviet Union and then feeding it back to SAC headquarters at Nebraska. Croughton is also the centre of AUTODIN, a network which links up computers, including those of the World-wide Command and Control System (WIMEX) responsible for a spectacular false alert on 6 June 1980. The United Kingdom is also central to US intelligence operations in Europe. Many of these facilities were created during the height of the 'special relationship' in the immediate post-war years when there was a generally uncritical acceptance of US military hegemony in Europe. The importance of the United Kingdom to US intelligence and communication operations is likely to increase as reliable political bedrocks from which to carry out such activities become harder to find, while at the same time the British government's knowledge of the extent of these operations seems, because of their nature, hazy.[28]

Other alternative models for the future of the US bases in the United Kingdom have been provided by the Alternative Defence Commission, who present a choice of no bases or the continuation of basing only in its conventional role.[29] The obvious problem with this approach is deciding which support facilities contribute to the nuclear option or to conventional defence (many do both), and deciding which bases or facilities are most likely to be targeted by the Soviet Union. Nor would Britain have any right to retain a conventional US presence *and* expect at the same time to be defended by the US strategic arsenal.

An option advocated by Peter Johnson[30] that addresses the wider identity of Anglo–American interest is that of neutrality for Britain. The premise behind this policy is wider than objections solely to the US nuclear presence in Britain. Peter Johnson argues that:

> The stance of alliance ties British policy closely to the policies of America. These are concerned with the security and well-being of America, not of Britain except as a secondary consideration. British security therefore now depends, not on any circumstances which we can control or influence, but on the precarious balance of the Soviet/American confrontation.[31]

A policy of 'neutralisation' (whereby formal undertakings are given in peacetime to be neutral during any conflict and not to allow foreign troops or bases on its soil, not to make warlike arrangements) would mean the removal of Britain's nuclear deterrent and US bases. Once Britain's importance as a strategic base is diminished it is difficult to see the attraction of an 'over-populated offshore island with slender resources, hard put to make our way in the world at all'[31] to any predatory power. A conqueror would thus find Britain more of a liability than as asset, unless of course her strategic position in relation to Europe were exploited. Although the neutralisation argument deserves more serious consideration that the confines of this study permits, there are from the start serious dangers and problems. The policy assumes an over-simplified model of international relations as well as Anglo–American relations. Britain's dependence upon the United States spills into many fields other than just the military sphere, and quite serious economic and political pressures could be applied against the adoption of such a policy.

SUMMARY

To summarise the debate over US defence bases in the United Kingdom, four propositions can be made for and against the continued American presence. The first argument for the continued United States presence is the 'coupling' argument, by which US forward base systems 'couple' European and American security by providing a sign of political and military solidarity and, more importantly, the implied threat that any war in Europe could escalate to the strategic level by involving the United States-based strategic arsenal. Some have objected that the GLCM and Pershing 2 deployments are potentially de-coupling, since they are not connected to the United States strategic arsenal but signify an unmistakable strategic nuclear threat to Russian territory. The second argument that could be forwarded is that if Britain demanded the withdrawal of bases, then she would forfeit any influence over American planning, with no guarantee that she would not be involved in any superpower nuclear exchange. The third argument, forwarded by the multilateralists opposed to any unilateral force reductions of the Mansfield type, is that the only condition for the withdrawal or reduction of US bases would be in the event of a reciprocal *and* verifiable concession from the Soviet Union. In practice this argument has proved weak because of verification problems and insufficient because of the increasing use of co-located bases and a sophisticated intelligence and communications 'infrastructure' that would presumably still provide important Soviet targets in the event of war. The final argument, and one forwarded by the Conservative government under Mrs Thatcher, in favour of the retention of the bases as they are, is that the United Kingdom derives benefits from the close relationship with the United States – both in terms of enhanced security (for example, the generous access to US intelligence and satellite facilities during the Falklands conflict), and considerable military expenditure for NATO's European security. The Alliance generally is seen as 'not-based on one-sided American idealism' and 'power or dominition' by the United States, but upon 'mutual respect and advantage'.[32]

The arguments employed against the presence of United States bases in the United Kingdom can also be summarised by four general propositions. The first, and most often employed, is that American bases and facilities should be removed because they provide targets for nuclear strikes in any war in which the superpowers are involved. Allied to this consideration is the feeling that American FBS nuclear weapons enable the United States to fight a nuclear war with the Soviet Union that is limited to Europe. However the procedure by which war could be limited in either a geographical or theatre sense is vague. The second argument holds that siting nuclear weapons so near the Soviet Union's border is provocative, that this includes the British deterrent, and that to remove them would decrease international tension. Those in favour of the GLCM deployments would no doubt point out that they were placed in Europe in response to the Russian threat implied by the presence of SS-20 missiles in Eastern Europe. The third argument could be called the unilateralist stance, claiming that the removal of all nuclear weapons (American and British) would set a precedent. To allow them to remain any longer would, by implication, merely serve to affirm the value of nuclear weapons and encourage proliferation. The weakness of this stance is that it ignores communication and intelligence centres that, while not nuclear bases, would presumably be major targets in the event of war. The final argument against the US bases is that they no longer serve British national interest or those of Europe, and that the dangers inherent in having such a presence outweigh the benefits to national security. The continued build-up of the US nuclear stakes in Europe is worrying when it is unaccompanied by a European conventional forces expansion. Fears have arisen that this pattern will lower the nuclear threshold of NATO's flexible response strategy and involve Europeans in an early nuclear exchange particularly where 'consultation' has proved indeterminate or even non-existent. This, combined with fears of a nuclear war being limited to Europe, has led to a growing distrust of US intentions. If there is an argument to be presented for an increased US presence in the United Kingdom, it is in the conventional, not nuclear, forces where NATO's need is most pressing.

The debate surrounding the presence of US bases in the United Kingdom is not, in the end, a question of whether facilities like Brawdy, Chicksands or Molesworth are in the interests of the United States or the United Kingdom. Nor is it a question of whether Britain wants cruise missiles or not. The question is whether the general interests of the United Kingdom (economic, foreign, political and defence) are any longer the same as those of the United States. There are certainly open difficulties with the relationship that call into question its 'special' label. The question should be addressed in the United States as well. One American observer argues that the United States gains little from the alliance with Western Europe and that withdrawal of US force is justified 'simply in the pursuit of America's long term strategic interests, taking account of any other realistic, attainable options'.[33]

The importance of the United Kingdom as an 'unsinkable aircraft carrier' to the United States is likely to be reassessed in the light of the cruise debate and the Libyan raid. However, in spite of this latest and most controversial chapter in the history of US bases in the United Kingdom, two smaller, but nevertheless significant, deployments took place that seem to confirm the continuing importance of the bases to the United States. The first was the unveiling of the new TR (Tactical Reconnaissance)-I spy plane, built at Lockheed 'Skunk Works' in California, at the 1982 Farnborough Air Show. The plane, now stationed in RAF Alconbury, is to fly along the East German border and in the Middle East, and without leaving NATO air space is able to see deep into Poland. SAC is basing its first squadron in the United Kingdom, which is to some a 'reminder of Britain's importance as an unsinkable US aircraft carrier off the shores of Europe'.[34] A decision in mid-December 1982 to allow the United States to set up an alternative military command headquarters near High Wycombe again seems to confirm the UK's continuing strategic importance to the United States. The unit would be an American Forces in Europe Command Post and not a NATO headquarters (the NATO headquarters are in Belgium), and would be of an administrative and logistic nature to provide support to US forces in Europe and to exercise control over US forces not committed to NATO. The placement of yet another major US facility in the United Kingdom is in part a measure of our strategic importance, but also a continued sign of political acquiescence.

If the United Kingdom is to remain America's 'airstrip one' it must be upon terms that are clearly understood by both sides.

Appendix 1: Documents

THE SPAATZ-TEDDER AGREEMENT

The precise form that the Spaatz-Tedder agreement took is still open to question. In character with later agreements it could merely have been a written undertaking without the formality of an agreement or, if it was a formal signed agreement, it remains classified.

During the course of the talks held on 25-28 June and 4-6 June 1946 the decisions reached were summarised in memoranda from Major-General Clayton Bissell (Military Air Attache in England) to General Carl Spaatz. During the first talks in June conservation was general and largely preparatory for the talks in July. The relevant points of the first meeting appeared in a memorandum entitled 'Reminder on decisions taken during London visit', 25-28 June 1946 from Bissell to Spaatz:

Item 6: Tedder stated that Zimmerman would be able to procure a copy of the [JCS] study on bases required for long range bombers to cover a possible future contingency. . . .

Item 8: Tedder agreed that Hollinghurst would confer with someone who would come over from Edward's command regarding RAF landing fields in England required for the execution of US emergency plans.

Item 10: Spaatz and Tedder discussed State Department's communication through US Embassy, London, reference facilities on route from US across Africa and India to support MacArthur in Japan. It was pointed out that in an emergency US would have to use its commercial air transport for this purpose, so that route would have to have radio and landing facilities useful for US and commercial aircraft. Spaatz and Tedder recognized desirability of standardized radar/radio for planes landing on airways and on landing fields in order to avoid situation that existed when US brought aircraft to suport GB during the war. Tedder made the point that there were certain technical matters that were difficult and would have to be worked out, but suggested that American and British technical experts get together in London. Tedder agreed to have forwarded to US; if possible, an agreement in principle that US should have use of landing fields and that necessary facilities should be authorized, with details to be worked out by technical group sent here for that purpose.

During the second visit, which gave rise to the bulk of what are known as the Spaatz-Tedder Agreements, Bissell again summarised the decisions taken:

Item 6: Spaatz stated Edwards would contact Bissell and then visit Williams to work out details of visit of American squadron from Germany.

Item 7: Spaatz and Tedder agreed matter must be handled as routine and not attract special attention. Spaatz agreed to have an officer familiar with the required special equipment [this refers to the visit made in August by

195

Colonel E. E. Kirkpatrick of the Manhattan district] come to England and report to Bissell. . . .

Item 8: There was further discussion regarding five installations needed for a certain type of activity. Tedder agreed that these requirements would be met without any difficulty and he would go ahead on them.

Item 9: No clear-cut decision was reached regarding the several aircraft of the two nations but there was complete agreement on the desirability of keeping the radio and other requirements of commercial aircraft in line with those of respective military aircraft.

Source for both extracts: NA: RG 341, DCS/O, TS AAG, File 23, Box 7, Memo for Gen. Spaatz from Clayton Bissell, Maj.-Gen., GSC, Milit. Air Attache, 8 Aug. 1946.

EXTRACT FROM THE VISITING FORCES ACT, 30 OCTOBER 1952

Section 2, para. 2

Subject to the Visiting Forces Act are:

a) members of any visiting force of that country;

b) all other persons, neither citizens of the United Kingdom and Colonies nor ordinarily resident in the United Kingdom, are for the time being subject to the service law of that country.

Section 3, para 1

A person charged with an offence against UK law *shall not be liable to be tried for that offence by a UK court* if at the time when the offence is alleged to have been committed he was a member of a visiting force or a civilian component of such a force and:

a) the alleged offence, if committed by him, arose out of and in the course of his duty as a member of that force or component, as the case may be, or;

b) the alleged offence is an offence against the person, and the person or, if more than one, each of the persons in relation to whom it is alleged to have been committed had at the time thereof a relevant association either with that force or with another visiting force of the same country, or;

c) the alleged offence is an offence against property, and the whole of the property in relation to which it is alleged to have been committed was at the time thereof either of the sending country or of an authority of that country or of a person having such an association as aforesaid;

Provided that this subsection shall not apply if at the time when the offence is alleged to have been committed the alleged offender was a person not subject to the jurisdiction of the service courts of the country in question in accordance with the last foregoing section.

Section 3, para. 3

Nothing in subsection (1) of this section shall prevent a person from being tried by a UK court in a case where the Director of Public Prosecutions, the Lord Advocate, or the Attorney-General for Northern Ireland certifies . . . that the appropriate authority of the sending country has notified him that it is not proposed to deal with the case under the law of that country.

Section 4

In the case where there is a charge of attempting or conspiring to commit an offence or of aiding, abetting or procuring or being an accessory to the commission of an offence paragraphs (b) and (c) of Section 3 sub-section 1 shall have effect as if references in those paragraphs to the alleged offence were references to the offence which the person charged is alleged to have attempted or conspired to commit.

Section 5, para. 1

None of the above provisions shall affect any powers of arrest, search, entry, seizure or custody exercisable under UK law with respect to offences committed or believed to have been committed against that law or . . . any power of any court to remand (whether on bail or in custody) a person brought before the court in connection with such an offence.

Section 5, para. 2

Where a person has been taken into custody by a constable without a warrant for such an offence as aforesaid and . . . he is subject to the jurisdiction of the service courts of a country to which this section applies . . . he can be detained in custody for a period NOT exceeding 3 days without being brought before a court of summary jurisdiction.

Section 18

Hereby repealed: Allied Forces Act 1940 and the United States of America (Visiting Forces) Act 1942.

Section 19

This Act may be cited as the Visiting Forces Act.

Appendix 2: Base Locations

Table A2.1 USAF Operating Locations

August 1950:	Third Air Division	
	Sculthorpe	Upper Heyford
	Marham	Brize Norton
	Burtonwood	Fairford
	Lakenheath	Manston
	Mildenhall	Ruislip

Total = 10 main operating locations

October 1953:	Third Air Force	
	Kirknewton	Bushey Park
	Blyton	South Ruislip (HQ)
	Prestwick	Colliers End Camp
	Alconbury	Stanstead
	Burtonwood	Woodbridge
	Chelveston	Bentwaters
	Sealand	Wethersfield
	Wimpole Park	Denham
	Chicksands	Bovingdon
	Croughton	Langham Camp
	Middleton-Stoney	Sculthorpe
	Burderop Park	Cranwick
	Shaftesbury	Molesworth
		Brigstock

	Seventh Air Division	
	Lindholme	Manston
	Waddington	Shepherds Grove
	Upper Heyford	Mildenhall
	High Wycombe	Lakenheath
	Brize Norton	East Kirby
	Fairford	Scampton
	West Drayton	Sturgate
	Greenham Common	

Total = 42 main operating locations

Source: Third Air Force Historical Brief, *Locations of United States Military Units in United Kingdom*, 16 July 1948–31 December 1967, Compiled by T.Sgt. Richard H. Willard, February 1968.

Table A2.2   Fluctuations in USAF Bases and Strength

| Date | USAF Bases | US Personnel | | | Mission Aircraft |
		Military	Civilian[a]	Total[b]	
June 1949	5	5 818	1 420	c	TDY only
June 1953	43	46 634	3 478	78 548	312
June 1961	Not available	37 689	Not available	82 174	381
December 1963[d]	23	26 817	6 337	71 297	329
December 1964[d]	13	23 459	5 540	62 010	315
December 1965[e]	9	20 959	5 043	57 726	244
December 1966	9	24 835	5 264	64 834	314
December 1967	9	26 079	6 279	66 981	308
June 1968	9	28 995	5 908	68 251	310
June 1969	9	23 473	6 897	64 061	330
June 1970[f]	8	21 283	6 322	59 744	275
June 1971	8	21 969	4 485	59 272	275
June 1972	8	21 205	4 941	59 413	275
June 1973[g]	7	22 552	5 213	61 413	274
June 1974	7	23 375	5 110	65 937	278
June 1975	7	22 562	5 200	62 485	274
December 1975	7	22 258	5 376	68 837	274
December 1976[h]	7	23 570	5 014	59 706	238
December 1977[i]	7	26 473	5 258	61 036	264
December 1978[j]	7	24 036	3 862	57 266	240
December 1979[k]	8	24 254	4 621	59 763	288
December 1980[k]	8	25 784	4 676	64 840	304
December 1981	8	26 830	5 521	63 637	304
December 1982[l]	9	26 584	5 755	64 894	298
October 1985	9	26 873	4 532	59 251	346[m]

Notes:
a. Includes US and UK civilians directly employed by American forces.
b. Includes dependents.
c. Does not include dependents.
d. Reduction in bases and personnel by closure of SAC bomber bases and inactivation of other units.
e. 81st TFW conversion from F-101 to F-4C aircraft temporarily lowered number of aircraft assigned.
f. 66th TFW inactivated; RAF Wethersfield reduced to Standby Deployment Base.
g. 3 AF H:Q. moved from South Ruislip; base inactivated.
h. Two squadrons of RF-4C's inactivated.
i. 527th TFTAS activated.
j. 48th TFW conversion to F-111s temporarily lowered aircraft assigned.
k. RAF Fairford activated; 81st TFW conversion to A-10s and the activation of three more squadrons, increased aircraft assigned.
l. 501st TMW activated at Greenham Common.
m. The mission figure is an estimate by the author and includes the TRIs at Alconbury assuming there are at least thirteen; the figure does however exclude GLCMs.

Appendix 3: Current Bases

Table A3.1 Current (1985) United States Air Force Installations in the United Kingdom, Third Air Force Main Operating Bases

Base	Unit	Aircraft	Mission
RAF Alconbury	*10th Tactical Reconnaissance Wing*		All-weather tactical air reconnaissance, distribute intelligence information
	1st Tactical Reconnaissance Sqdn	20 RF-4C Phantom	
	527th Tactical Fighter Training 'Aggressor' Sqdn	18 F-5E Tiger IIs	INFORM Net Station and standby nuclear storage capacity
	17th Reconnaissance Wing: (SAC)		
	95th Reconnaissance Sqdn	13 TR-1	Day/Night high altitude surveillance of battle areas

200

Base	Unit	Aircraft	Mission
RAF Bentwaters/ Woodbridge	*81st Tactical Fighter Wing:* Woodbridge: 78th/91st Tactical Fighter Sqdn's Bentwaters: 92nd/509th 510th/511th Tactical Fighter Sqdn's	108 A-10 Thunderbolt II	Tactical operations and aerospace rescue and recovery. A-10s provide close air support for NATO central front
	Woodbridge: 67th Aerospace Resuce and Recovery Sqdn	6 H-130 Hercules 5 HH-53 Super Jolly Green Giant Helicopters	Combat/peace search and rescue for NATO
RAF Chicksands	*7274th Air Base Group:* 6950th Electronic Security Group (Electronic Security Command Unit)		Provide rapid radio relay and secured communication for defence of US and allies

Base	Unit	Aircraft	Mission
RAF Fairford	11st Strategic Group (SAC):	18 KC-135 Stratotankers	Aerial refuelling for USAFE/NATO aircraft in the European theatre
	7020th Air Base Group: (TAF)		
	7020th Civil Engineering Sqdn 7020th Security Police Sqdn 7020th Supply Sqdn 66th Contingency Hospital (RAF Little Rissington)		Provide for operation and maintenance of Fairford in support of 11th Strategic Group.
			INFORM Net Station (Stand by)
RAF Greenham Common	501st Tactical Missile Wing:	96 GLCM (proposed)	Operate, maintain GLCM and all associated facilities, vehicles and equipment
RAF Lakenheath	48th Tactical Fighter Wing:	66 F-111F (In addition 22 replacement training unit of F-111s)	Train for and conduct tactical air operations in support of NATO
	492, 493, 494, 495th Tactical Fighter Sqdn's		INFORM Net Station (Stand by)

Base	Unit	Aircraft	Mission
RAF Mildenhall	*513rd Tactical Airlift Wing:* Bravo Sqdn:	approx 16 C-130 Hercules approx 15 KC-135 refuelling tankers	Operation of the base and provision of mission-ready EC-135H aircraft and flight crews for US European Command's
	10th Airborne Command and Control Sqdn	4 EC-135 H airborne command aircraft for USEUCOM (Silk Purse)	Airborne Command and Control Operation. Also supports over half of the tactical airlift in USAFE
			INFORM Net Station
	627th Military Airlift Support Sqdn:	provides for transiting C-141 Starlifters and C-5 Galaxies	
	6988th Electronic Security Sqdn:	SIGINT/ELINT specialists in RC-135s	
	Detachment: 9th Strategic Reconnaissance Wing	occasional visit from Beale AFB (Calif) in SR-71	
RAF Upper Heyford	*20th Tactical Fighter Wing:*		Long-range, all-weather tactical fighter and electronic combat sorties for NATO
	55, 77, and 79th Tactical Fighter Sqdns	66 F-111E	
	42nd Electronic Combat Sqdn:	22 EF-111A	Electronic counter-measure support for NATO
			INFORM Net Station (Stand by)

Standby Deployment Bases

RAF Sculthorpe: Detachment 1, 48th Tactical Fighter Wing
(subsidiary to Lakenheath).

RAF Wethersfield: Detachment 1, 10th Tactical Reconnaissance Wing
819th Civil Engineering Squadron (Red Horse)
INFORM Net Station (Stand by).

Co-located Operating Bases

Abingdon	likely use:	munitions store.
Bedford	,, ,,	F-111s.
Boscombe Down	,, ,,	F-111s.
Coltishall	,, ,,	RF-4 Phantoms.
Finningley	,, ,,	F-4 Phantoms.
Leeming	,, ,,	F-4 Phantoms.
Waddington	,, ,,	A-7 Corsairs.
Wittering	,, ,,	A-7 Corsairs.

USAF Communication Facilities

1. RAF Barford St. John
2. RAF Barkway
3. Botley Hill Radio Relay
4. Bovingdon Radio Relay
5. RAF Chicksands
6. RAF Christmas Common Radio Relay
7. Cold Blow Radio Relay
8. RAF Croughton (Global Command and Control Station)
9. Daventry Radio Relay
10. RAF Dunkirk Communications Station
11. Great Bromley Radio Relay
12. High Wycombe Air Station Static War Headquarters, US European Command and HQ, UK Air Forces Command and cruise missile targeting centre
13. Hillington
14. RAF Martlesham Heath Radio Station
15. Mormond Hill Communications Station (Scotland) – 'Silk Purse' ground communications station
16. RAF St. Mawgan's Communications Station
17. RAF Swingate Communications Station
18. RAF Wethersfield
19. Flyingdales Moor (BMEWS) Det 1: 12th Missile Warning Sqdn.

Other USAF Installations

RAF Brize Norton: B-52 Forward operating base

RAF Feltwell: Support Installation of RAF Lakenheath

High Wycombe Air Station: Detachment 1, 20th Tactical Fighter Wing

RAF Marham: B-52 Forward operating base

RAF Molesworth:	Defence Property Disposal Office UK (DoD)
RAF Welford:	7551st Ammunition Supply Squadron

In addition ranges at Cowden, Holbeach, Jurby and Wainfleet are used for air-to-ground nuclear bombing training.

US Navy

See Appendix 3, Table A3.2

US Army

Burtonwood:	Depot, Army Material Command (POMCUS) 47th Area Support Group
RSA Caerwent and RSA Hythe:	Subsidiary munitions store to Burtonwood; part of 60th Ordnance Group
Felixstowe:	US Army Terminal
Chessington:	Army Medical Storage Facility

US military personnel UK

Air Force:	27 906[a]
Navy/Marine Corps:	3 775[b]
Army:	57[c]
	31 738[d]

a. This figure represents approx. one-fifth of all USAF personnel abroad and includes US civilian members, without civilian members to the figure is 26 221.
b. This figure is approximate since precise USN figures for the Headquarters of the C-in-C, US Naval Forces, Europe in London are unavailable. Precise figures are also unavailable for RAF Macrihanish, Scotland.
c. Includes only RAF Burtonwood.
d. Figures accurate as of October 1985.

The information shown here was compiled in part by John Baylis in his book *Anglo–American Defence Relations 1939–80*, Appendix 16, with additional information from a Congressional Research Paper, *US Foreign Policy Objectives and Overseas Military Installations* (April 1979), the Department of Defense *Base Structure Annex* including an index of installations in the *Manpower Requirements Report for FY 85* prepared by the Office of the Assistant Secretary of Defense, and lastly from information supplied by *A Guide to the Third Air Force*, RAF Mildenhall, Suffolk. 3AF Public Affairs Office.

Major United States Naval Bases in the United Kingdom

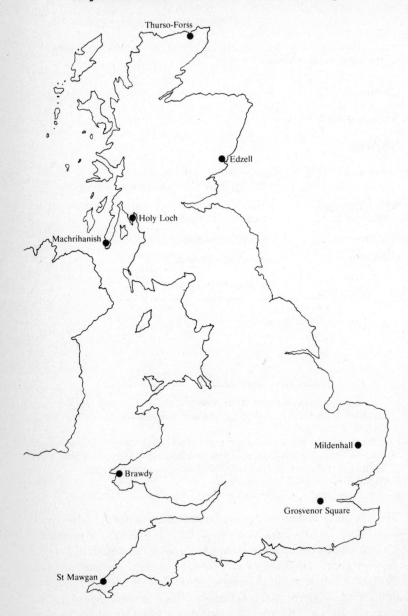

Key to Main Third Air Force/Seventh Air Division Bases in the United States **(map on next page)**

(Main bases indicated in capitals.)

1. Kirknewton
2. Sturgate
3. Scampton
4. Waddington
5. Upwood
6. ALCONBURY
7. Sculthorpe
8. Coltishall
9. Walton
10. LAKENHEATH
11. MILDENHALL
12. BENTWATERS
13. Woodbridge
14. Wethersfield
15. Stanstead
16. Colliers End Camp
17. Manston
18. Denham
19. Bovingdon
20. Bushy Park
21. South Ruislip
22. West Drayton
23. High Wycombe
24. GREENHAM COMMON
25. WELFORD
26. Burderop Park
27. FAIRFORD
28. Brize Norton
29. Chicksands
30. UPPER HEYFORD
31. Middleton Stoney
32. Croughton
33. Chelveston
34. MOLESWORTH
35. Burtonwood
36. Blyton
37. Lindholme
38. FYLINGDALES (EWS)
39. Prestwick

208

Main Third Air Force/Seventh Air Division Bases in the United Kingdom

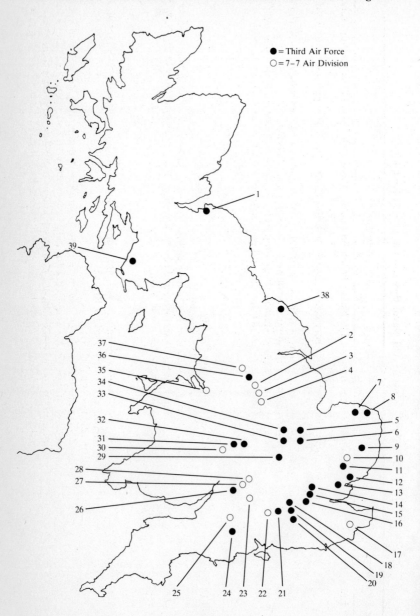

Source: Third Air Force Office of Information.

Table A3.2 Current US Naval Bases in the United Kingdom

Base	Description
Holy Loch	Submarine Squadron 14, US Navy; Poseidon nuclear missile; sub-squadron headquarters. *Staff*: 1800 personnel *Equipment*: 10 SSBN's services by one submarine tender (USS Hurley) and one dry dock (USS Los Alamos). *Function*: administration of refit site 1 at Holy Loch and to provide operational, material and logistic readiness of the nuclear-powered ballistic missile submarines. USS Hurley and USS Los Alamos: shore support by US naval activities at Holy Loch and Glen Douglas, which is a NATO nuclear and conventional weapons store for Holy Loch.
Edzell (Scotland)	Naval Security Group Facility *Staff*: approximately 630 personnel *Function*: primary function is communication and relay support, including communications relay, communications security, and communications manpower assistance to the Navy and other defence elements in the area.
Thurso (Forss)	US Navy microwave communications link station (LORAN radio navigation system for nuclear submarines). Jointly used by British. *Staff*: 135 personnel (US) *Function*: manages, operates, and maintains facilities and equipment, devices and systems necessary to provide the required information for command and operational and administration of the naval establishment; primary communications link to Polaris submarines in the Norwegian sea area, for which purpose the station was built in 1963. Until 1977 it shared its job with a similar US Navy station near Derry (N. Ireland).

Base	Description
Brawdy (S. Wales)	US Navy Sonar Surveillance Centre *Staff*: 280 personnel *Function*: officially given as 'oceanographic observations in selected areas to provide extensive information on oceanographic conditions'. More likely it was part of 'Project Caesar' designed to plot submarine and vessel movements. The station was completed in 1973 mainly to cover the movements of Soviet 'Charlie'-class submarines.
Grosvenor Square	US Naval Headquarters Europe and US Eastern Atlantic (UNCOMEASTLANT) naval commander in command of US Sixth Fleet (originally Eisenhower war-time command centre; also houses SUSLO (Special US Liaison Office) intelligence offices and communications centre). *Staff*: approximately 800 personnel *Function*: overall command and operational control of US navy forces, assignments, responsibilities, and navy components, and a unified command enabling the Commander-in-Chief and direct subordinate of the Chief of Navy operations and area command under USS command NATLAND to function. Also houses WMCCS (Worldwide Military Command and Control System) which includes access to Nuclear Weapons capabilities Plan and Nuclear Weapons Accounting System and FOSIC (Fleet Ocean Surveillance Information Centre).

Support Centres

Lime Grove/Eastcote, Ruislip	Annex to Grosvenor Square HQ; USN administrative offices as well as Naval Intelligence Staff and regional contracting centre.
St Mawgan (Cornwall)	USAF Communications Centre and US Navy Air Facility (USCOMEASTLANT) *Staff*: 35 US Navy Personnel *Function*: to maintain prescribed contingency capability to receive, store, monitor, maintain, issue, and trans-ship munitions and aviation ordnance in support of US Navy and NATO operations.

Base	Description
Macrihanish	Naval Aviation Weapons Facility Det. (USCOMEASTLANT), 'Crisis' base for US anti-submarine aircraft and permanent nuclear weapons store est'd July 1967. *Staff*: 12 enlisted men and 8 officers *Functions*: (i) Mobile Mine Assembly Group, detachment II: maintenance and assembly of underwater mines for NATO use; (ii) Naval Special Warfare Unit II (20 personnel): at readiness to conduct operations in support of NATO in time of war by conducting training and exercises in a local area with similar units from other countries. (iii) US Naval Aviation Weapons Facility Detachment (20 personnel).
Mildenhall	Naval Air Facility *Staff*: 35 personnel *Function*: to provide services, material and support the operations of aviation units and other naval activities and units of US Navy in North European area.
Northwood	HQ, Eastern Atlantic Command (EASTLAND), SACLANT: NATO Command including Submarine Forces of Biscay Subarea. HQ, Allied Command Channel (CHINCHAN): NATO and UK national command – as national command (CINCFLT) it controls UK Polaris force and as one of the three main commands of NATO includes Maritime Air Forces Channel Command (COMMAICHAN).
Pitreavie	HQ, Northern Subarea, EASTLAND: NATO Command inc. Maritime Air Forces. HQ Northern Channel Command (COMNORECHAN) and Maritime Air Forces North Channel Command.

US Navy list compiled with the help of Captain Jerry Pape of US Naval Authority (Grosvenor Square), to whom my thanks are due.

Appendix 4

Bomber Bases Base	UK Contribution	US Labour	US Contribution	Total
Brize Norton	15 670	2 892	19 063	37 625
Fairford	9 071	1 986	19 134	30 191
Greenham Common	9 243	3 947	13 448	26 638
Upper Heyford	15 013	2 631	16 043	33 687
Total	48 997	11 456	67 688	128 141
Average	12 249	2 864	16 922	32 035
Fighter Bases Base	UK Contribution	US Labour	US Contribution	Total
Bentwaters	3 901	—	8 132	12 033
Manston	8 312	—	6 298	14 610
Shepherds Grove	3 510	—	6 746	10 256
Wethersfield	3 902	—	7 339	11 241
Total	19 625	—	28 515	48 140
Average	4 906	—	7 129	12 032

Source: *A Matter of Decision*, prepared by Directorate of Plans and UK Financial Arrangements, ACS/Comptroller, HQ, 3AF, London.

Notes and References

Guide to Notes

PRO   Public Record Office, Kew, London.
NA   National Archives, Washington, DC.
                     Included in the National Archives Collection are:
                     NSC – National Security Council Reports.
                     RG 18 – Records, Army Air Force, Air Adjutant General, Records of AAR.
                     RG 107 – Office of Assistant Secretary of War for Air, Records Office of Secretary for War.
                     RG 165 – Office of Chief of Staff, Records of War Department General and Special Staffs.
                     RG 128 – Records of the Joint Chiefs of Staff (JCS).
                     RG 319 – Records, Plans and Operations Division, Records of War Dep't, Gen. and Special Staff.
                     RG 330 – Records of the Office of the Secretary of Defense.
                     RG 341 – Air Force Plans and Operations Division, Records of HQ USAF, 1942–56.
                     'Hot File' – Signifies recently declassified material yet to be categorised.
                     ORE – CIA reports.
FRUS   Annual collection of State Department Papers until 1953 published under the title *Foreign Relations of the United States*.
WNY   Archives at Washington Navy Yard, Washington, DC.
BOLLING AFB   Historical Archives, United States Air Force, Bolling Air Force Base, Washington, DC.

Postscript

1. *Aviation and Space Technology*, 21 April 1986, p. 24.
2. *Ibid.*, p. 25.
3. House of Commons Debates, 6th Series, (HC Deb.[6]), 16 April 1986. Col. 889.
4. *Ibid.*, Col. 893–4.
5. *Ibid.*, Col. 943 (emphasis added).
6. *Ibid.*, Col. 892.
7. *Ibid.*, Col. 891.
8. HC Deb.[6], 28 April 1986 (written answers) Col. 271–2.
9. HC Deb.[6], 16 April 1986, Col. 954–5.
10. *Ibid.*, Col. 885.
11. *Aviation and Space Technology*, 21 April 1986, p. 22.

Introduction

1. Figures from a Third Air Force Brief prepared by Staff Sergeant R. W. Hillard, Historical Division, Office of Information, 3AF, *Installation of USAAF Combat Units in the UK 1942–5* (February 1967).
2. A phrase to describe the intimacy of Anglo–American relations, first used by Winston Churchill at Westminster College, Fulton, Missouri, on 5 March 1946.
3. George Stambuk, *American Military Forces Abroad*, p. 9.
4. House of Commons Debates 5th Series (HC Deb.⁵), 454, col. 123 (Written Answer), 28 July 1948.
5. LtCol D. J. Alberts (USAF), 'Deterrence in the 1980s: Pt. II The Role of Conventional Air Power', p. 13.
6. *The Guardian*, 24 January 1983 (Marplan poll).
7. See *Sanity*, December 1982.
8. See 'Sources' below.
9. *The Times*, 17 July 1948.
10. Two recent publications that have been of help and also reflect the growing interest in US bases in the United Kingdom are Duncan Campbell's *The Unsinkable Aircraft Carrier: American Military Power in Britain* and Malcolm Spaven's *Fortress Scotland: A Guide to the Military Presence*.

1 Defining 'Bases'

1. HC Deb.⁵, 986, 18 June 1980, col. 587 (written answers).
2. HC Deb.⁵, 988, 7 July 1980, cols. 54–5 (written answers).
3. HC Deb.⁵, 990, 8 August 1980, col. 481 (written answers).
4. Duncan Campbell, 'Target Britain', *New Statesman*, 31 October 1981, p. 6.
5. Definitions are based on those by Hans W. Weigert, 'Collective Security', *Foreign Affairs*, vol. 25, January 1947, pp. 250–60.
6. See Appendix II, Table A2.1.
7. See Appendix III, Table A3.2.
8. Nils P. Gleditsch and Owen Wilkes, *Intelligence Installations in Norway: their number, location, function and legality*. The claim that the intelligence installations safeguard the sea lanes in the North Atlantic is challenged when they say there is a 'covert awareness that what they would really be safeguarding is the US SLBM forces in the North Atlantic.' p. 63.
9. Hans Weigert, p. 256.
10. See Lawrence Freedman, *The Evolution of Nuclear Strategy*, pp. 71, 242 and 383.
11. For a fuller discussion, see Vincenzo Tornetta, 'The Nuclear Strategy of the Atlantic Alliance and the "no-first-use" debate', *NATO Review*, vol. 30 no. 5, 1982, pp. 1–7.
12. Roy Allison, *Finland's Relations with the Soviet Union*, quoting M. Lazarev, *Imperialist Military Bases on Foreign Territories and International Law*, p. 39.

13. See Hearings before the Sub-committee on Arms Control, International Law and Organization of the Senate Committee on Foreign Relations, *US Forces in Europe*, 93 Congress, 1st session, 25 and 27 July 1973, pp. 40 and 63.
14. Michael Heseltine, UK Secretary of State for Defence, 'the Atlantic Alliance, an agenda for 1984', *NATO Review*, No. 1, 1984, Vol. 32, p. 1.
15. *The Economist*, 12 April 1952, p. 82.

2 Visits of Goodwill and Training Purposes

1. National Archives, Washington DC (NA), RG 218 (US JCS), 28/12/42 – JCS 183, Section 1, CCS 360 (19–9–42).
2. Michael S. Sherry, *Preparing for the Next War (America's Plans for Postwar Defense 1941–5)*, p. 42.
3. NA, RG 218, JCS 71st meeting, 30 March 1943: CCS 360 (12–9–42), Section 1.
4. Michael Sherry, p. 43.
5. NA, RG 218, JCS (undated) file CCS 360 (General Arnold to President Roosevelt) (12–9–42), Section II.
6. Library of Congress, Manuscripts Division, Washington DC, Arnold file 1932–46: Box 44, Letter from Commanding General, AAF, H. H. Arnold to Commanding General, U.S. Strategic Forces in Europe, Spaatz: APO 633. 6 November 1944.
7. NA, RG 218, JSP/215th mtg. 22 August 1945 in CCS 360 (12–9–42) Section VII, JCS.
8. Library of Congress, Manuscripts Division, Washington DC, Arnold file, letter to General Norstad, *Post-War Air Bases*. 22 August 1945.
9. NA, RG 353. Spaatz to Commanding General, AAF: *Occupation Period requirements of US Air Forces in Europe*. 10 April 1945, Enclosure to JCS 1332, 30 April 1945, file SWNCC 134 series, 323.3 'Air Bases/Europe', Box 24. SWNCC/SANCC.
10. NA, RG 341, Record of the HQ USAF: Box 7, entry 337. Deputy Chief of Staff, Operations to Director of Plans, Executive Office. General File 1944–53. Folder TS 21.
11. John Greenwood, 'The Emergence of the Postwar Strategic Air Forces, 1945–53', in *Proceedings of the Eight Military History Symposium* (USAF Academy, 1978). pp. 224–5.
12. NA, RG 341. Box 7, Entry 337: Memorandum for Deputy c/o. General, AAF, *Occupation Air Force Troop Basis* AAF D-700. September 1945.
13. Library of Congress, Manuscripts Div. *Briefing Materials for European Trip*, Box 265, prepared by AC/AS-4 for General Carl Spaatz , CG/AAF. Spaatz files. pp. 1–7.
14. *Ibid.*, p. 8.
15. *Ibid.*, p. 9.
16. *Ibid.*, p. 12.
17. The headquarters United States Continental Air Forces was redesignated Strategic Air Command at the start of 1946 and charged with the mission of 'concluding long range operations in any part of the world at any time'. The SAC motto later became 'Peace is our Profession'.

18. NA, RG 18 (Records of Army Air Force), Box 605, Entry 1. Air A/Gen Mail Records Division, Classified Records Section, Decimal File 1946–7. Folder 322, Organization and Tactical Units, Vol. 1. Letter from Requirements Div. AC/AS-3 (Brig-Gen. Alfred R. Maxwell) to AC/AS-3 Op's Div. (Lt-Col Sowers). 6 September 1946.

19. John Robertson, 'Looking back at SAC–UK', *Air Britain Digest*, July 1968, p. 198.

20. Britain was in fact never wholly free of an American military presence between 1945–8 since the United Kingdom remained host to the US Navy headquarters for Europe in London as well as a few radio transmitters and facilities.

21. Perry McCoy Smith, *The Air Force Plans for Peace 1943–5*, p. 75.

22. NA, RG 218 (Records of JCS). JSSC, *The Overall Effect of the Atomic Bomb and Military Organization*: JCS 1477, 26 October 1945, c 119531 – Section 29.

23. NA, ABC 092. Proceedings of the meeting of JSSC, JWPC, JPS, JPWC. 18 July 1945. Section 1.

24. NA, RG 218. JCS 570/2. 10 January 1944, CCS 360 (12–9–42), Section 2.

25. James F. Schnabel, *History of the JCS*, Vol. I, 1945–7. [Hist. Div.: Joint Secretariat, JCS], p. 305.

26. Lt-Col John W. Keeler (Director of Information), *Third Air Force Historical Brief*, Vol. II, 16 July 1948 – 31 December 1967: Foreword. (Historical Division, Office of Information, 3AF, USAFE).

27. John Greenwood, p. 225.

28. *Ibid*.

29. Library of Congress, Manuscripts Division, *Briefing Material for European Trip* prepared by AC/AS-4 for Gen. Carl Spaatz, CG/AAF. 20 June 1946. Box 265 in Spaatz files.

30. NA, RG 341, DCS/O, AAG, File 23, Box 7: Gen. I. Eaker, Dep. CG/AAF to Air Staff, *Decisions reached in London between General Spaatz and the Air Ministry*. 28 June and 6 July 1946. (For further details see Appendix 1). And NA: RG 218, JWPC 474/1, file CCS 092 USSR (3–27–45), Sect. 20, *Strategic Study of Western and Northern Europe*, 13 May 1947.

31. *The Times*, 23 February 1946.

32. In January 1946 the USAAF named the 58th Bomb Wing and its three bomb groups, albeit unofficially, as its strategic bomber force.

33. Library of Congress, Manuscripts Division, Washington, DC, Papers of Gen. Carl Spaatz, CCAF. Box 265, *Briefing Material for European Trip*, 21 June 1946 – prepared by Brig-Gen. F. F. Everest. (Emphasis added.)

34. NA, RG 341. DCS/O, TS AAG, File 23, Box 7. *Letter from Carl Spaatz (C/Gen AAF) to Maj-Gen Bissell* (Military Air Attache, London Embassy), 8 August 1946.

35. John Greenwood, p. 226.

36. Margaret Gowing, *Independence and Deterrence: Britain and Atomic Energy 1945–52*. Vol. 1: Policy Making, p. 185.

37. NA, RG 218 (US JCS). Combined Chiefs of Staff, Decimal File 1942–5, File CCS 381 (5–13–45), Section 2, Box No. 293.

38. NA RG 218, CCS 092 USSR (3–27–45), Section 20, JWPC, *Strategic*

Study of Western and Northern Europe, 13 May 1947, p. 3.

39. JWPC, *Strategic Study of Western and Northern Europe*. p. 30.
40. NA, RG 218. CCS 381 USSR (3–2–46), Section 2. *JWPC 432/5*, 10 June 1946.
41. *JWPC 432/5*, Appendix b to Appendix B.
42. NA, RG 218. CCS 381 USSR (3–2–46), *Enclosure B, JWPC 432/6*, 10 June 1946.
43. Sgt. E. James, Office of History, HQ USAFE, *Historical Highlights, USAFE 1945–8*, 1 May 1980, p. 2.
44. NA, RG 341. DCS/O TS AAG, File 23, Box 7. Memorandum for Gen. Spaatz from Maj.-Gen. Clayton Bissell, Air Attache, London. 'Reminder on decisions taken during London visit. July 4–6, 1946.' Item 6–9. (See Appendix 1).
45. NA, RG 341, DCS/O TS AAG, File 23, Box 7, Memorandum for CG/AAF, *Rotation of VHB Groups to ETO*, June 1946.
46. Interview with author, 10 May 1984, Washington, DC.
47. NA, RG 341, DCS/O TS AAG, File 23, Box 7. Letter, J. McCloy to Dean Acheson, 19 September 1945.
48. NA, RG 341, DCS/O TS AAG, File 23, Box 7. *Letter from Dep Co, AAF (Ira C. Eaker) to Lauris Norstad (Maj-Gen. USA ACAS-5)*, 10 September 1945 (with included memo from Mr. Lovett). See also NA, RG 330 (Secretary of Defense) Office Administrative Secretary, Numerical File, September 1947–June 1950, Box 119. Memo for Secretary of Defense, *Base Rights for the US in return for Military Aid to foreign nations*, from William D. Leahy, Fleet Admiral, USN 21 December 1948. In the memorandum Leahy put forward a JCS suggestion that: 'First, that it would be a wholly logical extension of mutual aid for the recipients to make our combat aid in war emergency more effective by granting appropriate base rights.
    Second, that it would, accordingly, seem appropriate that normally the granting of military aid should be coupled with negotiations for the consideration of US base rights requirements.'
49. NA, RG 341, DCS/O, TS P&O, PD381 Russia (PINCHER), Box 949, Memorandum for Brig-Gen. F. F. Everest from Col A. R. Leudecke. 6 September 1946, quoted in John T. Greenwood, 'The Emergence of the Postwar Strategic Air Force, 1945–53', *Air Power and Warfare: Proceedings of the Eight Military History Symposium*.
50. James F. Schnabel, *History of the Joint Chiefs of Staff*. Vol. II, 1947–9. p. 284.
51. NA, RG 218, CCS 381 USSR (3–2–46), *PM-573 to JWPC*. 29 August 1947.
52. James F. Schnabel, vol. 2, pp. 284–5.
53. *Ibid.*, p. 290.
54. NA, RG 218. Records of JCS, CCS 381 USSR c32–36. Section 10. *JSPG 496/4. Broiler*, 11 February 1948.
55. See Harry Borowski, *A Hollow Threat, Strategic Power and Containment before Korea*, p. 102.
56. Estimates on this point vary; most are between 25–35. David A. Rosenberg, in the Journal of American History (*American Atomic*

Strategy and the H-Bomb decision, Vol. 66, 1979), suggests that there were no more than twenty-nine atomic weapons in the American arsenal by mid-1947. Duncan Campbell, in *The Unsinkable Aircraft Carrier*, p. 28, suggests there were nine B-3 type bombs available in July 1946 and fifty available two years later. The figure here is taken from Harry Borowski, *A Hollow Threat, Strategic Power and Containment before Korea*, p. 104.

57. Richard Ned Lebov, 'Windows of Opportunity: Do States Jump Through Them?, *International Security*, Summer 1984, vol. 9 no. 1, p. 154.

58. John Greenwood, p. 28. Again, figures differ. Norman Polmas, *Strategic Air Command, People, Aircraft and Missiles*, p. 12, suggests that of the 148 B-29s first operating with SAC, thirty were SILVERPLATES.

59. H. Borowski, p. 106.

60. Fact Sheet, USAF Public Affairs Office, 20th Tactical Fighter Wing, RAF Upper Heyford, *Third Air Force History*, May 1982.

61. Directorate of Plants and UK Financial Arrangements, HQ 3AF; *A Matter of Decision*, p. 2.

62. *Ibid.*

63. *Ibid.* p. 3.

64. FRUS 1948, Vol. 2. Marshall to Douglas. 27 June 1948. pp. 926–7.

65. NA, RG 330, CO 6–2–9: Memorandum for Mr Forrestal from W. Stuart Symington, 25 June 1948, enclosing memo. for Mr Symington from Lt-Gen. Lauris Norstad (Deputy COS Operations). 24 June 1948.

66. PRO, FO 371, c 7517/3/18 G, 28 June 1948.

67. *Ibid.*

68. Avi Shlaim, *The United States and the Berlin Blockade 1948–9: A Study in Crisis Decision Making* p. 137.

69. Andrew Pierre, Nuclear Politics, *The British Experience with an Independent Strategic Force, 1939–70* p. 79.

70. Typescript of Forrestal's Diaries, memo JFT : FJT – record of meeting between Secretary Forrestal, Secretary Marshall and the President, *Sending B-29's to Britain* p. 2364.

71. Gregg Herken, *The Atomic Bomb in the Cold War 1945–50* p. 258.

72. NA, *Berlin 'Hot File'*. Plans and Operations of the Army General Staff, JCS Records, 28 June 1948.

73. PRO, FO 371, 70502, C/5740: Gen. Robertson to FO, 16 July 1948.

74. Harry S. Truman Library, President's Secretary Files. Minutes of 15th Meeting of the NSC (Decision 13), 15 July 1948.

75. *New York Times*, 16 July 1948.

76. *The Times*, 17 July 1948.

77. PRO, FO 371, C7517/3/18G, Memorandum from Arthur Henderson (Air Ministry) to Bevin, 27 July 1948.

78. *A Matter of Decision* pp. 4–5.

79. PRO, FO 371, C7517/3/18G. 28 June 1948.

80. *New York Times*, 29 August 1948.

81. *Ibid.*

82. *Keesing's Contemporary Archives* 16 July 1948, p. 9413.

83. HC Debs., 454, col. 123 (written answers). 28 July 1948.

84. PRO, Cab. 131/6, DO (48) 59th Mtd. *Cabinet memo. from Secretary of State for Foreign Affairs.* 10 September 1948.

85. Coral Bell, *The Debatable Alliance: an essay in Anglo–American relations* p. 278.
86. Walter Millis (ed.), *The Forrestal Diaries*, extract from diary, 3 October 1948, p. 491.
87. JCS 570/120.
88. Duncan Campbell, *The Unsinkable Aircraft Carrier: American Military Power in Britain* p. 30.
89. *New York Times*, no. 38, 15 September 1948, p. 18.
90. Margaret Gowing is emphatic that although the B-29s were potential carriers of nuclear weapons those based in England in 1948 had not been modified to do so. See *Independence and Deterrence: Britain and Atomic Energy* Vol. 1, pp. 311 and 311n. See also Kenneth W. Condit, *The History of the JCS* Vol. 2, 1947–9. (Washington, DC, Hist. Div., Joint Secretariat, JCS, 1976) in RG 218, National Archives, Washington, DC, who is also emphatic that the B-29s were not of the modified configuration or carrying A-bombs. p. 139.
91. Washington Navy Yard, Washington, DC: *Typescript of Forrestal's Diaries*, Vol. 12, 1 August–30 September 1948, p. 2501.
92. *Ibid*. Conversation with General Norstad, 17 September 1948, p. 2502.
93. Harry Borowski, *A Hollow Threat: Strategic Air Power and Containment before Korea* p. 127.
94. See Philip Windsor, *City on Leave: A History of Berlin 1945–62* pp. 98–126; Bernard Brodie: *Escalation and the Nuclear Option* pp. 44–6; and Daniel Yergin: *Shattered Peace: The Origins of the Cold War and the National Security State* p. 380.
95. Avi Shlaim, pp. 239–40.

3 Consolidation Part 1 – 1948–50

1. HC Deb.[5], 5th Series, col. 893, Statement by Secretary of State for Air, 3 November 1948.
2. Figure from, Notes of the Month, *World Today*, August 1960, p. 322.
3. Figure from, *The Times*, announced by Mr C. Attlee, 25 July 1950, in the House of Commons in response to a question by Mr S. O. Duncan requesting details on the nature and equipment of 'foreign' armed forces on British soil.
4. NA, RG 341. Box 443: *Memo from Secretary of Defense to Secretary of State*, 8 October 1948.
5. George Orwell, *Nineteen Eighty-Four* p. 29, 'everything had been different then . . . Airstrip One, for instance, had not been so called in those days; it had been called England or Britain.'
6. NA, ORE–58–48, *The Strategic value to the USSR of the Conquest of Western Europe and the Near East, prior to 1950* 30 July 1948.
7. Margaret Gowing, *Independence and Deterrence: Britain and Atomic Energy 1945–52* Vol. 1, Policy Making, p. 310.
8. Robert Futrell, *Ideas, Concepts, Doctrine. A History of Basic Thinking in the USAF 1907–64* p. 156.
9. *Articles of Agreement governing collaboration between the authorities of*

the USA and the UK in the matter of Tube Alloys, HMSO, April 1954, CMD. 9123.

10. *Foreign Relations of the United States [FRUS]*, 1945, Vol. 2 Memorandum by the Commanding General, Manhattan Engineer District (Groves) and the Chairman, British Advisory Committee on Atomic Energy (Anderson) to the Chairman of the CPC (Patterson), pp. 75–6.

11. See Gowing, vol. 1, pp. 104–12.

12. Richard G. Hewlett and Francis Duncan, *History of the United States Atomic Energy Commission. Atomic Shield 1947–52*, vol. 2, p. 263.

13. *Ibid.*, p. 275.

14. Vandenberg, Jnr. (ed.), *The Private Papers of Senator Vandenberg* p. 361.

15. Andrew Pierre, *Nuclear Politics. The British Experience with an Independent Strategic Force 1939–70* p. 129.

16. Gowing, vol. 1, p. 250.

17. Pierre, p. 129.

18. As laid out in Cabinet papers 134/21, 22–5 and 26.

19. Hewlett and Duncan, p. 280.

20. Gowing, Vol. 1, pp. 266–72. The agreements between Britain and the United States that were thus nullified were the Quebec Agreement of 1943, the Hyde Park Memorandum of 1944, and the Truman–Attlee–King concordant of 1945.

21. Gowing, p. 252.

22. Interview with Lord Sherfield. 21 February 1984.

23. Gowing, p. 251. Professor Gowing does point out one notable abstainer from this view. Vice Chief of the Air Staff, Sir William Dickson, thought that if Britain retained the veto, the British might be a 'restraining influence' in the event of an emergency.

24. Gowing, p. 253.

25. Interview with Lord Sherfield, London 21 February 1984.

26. Gowing, p. 251.

27. NA, RG 319. Records of the Army Staff: P & O 373 TS (Sect. I) (Case I). JCS 1952/10. *Memorandum for Dir., WSEG re JCS 1952/9.* 10 October 1949, p. 146, Sect. 2.

28. *Ibid.*, pp. 146–7, Sect. 3. (In Section (c) no mention was made of which three airfields.)

29. PRO, FO 371: DO (49) 13th Mtd. 13 May 1949.

30. PRO, FO 371: Telegram No. 1628 from Foreign Secretary to Sir O. Franks. Washington, DC, 26 November 1949.

31. Harry S. Truman Library, Papers of Harry S. Truman President's Secretary Files, *NSC 20/4*, Sect. 4., 23 November 1948.

32. NA, RG 319, Records of the Arms Staff. Plans and Operations (P & O) Sect. I (Case I) JSPC 877/59 *Offtackle.* 26 April 1949. Enclosure p. 29, Sect. 27a.

33. *Ibid.*, Sect. 27b, *Base Operations.*

34. Figures from James Schnabel, *The History of the Joint Chiefs of Staff and National Policy*, Vol. 2, p. 301.

35. *Ibid.*

36. NA, RG 319. Records of the Army Staff: P & O 373 TS (Section 1) Case 1. JCS 1952/9, memo on *Inadequacy of Bases Provided for Strategic Air*

Offensive, prepared by Lt-Gen. J. E. Hull, Dir. WSEG. 13 September 1949. p. 143, Sect. I.

37. NA, RG 319. Records of the Army Staff: P & O 373 TS (Sect. I) (Case I). JCS 1952/10. *Memorandum for Dir, WSEG re JCS 1952/9*, 10 October 1949, p. 147, Sect. 6.
38. Harry S. Truman Library, Papers of Harry S. Truman: President's Secretary's Files, *A Report to the National Security Council by the Sec. of Defense on Airfield Construction*, NSC 45, 17 March 1949.
39. NA, RG 319, Records of the Army Staff, 1949 'HOT FILE', p. 20, 600.1 TS. *Memorandum for the Secretary of the Army: Airfield Construction (NSC 45)*, 22 March 1949.
40. NA, RG 319, Records of the Army Staff, P20, 373 TS (Section 1) (Case 1) *JCS 1952/10*, p. 148. Section 7.
41. These proposals were put forward in a letter from the Secretary of Defense to the Secretary of State, 1 September 1949, as an appendix to JCS 1952/10.
42. FRUS, vol. 1 (National Security Affairs). *Foreign Policy Paper approved by Foreign Assistance Correlation Committee – Military Rights*, 20 May 1949, p. 312.
43. FRUS, vol. 1, *Staff Paper Prepared for the National Security Resources Board and NSC by an Interdepartmental Working Group*, Washington, DC, 1 June 1949, p. 339, Section (C).
44. James Schnabel, vol. 2, p. 523.
45. Carl Spaatz, General USAF, 'If We Should have to Fight Again', *Life Magazine*, 5 July 1948, p. 39.
46. Thomas K. Finletter (Chairman), *Survival in the Air Age: The Presidents Air Policy Commission Report*: Washington, DC, US Government Printing Office, 1948 (known as the Finletter Report), Senator Stuart Symington told the Mahon Committee in 1950 that Moscow would not have sufficient weapons to conduct an attack before 1952 (in Warner R. Schilling, Paul Y. Hammond, and Glenn H. Snyder, *Strategy, Politics and Defense Budgets*, p. 83).
47. George F. Kennan, *Memoirs* 1950–63, pp. 91–2. For a more general discussion see John Lewis Gaddis, *Strategies of Containment: A Critical Appraisal of Postwar American National Security Policy*, pp. 86–126.
48. J. Robert Oppenheimer, *The Open Mind*, p. 70.
49. NA, RG 330 (Sec. of Defense) Office Administrative Secretary, Numerical File, September 1947–June 1950, Box 119. *Memo for British in Connection with MDAP Bilateral*, 11 January 1950, Para. 8.
50. PRO, Cab. 131/8. DO (50) 4th mtg., 15 March 1950.
51. *Ibid.*
52. *Ibid.*, quoting Memorandum dtd. 29 December 1948 from Gen. Leon Johnson to the Hon. Stuart Symington, Sec. of the Air Force.
53. *Ibid.*, p. 54.
54. *Ibid.*, memorandum from Gen. L. Johnson, CG TAD, to the US Ambassador, American Embassy, London, 'Airfield Construction in the UK for use by the USAF', 4 May 1949.
55. *Ibid.*, p. 57, memorandum from Gen. L. Johnson, CG TAD, to Mr. H. H. Halaby, Director, Office of Foreign Affairs, US Dept. of Defense 9

November 1949.
56. *Ibid.*
57. NA, RG 330, Records of the Office of the Secretary of Defense. CD 092.3 NATO (General) 1949–50. *Memo by JCS to Sec. of Defense*, 16 April 1949.
58. *Ibid.*, 'British Isles', Section 3. (Emphasis in original).
59. NA, RG 330. *Letter from Air Chief Marshall Slessor, Chief of the Air Staff, Air Ministry, to General Hoyt S. Vandenberg (Ch. HQ USAF)*, 3 February 1950.
60. NA, RG 330. Folder 'United Kingdom' 3/49 through 3/52, Box 162. Memorandum from A. C. Murdaugh to Mr Halaby, *Possible Financial Demands on the British*, 29 December 1949. (Emphasis added).
61. *A Matter of Decision*, letter from Mr Aidan Crawley to Mr Louis Douglas, US Ambassador, American Embassy, London, 28 March 1950, p. 64.
62. *Ibid.*
63. *Ibid.*
64. *Ibid.*, p. 65.
65. *Ibid.*, p. 66.
66. *Ibid.*, Letter from Aidan Crawley to Louis Douglas, American Embassy, London, 15 April 1950.
67. When the USAF were deployed to the United Kingdom at the outbreak of the Berlin Crisis the pound sterling was worth $4.03, but after a devaluation in September 1949 it was reduced to $2.80.
68. PRO, Cab. 131/8, *DO (50) 4th mtg.*, 15 March 1950: comments by the Rt Hon. E. Shinwell and the Prime Minister were made at the same meeting.
69. *Ibid.*
70. The Third Air Division became a major command reporting directly to headquarters USAF, rather than headquarters USAFE, on 3 January 1949. It assumed all the functions of a major command except court martial jurisdiction. The headquarters, Third Air Division, was transferred from Bushy Park to South Ruislip on 15 April 1949.
71. Harry S. Truman Library, Records of the JCS, JCS 1906/18, Memo by the Chief of Staff, USAF, on 'Strengthening US Air Force capabilities in the United Kingdom', 8 July 1950, pp. 30–1.
72. *Ibid.*
73. NA, RG 330, Records of the Office of the Secretary of Defense: Folder, 'United Kingdom' 3/49 through 3/52. Box 162 Entry 19B. Assistant Secretary of Defense (International Security Affairs) DOS, Office of Public Affairs. 'The Role of the United Kingdom in the World Today, Information Memo, 30 June 1950.
74. 478, HC Deb.[5], Series, question by S. O. Davies, 24 July 1950, col. 26. (These figures roughly double those for the year before. See Table A2.2.)
75. NA, RG 330, CD 092.2, UK (1950) Memorandum for Secretary Johnson from Thomas K. Finletter, 7 July 1950.
76. *Ibid.*
77. *Ibid.*
78. NA, RG 330, CD 6–4–18, UK (1950). Memorandum for Secretary Johnson: Strategic Air Offensive requirements for Alternate Bases, 27 March 1950, Sec. 1–2.

79. *Ibid.*, Sec. 4.
80. PRO, FO 371/90966: WU 11913/70G. Flag F: in a memo by J. N. Henderson, 31 August 1951.
81. Andrew Pierre: *Nuclear Politics: The British Experience with an Independent Strategic Force 1939–70*, p. 148.
82. FRUS, Dept. of State, vol. IV, 1949 (Western Europe), p. 108.
83. NA, RG 330. Folder: United Kingdom 3/49 through 3/52, Box 162, Entry 19B. Assistant Secretary of Defense (Int. Security Affairs) Office of Foreign Military Affairs. Office of Public Affairs, DOS, Information Memorandum no. 85, 'The Role of the United Kingdom in the World Today', 6 June 1950, p. 5.

4 The Agreements – 1950–2

1. FRUS, 1950, Vol. 7 (Korea). Subannex in a Position Paper prepared for the Truman–Attlee talks, *Use of the Atomic Bomb*, p. 1261.
2. Harry S. Truman, Vol. 2, *Years of Trial and Hope*, pp. 419–20.
3. FRUS, 1950, vol. 7 (Korea), p. 1464.
4. See for instance John Baylis, *Anglo–American Defence Relations 1939–80*, who talks of 'Clement Attlee's visit to Washington in December 1950 to caution President Truman on the use of nuclear weapons in Korea' (p. 50). Duncan Campbell in *The Unsinkable Aircraft Carrier* expresses the same idea when he observed that 'the fears of backbench MPs that Britain might face annihilation without consultation were sharpened by the overt threat to use atomic weapons in Korea which President Truman made at a press conference.' (p. 33).
5. Margaret Gowing, *Independence and Deterrence: Britain and Atomic Energy, 1945–52*, vol. 1: Policy Making, p. 312.
6. *Ibid.*
7. *The Public Papers of Harry S. Truman, 1950* 31 November 1950, Special Message to Congress requesting Additional Appropriations for Defense on 1 December 1950, pp. 724–31.
8. NSC-68 was presented to the NSC in April 1950 and its main purpose was to impress upon its audience the threat to world peace and stability caused by the Soviet Union. Lawrence Freedman, in *The Evolution of Nuclear Strategy*, comments that one of the presumptions of NSC-68 was that if war did come it was hardly conceivable that the Soviet leaders would refrain from use of atomic weapons unless their objectives could be attained by other conventional means. NSC also 'accepted the propositions that the natural way to fight a war was to get in a surprise attack and that totalitarian states enjoyed a comparative advantage over open societies in the ability to strike swiftly and with stealth' (p. 70). The thought that two atomic powers could co-exist under some form of mutual deterrence was not accepted by the report.
9. Anthony Cave Brown, *Dropshot*, p. 21.
10. *Ibid.*, p. 77.
11. Richard G. Hewlett and Francis Duncan, *History of the USAEC, II. Atomic Shield 1947–52*, pp. 521–2.

12. PRO, Cab 128/18: CM (50) 80th, conclusions. Meeting of the Cabinet held in PM's room, House of Commons, 30 November 1950 at 6.45 pm.
13. *Ibid.*
14. Kenneth Harris, *Attlee*, p. 463.
15. Interview with Lucius D. Battle, Special Assistant to the Secretary of State, Washington, DC, 10 May 1984.
16. FRUS, Vol. 7 (Korea). Memorandum by the Ambassador at Large (Philip Jessup), 7 December 1950, p. 1462.
17. Kenneth Harris, p. 464.
18. Dean Acheson, *Present at the Creation*, p. 484.
19. FRUS, Vol. 7, Truman–Attlee conversations, 8 December 1950, p. 1479.
20. Department of State, *Bulletin*, vol. 23, 18 December 1950, p. 961.
21. Harry S. Truman, President's Secretary's Files, *Draft Communiqué*, 8 December 1950.
22. Dean Acheson talks to Kenneth Harris, *Listener*, 8 April 1971 (author's emphasis).
23. Interview, Lord Sherfield (London), 21 February 1984.
24. PRO, Cab. 128/18, Cabinet 85 (50). Meeting of the Cabinet held at Downing Street, 12 December 1950 at 11.30 am, p. 225.
25. 482 HC Deb.⁵, 14 December 1950, col. 1356.
26. Interview, Lucius D. Battle (Special Assistant to the Secretary of State under Acheson), Washington, DC, 10 May 1984.
27. *Ibid.*
28. Margaret Gowing, p. 313.
29. *Ibid.*
30. Walter S. Gifford, US Ambassador to the United Kingdom.
31. FRUS, Vol. 2 (1951), National Security Affairs, p. 802.
32. *Ibid.*
33. FRUS, vol. 2 (1951), Letter from the British Secretary of State for Foreign Affairs to the Secretary of State, 14 January 1951, p. 822.
34. Margaret Gowing, p. 315.
35. A. H. Vandenberg, Jnr., *The Private Papers of Senator Vandenberg*, p. 361.
36. FRUS, vol. 1 (1951), Extract of Memorandum by Director of Policy Planning Staff, Washington, 13 September 1951, p. 886.
37. Margaret Gowing, p. 316.
38. *Ibid.*
39. *Ibid.*, p. 317.
40. *Ibid.*, p. 318.
41. A. J. R. Groom, *British Thinking about Nuclear Weapons*, p. 51.
42. Margaret Gowing, p. 407.
43. 482, HC Deb.⁵, 14 December 1950, col. 1369.
44. *The Times*: speech made at the Lord Mayor's banquet, 10 November 1951, p. 6.
45. *New York Times*, 21 April 1951, p. 4.
46. *The Times*, 13 November 1951, p. 4.
47. John Robertson, Looking Back at SAC–UK, *Air Britain Digest*, July 1968, pp. 198–201.
48. Laurence R. Benson, USAFE Historical Monograph, *USAF Basing in*

Europe, Africa and the Middle East, 1945–80.

49. *Historical Data*, HQ 3AD, APO, 125 (USAF), 1 January–30 April 1951, p. 6.
50. *Historical Data*, HQ 3AD, APO, 125 (USAF), Vol. 1, no. 1. Message from the Inspector General, 1 May–31 December 1951, p. 18.
51. See Chapter 5.
52. *Keesing's Contemporary Archives*, (1948–50), p. 10107 A.
53. Figure from *SIPRI Yearbook 1982*, p. 4.
54. G. Sviridov, 'American Military Bases in Britain', *New York Times*, no. 19, 1952, pp. 12–14.
55. Raymond Daniel, 'US Air Bases in Britain', *New York Times*, Pt. IC, 2 December 1951, p. 4.
56. The phrase used by Daniel quoting Churchill was first used by the Prime Minister in response to a question by Emrys Hughes, the well-known pacifist, who asked if the Prime Minister would 'terminate the arrangement by which United States atom bombers are based in this country, in view of the dangers of retaliatory bombing to the people living in the crowded cities in Britain?' The Prime Minister replied: 'Certain bases and facilities in the United Kingdom were made available by the late government for the common defence of the United Kingdom and other countries who are parties to the North Atlantic Treaty. This arrangement will continue so long as it is needed in the general interests of world peace and security.' 494, HC Deb.⁵, 21 November 1951, col. 376.
57. *Records of the JCS: Europe and NATO*, Pt. 2 (1946–53), Microfilm Reel II, Frame 0391, DOS Position Paper, 'Essential Elements in the US–UK relationship' (FM, D-16 b).
58. *Ibid.*
59. *The Times*, 7 December 1951.
60. *New York Times*, 9 December 1951, Section 4.
61. 496, HC Deb.⁵, written answer in response to a question by Mr S. Silverman, 6 December 1951, col. 280 (emphasis added).
62. Harry S. Truman Library, Papers of Harry S. Truman, President's Secretary's Files: Steering Group for talks between the President and Prime Minister Churchill, 'Nature of the US–UK Relationship', 28 December 1951, TCT D-2/16, p. 1.
63. *Ibid.*, p. 5.
64. Harry S. Truman, Papers of Harry S. Truman, President's Secretary's Files, Talks between the President and Prime Minister Churchill, negotiating paper: 'Technical Cooperation in Atomic Energy', 3 January 1952 (prepared by R. Gordon Arneson, Special Assistant to the Secretary of State), pp. 2–3 (TCT D-2/8).
65. Harry S. Truman Library, President's Secretary's Files. Steering Group for talks between the President and Prime Minister Churchill: 'Approach and Objectives for Churchill Talks', TCT Memo 3b, 21 December 1951, p. 5, para. (b).
66. PRO, FO 371/97592, doc. Au 1051/12. From Washington to Foreign Office, Sir O. Franks, No. 77, 9 January 1952, text of communiqué.
67. Department of State Bulletin, Vol. 26, no. 656, 21 January 1952, joint communiqué, p. 83.

68. PRO, PREM 11/431, 56513: 'Mr Truman's Statement to Messrs. Churchill and Eden', 7 January 1952.

69. PRO, FO 371/97588, 041605, AU 1021/6. Comments on survey of American press and radio on Churchill's visit from Sir O. Franks, Washington, to the Foreign Office, 16 January 1952.

70. Congressional Record (House), 'Agreement of understanding between the President of the United States and the Prime Minister of Great Britain', (Letter from Jack K. McFall to Hon. James P. Richards, 1 February 1952), 20 February 1952, p. 1205. (Emphasis mine, both above and below.) In spite of the statement by Jack McFall, Mr Richards, during a debate on HR 514, later said that: 'personally, I think the executive went further than was proper in the communiqué, because Russia and the world are told that we agreed to do certain things that it might have been wiser not to publish. One of the disclosures is the agreement with Great Britain that *our planes would not take off from their airfields to bomb Russia without prior British consent.' (Ibid.*, 20 February 1952, p. 1210). Churchill would have loved such a return to the Quebec Agreement's 'consent clause', although this did of course only cover the A-bomb since the US government's decision to proceed with development of the H-bomb was not taken until 1950.

71. Sir Oliver Franks in an earlier telegram had informed the Foreign Office that: 'Throughout our talks we have been impressed by the need to strengthen the North Atlantic Treaty Organisation by every means within our power, and in full accord with our fellow members we are resolved to build an Atlantic Community, not only for immediate defence, but for enduring progress.' (PRO: FO 371/97592 041605: AU 1051/12. *F.O. Telegram No. 77*, Sir O. Franks to Foreign Office, 9 January 1952).

72. Press extracts from FO 371/97588 041605, AU 1021/6, *Survey of American Press and Radio Comment*, Sir O. Franks, Washington, to Foreign Office, 16 January 1952.

73. David Henshaw, 'Whose Finger on the Button?', *The Listener*, 2 June 1983.

74. Interview, Lucius D. Battle, 10 May 1984, Washington, DC.

75. Interview, Dr James Schlesinger, 19 June 1984, Washington, DC.

76. *Ibid.*

77. *The Listener*, 2 June 1983, p. 3.

78. PRO, PREM 11/431 56513, 'From Foreign Secretary on board RMS Queen Elizabeth to FO'. Addressed to FO telegram No. 22 of 2 March 1953. Truman had assured Churchill and Eden on 7 January 1952 that he was 'just as reluctant as HMG to see atomic weapons used . . . nevertheless this feeling would not prevent his taking the decision if and when it proved to be necessary. In any case, those countries 'lined-up' with the US should be consulted first.'

79. PRO, PREM 11/431 56513, 'Visit of Foreign Secretary and Chancellor to USA', record of meeting at the State Department at Washington on Friday 4.45 pm, 6 March 1953.

80. PRO, PREM 11/431 56513. Record of Meeting with the President of the United States in the White House in Washington at 10 am, Monday 9 March 1953 – in Washington telegram to Foreign Office no. 531 of 9 March 1953.

81. *Ibid.*
82. Dwight D. Eisenhower Library, Dwight D. Eisenhower Papers as President of the United States 1953–61 (Ann Whitman File). International File, Box 17, Churchill–President, January–June 1954. Entry no. 9, 'Embassy's Comments on H-bomb debate in the House of Commons, April 5', From London (Aldrich) to Secretary of State, no. 4384. 6 April 1954, 5 pm.
83. Congressional Research Service (CRS), Report prepared for Subcommittee on International Security and Scientific Affairs of the Committee on International Relations, 'Authority to Order the use of Nuclear Weapons', 1 December 1975, p. 1. (Emphasis mine.)
84. *Ibid.*, p. 6.
85. 42, HC Deb.⁶, 12 May 1983, col. 433 (written answer).
86. Transcript of BBC 'Brass Tacks' programme, *A Matter for Joint Decision*, broadcast May 1983, p. 2.

5 The US Presence Consolidated – America Builds up Her Military Presence in the UK: The Developing Years

1. James F. Schnabel, *The History of the Joint Chiefs of Staff*, vol. 2, 1947–9, pp. 298–9.
2. *Ibid.*
3. Bolling AFB, Washington DC, Letter from General Leon Johnson, CG TAD to the Under Secretary of State for Air, Air Ministry, 3 August 1950.
4. Bolling AFB, Washington DC, Letter from Air Marshal Sir William F. Dickson, Air Ministry, to General Leon Johnson, CG TAD.
5. Duncan Campbell, *The Unsinkable Aircraft Carrier: American Military Power in Britain*, p. 39.
6. Bolling AFB, Letter from Gen. Johnson to Air Marshal Dickson, Air Ministry, 31 August 1950, in *A Matter for Decision*, prepared by Director of Plans and UK Financial Arrangements, ACS/Comptroller, HQ 3AF, p. 95.
7. *Ibid.*, Letter from Air Marshal Sir William Dickson, Air Ministry, to General Leon Johnson, CG TAD, 11 December 1950, p. 97.
8. Air Marshal Sir William F. Dickson was promoted to Air Chief Marshal on 8 January 1951.
9. *Ibid.*, p. 105.
10. The eight bomber bases were at Brize Norton, Upper Heyford, Lakenheath, Fairford, Greenham Common, Chelveston, Sculthorpe and Mildenhall. In addition it was realised that bombers would require escorts, so a Fighter Escort Wing was transferred to the UK in January 1951 and soon a permanent station was established at Bentwaters.
11. Duncan Campbell, p. 39.
12. RAF Mildenhall, TAF HQ, 'Transfer Agreement and Delineation of Responsibilities between USAFE and SAC in the United Kingdom', 11 September 1951.
13. Bolling AFB, Director of Plans and UK Financial Arrangements, ACS/Comptroller, HQ 3AF, *A Matter for Decision*, p. 135.
14. *Ibid.*
15. *Ibid.* Letter from Air Marshal Sir J. Slessor, Chief of the Air Staff, to

General Hoyt S. Vandenberg, COS HQ USAF, 8 October 1951.

16. Bolling AFB, Memorandum by UK on Works Services for the USAF, 1 April 1952, p. 138.

17. The Seventh Air Division supervising the SAC rotational tours was originally under General Paul T. Cullen, whose C-124 crashed somewhere in the Atlantic en route to the United Kingdom to take up his new command. On 26 April 1951, Major-General Archie J. Old, Jnr, assumed temporary command, to be replaced a month later by Major-General John P. McDonnell.

18. Bolling AFB, Washington, DC, 'Outgoing message from 3AF S. Ruislip, England to HQ USAF Washington DC', DCG N-1545, 16 May 1952.

19. *Ibid.*

20. Bolling AFB, DEPTEL No. 1556 (State Dept.) to American Embassy, London, 4 September 1952.

21. Bolling AFB, Disposition Form signed by Col Edward J. Hopkins, ACS/Comtroller, Hqs TAF to Commander TAF, *Cost Sharing Negotiations*. 7 August 1953.

22. *The Times*, 1 February 1954.

23. *A Matter for Decision*, pp. 164–5.

24. *Ibid.*

25. See Appendix 4, Table A4.1

26. Figures from Sgt Richard H. Willard, *Third Air Force Historical Brief*, 'Installations and USAF combat units in the UK: 1945–1965', Hist. Div., Office of Information, 3AF, USAFE, pp. 70–2.

27. Walter S. Poole, *History of the Joint Chiefs of Staff. JCS and National Policy*, vol. 4, 1950–2, p. 170.

28. Bolling AFB, *Letter from US Ambassador, London, Winthrop Aldrich to the Rt Hon. The Lord De L'Isle and Dudley, Secretary of State for Air.* Para. 4, Section e. 9 September 1953.

29. *Ibid.*, Paragraph 11.

30. Bolling AFB, Letter signed for Lord De L'Isle and Dudley by George War, Parliamentary Under-Sec. of State for Air, Air Ministry, to the Hon. Winthrop Aldrich, US Ambassador, 9 September 1953.

31. PRO, FO 371/90966, AU 1194/11G, Minute by JNO Curle, 25 August 1951.

32. *Ibid.*

33. *Ibid.*

34. *Ibid.* Letter dated 20 February 1951 to Foreign Office quoted in minute by JNO Curle.

35. *Ibid.*

36. See Appendix 2, Table A2.2.

37. PRO, FO 371/90966: Memorandum for JNO Curle from R. Cecil, 27 August 1951.

38. The list of military requirements for the United Kingdom were set out in late 1950 as main bomber bases at Brize Norton, Upper Heyford, Fairford, Chelveston, Sculthorpe, Mildenhall and Lakenheath (Greenham Common should have been included). The main fighter base requirements were at Carnaby, Manston and Woodbridge. Transport bases for the Military Air Transport Service or SAC were required at

Heathrow, Nutts Corner (Northern Ireland), Prestwick, Stornoway and Valley, and lastly depots at Burtonwood and Alconbury. The US also set out a plan for long-range navigation (LORAN) facilities and extensive military rights. (NA, OSD Papers, sect. 092.2 (Saudi Arabia), 'List of US requirements for military rights in NATO countries and their territories', 26 December 1950.

39. PRO, FO 371/90966, Memorandum to W.O. Department by JNO Curle, 7 September 1951.

40. PRO, FO 371/90966, AU 1194/14G, *Comments on the obscurity about the future strength of the US forces in the UK*, R. Cecil, 12 September 1951.

41. Alvin J. Cottrell and Thomas H. Moorer, *US Overseas Bases: Problems of Projecting American Military Power Abroad*, p. 7.

42. PRO, FO 371/90966, AU 1194/25: Memorandum from A. Lawson OBE (Air) to P. T. Hayman (MoD), 31 December 1951.

43. Washington Navy Yard, USN Historical Branch, Bldg 57, File A12-1, *C/O US Naval Forces East Atlantic and Mediterranean to Dir. of Naval History*, 1 October 1946 – 1 April 1947, p. 28.

44. Washington Navy Yard, USN Historical Branch, Bldg 57, File A12-1(i), *Quarterly Summary of US Naval Forces E. Atlantic and Mediterranean*, 1 April 1947 – 1 July 1947, Co USN E. Atlantic and Mediterranean to Dir. Naval History, pp. 1–3.

45. Testimony of Secretary of State Dean Acheson: Hearings of the Senate Foreign Relations and Armed Services Committee, *Assignment of Ground Forces of the United States in the European Area*, February 1951.

46. George Stanbuk, *American Military Forces Abroad*, p. 9.

47. A. J. Cottrell and T. Moorer, *US Overseas Bases: Problems of Projecting American Military Power Abroad*, p. 6.

48. Subcommittee on Military Public Works, 82nd Congress Senate, *Overseas Construction in the North Atlantic and Mediterranean Areas*, 2 January 1953, p. 9.

49. The first British A-bomb was exploded in Australia at the Monte Bello Test site on 3 October 1952. The research and development cost amounted to almost £150 million.

50. Margaret Gowing, p. 441.

51. Walter S. Poole, *History of the Joint Chiefs of Staff*, vol. 4 (1950–2), SAC Emergency War Plan quoted in Peter Pringle and William Arkin, *SIOP: Nuclear War from the Inside*, p. 35.

52. Robert E. Harkavy, *Great Power Competition for Overseas Bases. The geopolitics of Access Diplomacy*, p. 154.

53. John Robertson, 'Looking Back at SAC–UK', *Air Britain Digest*, July 1968, p. 199.

54. Robert E. Harkavy, p. 116.

55. Senate Committee on Foreign Relations, *Report on Security Agreements and Commitments Abroad* (Gov' Printing Office, Washington, DC), 21 December 1970, p. 19.

56. Bernard Brodie, 'Nuclear Weapons: Strategic or Tactical?', *Foreign Affairs*, vol. 32, no. 2, January 1954, p. 222.

57. Sir John Slessor, 'The Place of the bomber in British strategy', *International Affairs*, vol. 34 no. 3, July 1953, pp. 302–3. Slessor also believed that

the 'Pax Atlantica depends as surely, and probably more permanently, on Anglo–American air power, of which the decisive expression is the long-range atomic bomber.' (*Ibid.*, p. 304). Slessor's belief in the importance of a strategic nuclear bomber force led to the creation of the British V-bomber force under Bomber Command.

58. Alvin J. Cottrell and Thomas H. Moorer, *US Overseas Bases: Problems in Projecting American Military Power Abroad*, p. 7.
59. *Ibid.*
60. American missile development was still in its infancy in 1953. The 'Redstone' project was still experimenting with adapted V-2 designs the first of which was fired in 1953 and a year later the Killan committee recommended concentration upon the development of a 1500-nautical-mile missile rather than an ICBM, a move which was to have great significance for American bases in Britain since the failure to develop an ICBM saw IRBM deployments in Britain, while the development of a nautical missile culminated in the Polaris base at Holy Loch. (Hearings, Subcommittee on the Air Force of the Senate Committee on Armed Services, statement by Maj.-Gen. J. B. Medavis (Co-Gen, Army Ballistic Missile Agency, Redstone, Al.), April 16–20, 1956).
61. 524, HC Deb.[5], 4 March 1954, col. 1503.
62. David Walker, 'How US urged nuclear strike on China', *The Times*, 2 January 1985.
63. Marshall A. Yeremenko; quoting Nikita Khrushchev in an address to the Fourth Session of the USSR Supreme Soviet, 14 January 1960, *Survival*, vol. 3 no. 2 March–April 1963, p. 62.
64. *Ibid.*, p. 64.
65. Henry A. Kissinger, *Nuclear Weapons and Foreign Policy*, p. 107.
66. *Ibid.*, p. 109.
67. Frank C. Nash, Report to the President, *United States Overseas Military Bases*, December 1957, Eisenhower Library, Kansas, File 152, p. 17.
68. *Ibid.*, p. 181.
69. *Ibid.*
70. H. L. Roberts and P. A. Wilson, *Britain and the United States: Problems in Cooperation*, p. 360.

6   A Political and Sociological Experiment

1. Robert H. Ferrell, *The Eisenhower Diaries* (New York: 1981), p. 189.
2. *The New York Times*, 1 September 1952.
3. *Ibid.*, 16 November 1952.
4. PRO, FO 371/97606 041605, Paper AU 1195/22: Letter from Selwyn Lloyd to Walter H. Ayres MP, 23 May 1952.
5. *Ibid.*
6. PRO, FO 371/97606 041605, Paper AU 1195/10.
7. *Financial Times*, 19 March 1953.
8. *New York Herald Tribune*, 9 November 1953.
10. *New York Herald Tribune*, 28 December 1953.
11. Financial Impact includes: salaries of national employees, personal expenditures survey, temporary lodgings allowance, local procurements,

civil engineering construction projects, operational and maintenance costs, dependent school wages and supplies, rates for base facilities and housing, local non-governmental wages and purchases, and private organisations. The figures *do not* include tourism generated by relatives etc. visiting the UK, or the purchase of the Ropier Missile Defence System. [Figures (current as of January 1986) prepared by 3rd Air Force Public Affairs, RAF Mildenhall]

12. House of Representatives, Committee on Appropriations, subcommittee on Military Construction, FY 1984, pt. 5, p. 253, quoted in Duncan Campbell's *The Unsinkable Aircraft Carrier*, p. 305.

13. Still under construction at time of writing. It will eventually have over 5000 beds.

14. Information from Dan Cragg, *The Guide to Military Installations*, pp. 323–38. The statue of RAF Lakenheath replaced a larger statue that the 48 TFW had at Chaumont before moving to Lakenheath. The Chaumont statue was made from the original molds. When the wing left France, the French Government refused to allow the statue out of France.

15. *The Economist*, 12 April 1952, p. 82.

16. Serge Lazareff, *Status of Military Forces under International Law*, pp. 18–19.

17. Congressional Record–House: vol. 1–2, 1955–6: extract from a speech by Hon. Frank T. Bow (Representative for Ohio), pp. 381–2.

18. *Ibid.*, quoting Lord Acton, p. 403.

19. NA, RG 341, Box 352, JCS 1824 series, JCS 1824/3, Memo to the Department of State from the British Embassy, 14 July 1950.

20. *Ibid.*

21. NA, RG 341, Box 443, Memo for Secretary Johnson from Thomas K. Finletter, 8 August 1950.

22. *House of Representatives hearings*, vol. 1–11, 1955–6, quoting Malemo Manuel v. Ministere Public, A.J. (1945/349), p. 226.

23. *Ibid.*, p. 266.

24. Judgement reached by the Permanent Court of International Justices on 7 September 1927 on conclusion of the 'S.S. Lotus' case.

25. H. Lauterpacht, *International Law*, vol. 1 (8th ed.) (London: 1955), p. 396.

26. NATO Status of Forces Agt., Article 7, 3a para. 2 (enacted by the Visiting Forces Act in Section 3, para. 1. See Appendix 1.)

27. *Ibid.*, Article 7, 2a.

28. *International Law Studies 1957–8*, US Naval War College (Newport, Rhode Island), vol. 52, pp. 100–12.

29. On January 1957 Army specialist 3rd Class William S. Girard and others were guarding a machine gun overlooking a manoeuvre area made available by the Japanese government for part-time use of the US Army. Japanese people frequently combed the ground for empty brass cartridge cases which could be sold locally. As a Japanese man approached the area, placing a brass shell case in his rifle grenade launcher, Girard fired a blank cartridge in the man's vicinity. The man fled. Then a Japanese woman approached and Girard, using the same makeshift equipment, fired again. The woman, Mrs Naha Sakai, fell dead. There ensued a long argument

between Japanese and American authorities over whether Girard had acted in the performance of official duty, and eventually the US authorities surrendered him in accordance with SOFA for trial. The SOFA also provided that either party could either 'waive' its jurisdiction if it so wished, which is what the US Army did, only to meet charges of abridgement of Girard's constitutional rights. On 1 July, the House of Foreign Affairs committee reported on a Joint House resolution introduced by Representative Frank T. Bow (Ohio) to revise SOFA and provide that foreign countries would have no criminal jurisdiction over US servicemen stationed within their boundaries. As President Eisenhower notes, 'Girard was later tried by a Japanese court and given a three-year suspended sentence. The abortive and unwarranted attack on our Status of Forces agreement was not forgotten.' (Dwight D. Eisenhower, *Waging Peace 1956–61. The White House Years*, vol. 2, pp. 140–44) Under an American–Japanese agreement of 23 September 1953, it stated that 'on-duty' could be seen as any duty or service required or authorized to be done by statute regulation, the order of a superior or military usage. It was however up to the sending state to decide if a member of the force was on 'official duty'.

30. G. A. Barton: *British Yearbook of International Law*, vol. 26 (1949) p. 358.
31. George Stambuk: American Military Forces Abroad, p. 125.
32. NA, RG 330, OSD File, 1952, Box 323, File on USAFE command, CD 092.2 (Europe).
33. Bolling AFB: HQ 3AF, APO 125, *History of the Third Air Force*, January–December 1954, vol. 1, p. 201.
34. See L. J. Blom-Cooper: *The Solicitor* (Journal), 1956–7 (vol. 23–4), November 1957, pp. 296–8.
35. D. W. Greig, *International Law*, p. 271.
36. NA, RG 330: Defence, Executive Office Files, 1953 (OSD), Box no. 14, CD 092.2, General, RS 01852, Memo for Secretary of Defense from Frank C. Nash, Assistant Secretary for International Security Affairs, 4 February 1953.
37. USA Status of Forces Agreement, *House of Representatives Hearings*, vols 2–3, 1955–6, 'Exercise of criminal jurisdiction by foreign tribunals over US citizens subject to military law', pp. 230–2.
38. Duncan Campbell, 'Outside the Law', *New Stateman*, 18 November 1983, p. 12.
39. *Ibid*.
40. *Ibid*.
41. *House of Representatives Hearings*, vols 1–2 (1955–6) US Status of Forces Agreements, p. 402.
42. Duncan Campbell, *New Statesman*, 18 November 1983, p. 12.

7 Consolidation: Part 2 – 1954–63

1. Roy Allison, *Finland's Relations with the Soviet Union*, pp. 37–8.
2. Strobe Talbott (ed.), *Khrushchev Remembers*, p. 446.
3. Roy Allison, p. 39.

4. 523, HC Deb.[5], question by Tom Driberg, 9 February 1954, col. 1000.

5. Public Law, 703, 83rd Congress. The Act was passed partly because the Soviet Union exploded a thermonuclear device in August 1953, thus demonstrating conclusively that the US no longer had a monopoly. Britain had also exploded her own device.

6. White Paper, *Articles of Agreement governing collaboration between authorities of USA/UK in the matter of Tube Alloys*, April 1954, Cmd. 9123.

7. The Lisbon Goals of 1952 set out a programme of massive conventional forces expansion for NATO forces so that by the end of 1952 NATO would have 50 Divisions and 96 by 1954.

8. The 'Matador' missile (and a later improved version 'Mace') was a jet-powered surface-to-surface missile with a range of about 500 miles and stationed in Europe between 1954–69. Mace had an increased range of between 700–1200 miles.

9. Harold Macmillan: *Riding the Storm*, p. 176. Letter quoted in full in J. Baylis, *Anglo–American Defence Relations 1939–80*, p. 57.

10. Treaty Series no. 14 (1958), 'Exchange of Notes between the Government of the United Kingdom, Great Britain and Northern Ireland and the Government of the United States of America concerning the supply to the United Kingdom of IRBMs.' (Washington, 22 February 1958). Cmnd. 406, signed by Christian Herter (the American Under Secretary of State) and the Ambassador for Britain, Sir Harold Caccia.

11. Permanent Secretary, Ministry of Defence.

12. Chairman of the United States Atomic Energy Commission.

13. Gregory Treverton: 'Nuclear Weapons in Europe', p. 5.

14. Statement by Dr. Morton H. Halperin (former Deputy Assistant Secretary of Defense for International Security Affairs), *Tactical Nuclear Weapons in Europe*, Subcommittee on Arms Control, International Law and Organization of the committee on Foreign Relations, US Senate, 93rd Congress, 2nd session on US nuclear weapons in Europe, 7 March 1974 and 4 April 1974, pp. 17–18.

15. 568 HC Deb.[5], 16 April 1957, col. 1760–1.

16. For a fuller exposition of the White Paper's contents see Andrew J. Pierre, *Nuclear Politics. The British Experience with an Independent Strategic Force, 1939–70*, pp. 95–101.

17. 'There is a wide measure of agreement that she [Britain] must possess an appreciable element of nuclear deterrent power of her own.' (Defence: Outline of Future Policy, 1957, Cmnd. 124, p. 3.)

18. Harold Macmillan, *Riding the Storm, 1956–9*, p. 474.

19. Cmnd. 406, 22 February 1958. (The missile was to be activated under a 'two key' or 'dual key' system which involved the participation of a RAF and USAF representative to activate the system. Recent reports do, however, cast doubt upon such nuclear safeguards. A letter to *The Times* (23 September 1974) from a retired RAF officer, Donald Hofford, who was observing a simulated launch of a Thor missile, reported that as zero hour approached a USAF officer had failed to arrive with his key. The situation was saved by an RAF officer 'whose adroit use of a screw-driver in the other key-hole enabled the simulated launch to take place.')

20. Harold Macmillan, *Riding the Storm, 1956–9*, p. 245.
21. Whilst the missiles were free under the Mutual Defence Assistance Programme, Britain was liable for missile base construction costs and deployment costs for the missiles. Much of the American deployment cost was passed off under the NATO Infrastructure Funds.
22. *New Statesman*, 4 January 1958. 'Buying Brooklyn Bridge' This figure was then upgraded to £30 million (*New Statesman*, 1 March 1958) when the true extent of the missile basing became evident.
23. Coral Bell, *The Debatable Alliance*, p. 59.
24. 88th Congress, 1st session, Department of Defense Appropriations for 1964, House of Representatives, pt. 5, pp. 974–976.
25. Robert F. Futrell, *Ideas, Concepts, Doctrine: A History of Basic Thinking in the USAF. 1907–64*, p. 319.
26. Jupiter was similar to Thor but was an Army-backed development and Thor the Air Force version.
27. Hearings before the Senate Appropriations Committee, Department of Defense Appropriations 1960, vol. 130, 26 May 1959, p. 704.
28. *Ibid.*
29. *Ibid.*, p. 705.
30. *Ibid.* Extract from Senator Symington's testimony following a visit to the first Thor squadron in Britain; 'It is going to be pretty hard to fire a missile if you cannot pull the shed off so you can elevate it. The British press was saying that the British military authorities denied the assertion of the American military authorities that the IRBMs were operational. . . . I said to this office [giving the demonstration], "This whole thing is a farce". He made no comment. Then I noticed how close the road was to the missiles. So I said "You know, all you would have to do is throw something in here out of an automobile with delayed action, or drop it from a Piper Cub you rented. It is all there. You can look down at these other bases like I did at these three sheds. All they have to do is throw something in." This fellow said, "You would not have to do that. Anybody with a .22 rifle who was any kind of shot could destroy them from this road." These are the facts. I think it is important that the American people know the facts and are not kidded as to what our retaliatory capacity is on that kind of item.'
31. House of Representatives Foreign Affairs Committee, *Mutual Security Act 1958*, Statement by Hon. Neil H. McElroy, Secretary of Defense, vol. 62, 27 February 1958, p. 319.
32. Hearings before the House Committee on Foreign Affairs, 85th Congress, 2nd Session, on Mutual Security Act 1958, Extract from Statement of Secretary of State, John F. Dulles, 26 February 1958, p. 211.
33. *Daily Worker*, 3 March 1958.
34. *The Daily Telegraph*, 27 February 1958, listed the Thor convoy as follows: 'Each individual Thor needs some two dozen pieces of heavy equipment, among them are a missile shelter, a ramp, a transporter-launcher, liquid oxygen tanks and transfer tanks, a hydro-pneumatic trailer, nitrogen storage and transfer systems, nose-cone handling equipment, a missile "checkout" trailer, electrical equipment check trailer, air conditioning, hydraulic power system and two gaseous oxygen storage trailers'

35. 568 HC Deb.[5], 17 April 1957, col. 1985.
36. House of Representatives, Foreign Affairs Committee; Statement by Mr Sprague (Assistant Secretary for Defense) *Mutual Security Act* 1958, vol. 62, 27 February 1958, p. 320.
37. Colonel Zinc is sometimes mis-spelled 'Zink' as in many press reports. For the sake of regularity the former will be used as it appears in Macmillan's memoirs.
38. 568 HC Deb.[5], 24 February 1958. (Duncan Sandys quoting Para. 4 of the IRBM agreement, Cmnd. 366.)
39. Harold Macmillan, *Riding the Storm*, p. 474.
40. 24 February 1958, Cmnd. 366. The language of the agreement reflected that of the earlier Truman–Attlee understandings proclaiming in Section 7 that 'the decision to launch the missiles would be a matter for joint decision by the two governments.'
41. 579 HC Deb.[5], 12 December 1957, col. 1420.
42. *Ibid.*, col. 1427.
43. A converted B-47, the 'R' denoting its reconnaissance task.
44. 626 HC Deb.[5], 12 July 1960, col. 1174.
45. '. . . we have made ourselves the target and perhaps the bull's eye of a Soviet attack.' (Mr Churchill, *Official Report*, 15 February 1951, vol. 484, col. 630)
46. 626 HC Deb.[5], 12 July 1960, cols. 1172–3.
47. *Ibid.*, col. 1173.
48. *Ibid.*, col. 1178 (emphasis added).
49. *The Times*, 13 July 1960.
50. Leonard Mosley, *Dulles*, p. 369.
51. 626 HC Deb.[5], 12 July 1960, col. 1174.
52. 627, HC Deb.[5], 19 July 1960, col. 251 (for the general debate on bases see cols. 245–51 and Macmillan's statement on the RB-47, cols. 251–262).
53. 661, HC Deb.[5], 26 June 1962, col. 958.
54. Dwight D. Eisenhower Library, *Review of United States Overseas Military Bases*, April 1960, White House Office of Special Assistant for National Security Affairs: Records 1952–61, Folder 'Base Rights' (1), Box 27, p. 1.
55. Dwight D. Eisenhower Library, *Basic National Security Policy*, 26 March 1962.
56. *Review of Overseas Military Bases*, p. 3.
57. Laurence R. Benson. *USAFE Historical Monograph, USAF Aircraft Basing in Europe, African and the Middle East, 1945–80*, Office of History, HQ USAFE, Ramstein, 23 April 1981, p. 30.
58. The first Polaris missiles had a range of about 1400 miles.
59. *The Times*, Letter to the Editor from E. M. Evans-Lombe, 15 January 1958.
60. Although the Clyde and the Gareloch adjacent were the best sites, several others were considered. Londonderry, Stornoway and Milford Haven were all considered but rejected in favour of the Clyde.
61. Washington Navy Yard, Washington, DC, Bldg. 57, Report of Operations and Conditions of Command, *1 July 1959 – 18 February 1960* From CINCNELM to Director of Naval Operations, p. 3.
62. Harold Macmillan, *At the End of the Day*, p. 342 (The guarantee was of

little practical value since the Royal Navy had no real desire for Polaris and no nuclear submarine capability.)

63. Harold Macmillan, *Pointing the Way*, p. 254.
64. John Baylis, *Anglo–American Defence Relations 1939–80. The Special Relationship*, p. 68. At the Nassau meeting of 18–21 December 1962, Prime Minister Macmillan reminded President Kennedy of Eisenhower's assurance that, in the event of Skybolt's failure, Britain might rely on obtaining Polaris. Kennedy was reluctant to uphold this 'gentleman's agreement', explaining the political difficulties that could be engendered by this offer and in particular the risk of upsetting France. The provision of Polaris to Britain would also upset proposals for some kind of nuclear sharing in NATO through a multilateral force.
65. Washington Navy Yard, *Reminiscences of Vice-Admiral Lawson P. Ramage, USN (ret'd)* pp. 342–4 (Interviewed 9 August 1973).
66. *Ibid.*
67. *Ibid.*
68. *Ibid.*
69. Washington Navy Yard, *Reminiscences of Admiral Arleigh A. Burke USN (Retd).* (Interview, 14 November 1972), pp. 135–6.
70. Washington Navy Yard, *Reminiscences of Vice-Admiral Lawson P. Ramage, USN (Retd).* (Interview, 9 August 1973), p. 345.
71. Emrys Hughes: *Polaris and the Arms Race* (1961).
72. *Ibid.*, p. 4.
73. At the time of the first arrival of Polaris submarines in Holy Loch during February 1961, there were no detailed arrangements for the use of Holy Loch. According to a background paper (Lyndon B. Johnson Library: Visit of Prime Minister Douglas Home, Holy Loch Arrangements, February 12–13 1964) there were delays in reaching agreements over rights of inspection and liability in the event of a nuclear accident. A memorandum of understanding was signed during Douglas Home's visit to Washington, DC, which was said to be 'entirely satisfactory' to the American delegation.
74. Washington Navy Yard: *Reminiscences of Admiral Alfred G. Ward USN (Retd).* (Interview, 19 August 1970) p. 228.
75. 629, HC Deb.[5], 1 November 1960, cols 37–8.
76. 629, HC Deb.[5], 8 November 1960, cols 831–2.
77. *Ibid.*
78. Emrys Hughes, op. cit., p. 14.
79. *Daily Express*, 9 November 1960.
80. 629, HC Deb.[5], 3 November 1960, col. 338.
81. The depot ship USS Proteus sailed out of Holy Loch on 23 October 1962 at the height of the Cuban missile crisis.
82. For a fuller account, see Malcolm Spaven: *Fortress Scotland*, pp. 135–42.
83. Duncan Campbell, *The Unsinkable Aircraft Carrier*, p. 211.
84. *Ibid.*, p. 212.
85. See Appendix 3, Table A3.2
86. Washington Navy Yard, *CINCNELM Annual Historical Report*, File FF1/NELM/5213, 24 February 1960.
87. WNY, *Command History, Edzell*, Ser. 249, US NAVSECGRUACT p. 7.

88. *NAVCOMMSTA LONDONDERRY Instruction 5400.1* (4 October 1971).
89. WNY, NRS/2, 5750, Ser. 09, *OP Nav Report, 5750–1 (Command History) Thurso*, 26 January 1970.
90. WNY, Ser. 102–69, *Command History: Machrihanish*, 7 February 1969 p. 213.
91. Congressional Research Service, *Authority to Order the Use of Nuclear Weapons*, (US, UK, France, Soviet Union, PRC), prepared for the subcommittee on International Security and Scientific Affairs of the Senate Committee on International Relations, 1 December 1975. During the meeting Andrew C. Mayer, Specialist in National Defense, Foreign Affairs Division, testified: 'A significant part of the British tactical nuclear arsenal can be employed only with the consent of the United States government because the warheads were supplied by the United States and, as required by United States law, remain under US control', p. 10.

8   1964–84: From MLF to INF

1. John Baylis, *Anglo–American Defence Relations 1939–80. The Special Relationship*, p. 81.
2. Harold Wilson, *The Labour Government 1964–70*, p. 82.
3. Andrew Pierre, *Nuclear Politics*, p. 280.
4. See 'Equality Among Allies', *The Economist*, 12 December 1964.
5. Norman Polmar (ed.), *Strategic Air Command: People, Aircraft and Missiles*, p. 5.
6. Helmut Schmidt, in *Defence or Retaliation* ironically warned that 'the stationing of enemy IRBMs, so to speak, on its very threshold [Russia] must produce the psychological effect of a provocation on any great power. One need only imagine how the Americas would react if the Soviets were to station IRBMs in Cuba.' Quoted in The Lunn Report p. 8.
7. The site at Fylingdales (Yorkshire) was the last of three stations built that collectively are known as the Ballistic Missile Early Warning Systems (BMEWS) chain. Fylingdales' partners are in central Alaska (Clear) and Greenland (Thule). Clear and Thule were operational in 1961, joined two years later by Fylingdales.
8. Paul Buteux, *The Politics of Nuclear Consultation in NATO 1965–80*, p. 63.
9. *Ibid.*
10. The NPG was originally put forward to America's European allies on the understanding that they would be consulted in the event of a crisis or emergency. In 1970 the Secretary for Defense emphasised that participation by the allies 'would only be meaningful if all the interested countries, on the highest political level, could be constantly kept informed about a developing crisis as well as factors which could play a role in a possible decision on the use of nuclear weapons.' (W. F. van Eekelen: 'Development of NATO's Nuclear Consultation', *NATO Letter*, July/August 1970, p. 3).
11. US House of Representatives: *Authority to Order the Use of Nuclear Weapons*, Report prepared for the Committee on International Re-

lations, by the CRS, Library of Congress, 94th Congress, 1st Session, Washington GPO, 1975, pp. 5–6.

12. Paul Buteux, p. 105.
13. Lyndon Baines Johnson Library; Department of State Files 277/2, Incoming Telegram Department of State from US Embassy, Paris, 23 November 1965.
14. *Ibid.*
15. *Morning Star*, 9 January 1967.
16. *Daily Telegraph*, 27 June 1967.
17. Duncan Campbell, *The Unsinkable Aircraft Carrier*, p. 81.
18. *Ibid.*
19. The remaining airmen would be involved either in SAC duties (like reconnaissance), visiting or training and MAC (Military Airlift Command) duties.
20. *The Times*, 18 August 1971.
21. Laurence R. Benson, Historical Monograph Series, 'USAF Aircraft Basing in Europe, Africa and the Middle East, 1945–80', Section on Air Staff's 'European Air Base Study', 31 October 1966. (Office of History, HQ USAFE, Ramstein, 23 April 1981).
22. S Res. 300, 31 August 1966 (amending S. Res. 99, 4 April 1951, which was a major Senatorial statement of foreign policy approving measures of support for the North Atlantic Treaty concluded two years earlier).
23. S. Res 292, 1 December 1969.
24. Henry Kissinger, *The White House Years*, p. 946.
25. The CSCE negotiations stated on 3 July 1973 in Finland at Helsinki. The MBFR conference started on 30 October 1973 in Vienna.
26. Charles R. Gellner, CRS, *The Mansfield Proposals 1967–74*, p. 25.
27. John Baylis, *Anglo–American Defence Relations 1939–80*, p. 103.
28. D. C. R. Heyhoe, 'The Alliance and Europe; Part 6, The European Programme Group', p. 2.
29. Richard M. Nixon, *Memoirs*, p. 928.
30. *Ibid.*, p. 940. The Soviet Union according to available sources did not alert its own nuclear forces. The US gambled on breaking the symmetry of escalation where before 24 October the American and Soviet diplomatic and military initiatives had balanced each other. The US gamble paid off but at the cost of an exercise in nuclear brinkmanship. See Amnon Sella: *Soviet Political and Military Conduct in the Middle East* (London: 1981), Ch. 3, The October War, pp. 72–104. US forces are normally at various stages of readiness known as Defence Conditions or 'Def Cons', of which there are five. Def Con I means 'War'; Def Con III means 'attack imminent'; Def Con II means 'increase readiness when *war is likely*'; and Def Cons IV and V are peacetime conditions. Forces are normally at IV or V except in the Pacific where, as a legacy of the Vietnam war, forces are permanently at Def Con III. All forces during the Middle East crisis of 1973 were at Def Con III except the US Sixth Fleet in the Mediterranean which was at Def Con II.
31. NA, CCS 3180, 'Emergency Readiness File', Box 19, JCS 1968/88, Letter, Secretary of Defense to Hon. H. Watkinson, 12 July 1960.
32. NA, CCS 3180, JCS 1968/30, 'Notification to other countries when the

readiness postures of US forces have been increased', 17 January 1963.

33. Dr James Schlesinger, interview with author, 19 June 1984.
34. Henry A. Kissinger, *Years of Upheaval*, p. 713 (emphasis added).
35. *Ibid.*
36. *New York Times*, 31 October 1973.
37. Henry A. Kissinger, *Years of Upheaval*, p. 712.
38. *Ibid.*, pp. 716–7.
39. CRS report for Subcommittee on International Security and Scientific Affairs of the Committee on International Relations, *Authority to Order the Use of Nuclear Weapons*, 1 December 1975, pp. 10–14.
40. Carl A. Ehrhardt; 'Disenchantment between Europe and America', *Aussenpolitik*, 4th quarter 1973, p. 392.
41. General Assembly Resolutions, 29th Session, vol. 1, Agenda Item 86, 3314, (XXIX), Report of the Special Committee on the question of defining aggression, A/9890, Article 3, Section (e), 14 December 1974, p. 143.
42. *Ibid.*, Article 3, Section (f).
43. *United Nations Yearbook*, 1974, p. 841.
44. See David Greenwood, 'Politics, Economics and European defense', RUSI, *Brassey's Defence Yearbook 1975–6*, pp. 120–3.
45. H. G. Hagerty, *Forward Deployment in the Seventies and Eighties*, National Security Affairs Monograph No. 77, National Defense University, Washington, DC, February 1977.
46. *Daily Telegraph*, 13 March 1979.
47. *The Times*, 14 September 1978.
48. Chapman Pincher, *Daily Express*, 17 May 1976.
49. Central Policy Staff, *Review of Overseas Representation*, p. 126.
50. *Strategic Survey*: 1976, 'Tactical Air Power in Europe' (IISS), p. 71.
51. Statement by Hon. M. R. Currie: 'Program of Research Development Test and Evaluation, Fiscal Year 1978', Dir DIE, 95 Cong: House, 95 Cong., p. 17.
52. See in particular Simon Lunn, *Modernization of NATO's LRTNF* prepared by Dir. of Military C'ttee, North Atlantic Assembly, Belguin, for the Sub-c'ttee on Europe and the Middle East for the CRS (Lib. of Congress), 31 December 1980 (hereafter referred to as the Lunn Report).
53. Charles Gellner, CRS, *Authority to Order the Use of Nuclear Weapons* (US, UK, France, Sov Union, PRC) prepared for the sub-committee on International Security and Scientific Affairs of the Senate Committee on International Relations, 1 December 1975. Appendix 1, Statement of Sec. of Defense, James R. Schlesinger, p. 24.
54. In fact the eventual stance was a compromise between the 'hawks' and 'doves'. Helmut Schmidt said that a balance could be reached with the Warsaw Pact in two ways: 'One would be a massive Alliance build-up of forces and weapons systems; the other for both NATO and Warsaw Pact to reduce their force strength and to achieve an overall balance at a lower level. I prefer the latter.' (H. Schmidt: *Survival*, January/February 1978, p. 4.)
55. *Jane's Weapons System 1984–5* have in fact identified a Soviet look-alike version of the GLCM called the SSC-X4 (land-based version). There are

also thought to be sea- and air-borne versions. The land version is substantially longer than the GLCM and is not necessarily nuclear armed. The Sea-based variant, (see *Soviet Military Power 1985*, p. 35) the SS-NX-21 is small enough to be fired from standard Soviet torpedo tubes.

56. *Lunn Report*, p. 36.
57. Laurence Martin, *The Two-Edged Sword*, p. 31.
58. *International Herald Tribune*: 15 September 1982, p. 6.
59. *Ibid*.
60. Quoted in G. Treverton: 'Nuclear Weapons in Europe', p. 16.
61. The dividing line between Theatre and Strategic forces is subject to continual debate. The US claimed the Soviet Backfire bomber was a strategic weapon and therefore accountable under SALT, assuming that it was recovered in a third country experts claimed it could be used against the US with a range of 3000 miles. The Soviet Union denied this arguing it was a medium-bomber. To many Soviet strategists the differences are academic and it has been made clear that whatever hits them will be considered 'strategic'.
62. HC Deb.⁵, Pt. 2, 20 December 1979, written answers, cols. 321–2.
63. *Lunn Report*, p. 60.
64. General George Brown (Chairman, JCS): 'Why the United States maintains Forces in Europe', *Commanders Digest*, 6 March 1975, p. 2.
65. *SIPRI Yearbook*, 1982, p. 24.
66. Andrew White, *Symbols of War; Pershing II and Cruise Missiles in Europe*, p. 7.
67. See H. Schmidt, 1977 Alastair Buchan Memorial Lecture, *Survival* vol. 20 no. 1. January–February 1978.
68. For a wider discussion of this point see Sverre Lodgaard 'Long Range Theatre Nuclear Forces in Europe', in *The Arms Race and Arms Control*.
69. *The Sunday Times*: 30 October 1983. (MORI interviewed a representative sample of 1032 adults aged 18 and over on 28 October in 52 constituencies.)
70. *Ibid*.
71. *The Washington Post*: Walter Pincus and Bradley Graham, 'The War-game: Battlefield Europe', 16 November 1981.
72. There are roughly 156 F-111s in the UK although some older models have been converted to carry out reconnaissance duties and the F-111E and F-111F models actually comprise the strike force, stationed at RAF Lakenheath and RAF Upper Heyford.
73. See *Aviation Week and Space Technology*, Special Report on US Air Forces in Europe: 1982, p. 16–17.
74. The TEL and LCC are based on a MAN M-1001 8 × 8 tractor and a large cross-country semi-trailer weighing 33 tons and 36 tons respectively.
75. *Military Enthusiast*, vol. 5 no. 32, p. 30.
76. *Observer Magazine*, 4 December 1983.
77. *The Times*, 3 November 1983.
78. The TERCOM system was not a new system built specifically for cruise. For a detailed description of TERCOM by E-Systems (the manufacturers) see *Aviation Week and Space Technology*. 10 March 1975.
79. Vladimir Zagladin (First Deputy Chief of the International Department

of the CPSU Central Committee) in *La Stampa*, 25 November 1979, quoted in the Lunn Report, p. 52.

80. Ustinov, *Pravda*, 25 October 1979, also quoted in the Lunn Report.
81. *Interim Report on Nuclear Weapons in Europe*, prepared by the North Atlantic Assembly's Special Committee on Nuclear Weapons in Europe, in a report to the Committee on Foreign Relations, Senate, 97 Cong., 1st Session, December 1981, p. 14.
82. *Ibid.*, p. 7, para. 25.

9 Conclusion

1. *Report on Defence. Britain's contribution to Peace and Security* Cmd. 316, para. 12.
2. Field Marshal Lord Carver: *A Policy for Peace*.
3. Report of the Committee Delegation to NATO submitted to the Committee on Armed Services, *NATO and United States Security* (House Report No. 93–9- 78). 95 Cong., 1st session, 25 May 1977.
4. *Aviation Week and Space Technology*, Special report on US Air Forces in Europe 1982, p. 37.
5. H. G. Hagerty, *Forward Deployment in the '70s and '80s*, pp. 29–30.
6. Senator F. Church, 'Reappraising American Policy', *Survival*, vol. 35, 15 May, p. 232.
7. *Ibid.*, p. 233.
8. See J. Newhouse; *American Troops in Europe*.
9. *Ibid.*, p. 13.
10. Alain C. Enthoven: 'US Forces in Europe: How Many? Doing What?' Foreign Affairs, vol. 53 no. 3, April 1975, pp. 513–32.
11. Robert L. Pfaltzgraff, Jnr, 'European–American Defence Budget Sharing', *Atlantic Community Quarterly*, vol. 12 no. 2, Summer 1974, p. 198–199.
12. See *Aviation Week and Space Technology*, Special Report on US Air Forces in Europe, 1982. p. 37.
13. Senate Committee on Foreign Relations, *Security Agreements and Commitments Abroad*, 21 December 1970, p. 20.
14. Brigadier C. N. Barclay (retd), 'What Happens to Europe if the Americans Leave?, *Army*, no. 11 November 1973, pp. 7–1. He concludes that: 'There is a general belief in Britain and other West European countries that a reduction in US forces in Europe is probable in the near future. The changeover to Long-service volunteer forces with its consequent reductions in numbers seems to make this inevitable. It is also thought there is little likelihood of a complete withdrawal.'
15. *The Times*, 7 March 1985.
16. Alain C. Enthoven, 'US Forces in Europe: How Many? Doing What?' *Foreign Affairs*, vol. 53, April 1975, p. 523.
17. *Ibid.*, p. 526.
18. Statement of Hon. Kenneth Rush (Deputy Secretary of State): Hearings of Subcommittee on Arms Control, International Law and Organization of Senate Committee on Foreign Relations, 93 Cong., 1st session, 'US Forces in Europe', 25 and 27 July 1973, p. 43.

19. See Paul Buteux: *The Politics of Nuclear Consultation in NATO 1965–80* (Cambridge, CUP, 1983). For a general review of the consultation procedure, see pp. 207–213 where Buteux concludes,' in time of crisis the opportunities for consultation would be limited, and that through their control of nuclear weapons the nuclear powers retain very considerable freedom of action to decide whether or not, or how, to use nuclear weapons. The obligation to consult before making a decision, if such consultations were judged to be both possible and politically and miltarily desirable, can at best only serve to influence the American President's decision . . . it cannot ensure that the ultimate decision will be satisfactory to the parties consulted.'

20. Statement by Dr Morton H. Halperin (Former Secretary of Defense for International Security Affairs), 'United States Foreign Policy Objectives and Overseas Military Installations' (CRS: Library of Congress), April 1979, p. 44.

21. Statement by Dr Stanley Hoffmann: Hearings before the Subcommittee on US Security Agreements and Commitments Abroad and the Subcommittee on Arms Control, International Law and Organization of the Senate Committee on Foreign Relations, *Nuclear Weapons and Foreign Policy*, 93rd Congress, 2nd session, 14 March 1974, p. 43.

22. Statement of General Goodpaster: Hearings before the Subcommittee on Military Applications of the Joint Committee on Atomic Energy, 'Military Applications of Nuclear Technology' 29 June 1973, p. 66.

23. See John Baylis, *Anglo–American Defence Relations, 1939–80*, p. 121.

24. K. Hunt, 'The Alliance and Europe: Part II – Defence with Fewer Men', p. 11.

25. Equil Ulstein, 'Nordic Security', pp. 9–10.

26. See David Henshaw, 'Whose finger on the Button?', *The Listener*, 2 June 1983, pp. 1–4.

27. Angel Vinas, in a talk entitled *The Experience of Spanish–American Bilateral Defence Agreements*, to the Instituto de Duestiones Internacionales, 24–27 April 1980 (unpublished transcript), p. 5.

28. For a fuller account of the intelligence and surveillance facilities operated jointly or solely by the United States in the United Kingdom, see Duncan Campbell: *The Unsinkable Aircraft Carrier: American Military Power in Britain*, pp. 118–204.

29. Report on the Alternative Defence Commission, *Defence Without the Bomb*.

30. Peter Johnson, *Neutrality: A Policy For Britain* p. 27.

31. *Ibid.*, p. 79.

32. Michael Heseltine, UK Secretary of State for Defence: 'The Atlantic Alliance, an agenda for 1984', *NATO Review*, vol. 32 no. 1/1984 p. 1.

33.. Ronald Nairn, 'Should the US pull out of NATO?', *Wall Street Journal*, 15 December 1981. See also H. Kissinger: 'Something is Deeply Wrong in the Atlantic Alliance', *Washington Post*, 21 December 1981.

34. *The Guardian*, 9 September 1982.

Bibliography

PRIMARY SOURCES

United States

National Archives, Washington, DC
See relevant footnotes.

Congressional and Congressional Research Service Reports
Report to the Committee on Foreign Relations and Committee on Armed Services, US Senate: *US Troops in Europe*, 15 October 1968 (Washington, DC, Government Printing Office).
Staff Report prepared for use of the subcommittee on US Security Agreements and Commitments Abroad of the Senate Foreign Relations Committee: *US Security Issues in Europe: Burden Sharing and Offset, MBFR and Nuclear Weapons*, 93 Cong: 1st session, 2 December 1973.
Report prepared for the subcommittee on International Security and Scientific Affairs of the Committee on International Relations by the CRS: *Authority to Order the Use of Nuclear Weapons* (US, UK, France, Soviet Union, PRC), 1 December 1975.
Congressional Research Service, Foreign Affairs Division: Background information on the use of US armed forces in foreign countries, *US Foreign Policy Objectives and Overseas Military Bases* (Washington, DC, Government Printing Office, 1975 revision).
Report of the Committee delegation to NATO submitted to the Committee on Armed Services (House), *NATO and US Security* 95 Cong: 1st session, 25 May 1977.
Congressional Research Service, Report by Simon Lunn (Director Military Committee, North Atlantic Assembly on detail to Foreign Affairs and National Defense Div.): *Modernization of NATO's LRTNF*, May 1979–September 1980.
Report to the Committee of Foreign Relations, US Senate: *Interim Report of the Special Committee on Nuclear Weapons in Europe*, December 1981.
Congressional Research Service, Report prepared by Dr Charles R. Gellner: *The Mansfield Proposal to Reduce US Troops in Europe, 1967–74*, 1 December 1982.

Presidential Reports
Frank C. Nash: Report to the President, *US Overseas Military Bases*, December 1957.
Review of Overseas Military Bases, April 1960.

Congressional Hearings

Subcommittee of Senate Committee on Foreign Relations, *US Economic and Military Assistance to Free Europe*, 7–23 July 1951.

Senate Appropriations Committee: *Financial Aid to Europe*, 26 May 1954.

Subcommittee on the Air Force of the Senate Committee on Armed Services, *Discussions on JCS War Plans*, 16–20 April and 2 July 1956.

Senate Foreign Relations, *Mutual Support Act*, 19–31 March 1958.

House Foreign Affairs: *Mutual Support Act*, 27 March 1958.

House Subcommittee on Europe, *US Relations with Europe in the Decade of the 1970s* February–April 1970.

Senate Foreign Relations, Subcommittee on US Security Agreements and Commitments Abroad: *Part 10 US Forces in Europe*, October 1971.

Joint Committee on Atomic Energy, Subcommittee on Military Applications: *Military Applications of Nuclear Technology* 29 June 1973.

Senate Foreign Relations, Subcommittee on Arms Control, *US Forces in Europe*, 25–27 July 1973.

Senate Foreign Relations, Subcommittee on US Security Agreements and Commitments Abroad and Subcommittee on Arms Control, International Law and Organization, *Nuclear Weapons and Foreign Policy*, 7, 14 March and 4 April 1974.

NATO Reports

Lunn, Simon: *Modernization of NATO's LRTNF* (Director, Military Committee, North Atlantic Assembly) May 1979–September 1980.

Cartwright, John and Critchley, Julian: *Interim Report of the Special Committee on Nuclear Weapons in Europe*, May 1983.

Also consulted

Department of State, *Bulletin*.

Documents on American Foreign Relations, vols 1–12 (Princeton, NJ: Princeton University Press).

Foreign Relations of the United States, Department of State, 1943–1952.

United States Department of the Army, Army Library, *US Overseas Bases*.

Present Status and Future Prospects, DA Pamphlet 20163 (Washington, DC: Government Printing Office, 1963).

House of Representatives, *Congressional Record*.

Status of Forces Agreements: House of Representatives Hearings, i–ii, 1955–6 (Washington, DC: US Government Printing Office, 1955).

Washington Navy Yard, Washington DC: *Command Histories* (Londonderry, Machrihanish, Edzell and Thurso).

Public Papers of the Presidents Series
  (i)   Papers of Harry S. Truman, 1952–3.
  (ii) Papers of Dwight D. Eisenhower, 1954.
  (iii) Papers of Dwight D. Eisenhower, 1958.
  (iv) Papers of John F. Kennedy, 1962.

Library of Congress, Manuscripts Division

General 'Hap' Arnold Files.

General Carl Spaatz Files.

General Le May Files.

Britain

Public Record Office, Kew, London
See relevant footnotes in text.

Command Papers
Cmnd. 7327 – Statement Relating to Defence, 1948.
Cmnd. 7895 – Statement of Defence, 1950.
Cmnd. 9123 – Articles of agreement governing collaboration between the authorities of the USA and United Kingdom in the matter of Tube Alloys, April 1954.
Cmnd. 366 – Report on Defence: Britain's contribution to Peace and Security, 1958.
Cmnd. 366 – Report on Defence, 1958.
Cmnd. 406 – Exchange of notes between the governments of the United Kingdom, Great Britain and Northern Ireland and the Government of the United States of America concerning the supply to the United Kingdom of IRBMs, 22 February 1958.
Cmnd. 1995 – Polaris Sales Agreement.

Other sources
Parliamentary Debates, 1945–85, House of Commons.
Parliamentary Debates, House of Lords.
Central Policy Review Staff: *Review of Overseas Representation* (London: HMSO, 1977).
Sixth Report from the Expenditure Committee, *The Future of the United Kingdom's Nuclear Weapons Policy*, Session 1978–9, no. 348 (London: HMSO, 1979).

SECONDARY SOURCES

Books

Acheson, D., *Present at the Creation* (New York: Norton, 1969).
Adomeit, H., *Soviet Risk Taking and Crisis Behaviour* (London: George, Allen & Unwin, 1982).
Aldridge, R. C., *First Strike. The Pentagon's Strategy for Nuclear War* (London: Pluto Press, 1983).
Alford, J. (ed.), *Arms Control and European Security*, Adelphi Library 11 (Hampshire: Gower, 1984).
Allen, H. C., Great *Britain and the United States. A History of Anglo–American Relations* (London: Odhams, 1955).
Allen, H. C., *The Anglo–American Predicament* (London: Macmillan, 1960).
Allison, R., *Finland's Relations with the Soviet Union* (London: St Antony's/Macmillan Series, 1985).
Arkin, W. and Pringle, P., *SIOP. Nuclear War From the Inside* (London: Sphere Books, 1983).
Ball, D., *A Suitable Piece of Real Estate* (Sydney: Hale and Iremonger, 1980).
Bamford, J., *The Puzzle Palace* (London: Sidgwick & Jackson, 1983).

Bartlett, C. J., *The Long Retreat. A Short History of British Defence Policy* (London: Macmillan, 1972).

Barton, G. P., *British Yearbook of International Law* 26 (1949).

Baylis, J., *British Defence Policy in a Changing World* (London: Croom Helm, 1977).

Baylis, J., *Anglo–American Defence Relations 1939–80* (London: Macmillan, 1981).

Bell, C., *The Debatable Alliance. An Essay in Anglo–American Relations* (London: Oxford University Press for Royal Institute for International Affairs, 1964).

Benson, L. R., *USAF Aircraft Basing in Europe, Africa and the Middle East, 1945–80,* USAFE Historical Monograph (Headquarters USAFE, Ramstein: Office of History, April 1981).

Borowski, H., *A Hollow Threat. Strategic Air Power and Containment before Korea* (Connecticut: Greenwood Press, 1982).

Bracken, P., *The Command and Control of Nuclear Forces* (New Haven: Yale University Press, 1983).

Brodie, B., *Strategy in the Missile Age* (Princeton: Princeton University Press, 1959).

Brodie, B., *Escalation and the Nuclear Option* (Princeton: Princeton University Press, 1966).

Brown, A. C., *Dropshot* (New York: The Dial Press, 1978).

Buchan, A., *NATO in the 1960s* (New York: Praeger, 1963).

Bullock, A., *Ernest Bevin. Foreign Secretary* (London: Heinemann, 1983).

Burrows, B. and Edwards, G., *The Defence of Western Europe* (London: Butterworth, 1982).

Buteaux, P., *Strategy, Doctrine and Politics of Alliance. TNF Modernization in NATO* (Colorado: Westview Press, 1973).

Buteaux, P., *The Politics of Nuclear Consultation in NATO 1965–80* (Cambridge: Cambridge University Press, 1983).

Calleo, D. P., *The Atlantic Fantasy. The United States, NATO and Europe* (Baltimore: Johns Hopkins Press, 1970).

Campbell, D., *The Unsinkable Aircraft Carrier. American Military Power in Britain* (London: Michael Joseph, 1984).

Campbell, J. C. and Stebbings, R. P., *The United States in World Affairs* (New York: Council on Foreign Relations, Harpers, 1977).

Carroll, J., *Secrets of Electronic Espionage* (New York: Dutton, 1966).

Carver, Field Marshal Lord, *A Policy for Peace* (London: Faber & Faber, 1982).

Conant, J. B., *Anglo–American Relations in the Nuclear Age* (London: Oxford University Press, 1952).

Condit, K. W., *The History of the JCS* vol. 2, 1947–9 (Washington DC: Historical Division, Joint Secretariat, JCS, 1976) (US National Archives: RG 218).

Cottrell, A. J. and Moorer, T. H., *United States Overseas Bases. Problems of Projecting American Military Power Abroad* Washington Papers No. 47 (London: Sage Publications, 1977).

Cragg, D., *The Guide to Military Installations* (Harrisburg: Stackpole Books, 1983).

Donovan, R. J., *Eisenhower. The Inside Story* (New York: Harper, 1956).
Donovan, R. J., *Conflict and Crisis. The Presidency of Harry S. Truman 1945–8* (New York: W. W. Norton, 1977).
Eden, A., *Full Circle* (London: Cassell, 1960).
Eisenhower, D. D., *Waging Peace 1956–61. The White House Years* vol. 2 (London: Heinemann, 1966).
Epstein, L. D., *Britain – Uneasy Ally* (Chicago: University of Chicago Press, 1954).
Ferrell, R. H., *The Eisenhower Diaries* (New York: W. W. Norton, 1981).
Fitts, R. E., *The Strategy of Electromagnetic Conflict* (California: Peninsula Publishing, 1980).
Freedman, L., *The Evolution of Nuclear Strategy* (London: Macmillan, 1982).
Funck-Bretano, T. and Sorel, A., *Precis du droit des gens* (Paris: 1877).
Futrell, R. F., *Ideas, Concepts, Doctrine. A History of Basic Thinking in the USAF 1907–64* (Alabama: Air University Maxwell Air Force Base, 1974).
Gaddis, J. L., *Strategies of Containment. A Critical Appraisal of Postwar American National Security Policy* (New York: Oxford University Press, 1982).
Gelber, L. M., *The Rise of Anglo–American Friendship* (London: Oxford University Press, 1938).
Gouré, L., Kohler, F., Harvey, M., *The Role of Nuclear Forces in Current Soviet Strategy* (Miami: University of Miami Press, 1974).
Gowing, M., *Independence and Detterence. Britain and Atomic Energy 1945–52*, vol. 1 (London: Macmillan, 1974).
Greenwood, D., *Politics, Economics and European Defence* (London: Brasseys, 1975).
Greig, D. W., *International Law* (London: Butterworth, 1976).
Groom, A. J. R., *British Thinking about Nuclear Weapons* (London: Frances Pinter, 1974).
Hackett, General Sir John, *The Third World War* (Glasgow: Sidgwick & Jackson, 1978).
Hammond, P. Y., Schilling, W. R. and Snyder, G. H., *Strategy Politics and Defense Budgets* (New York: Columbia University Press, 1962).
Harkavy, R. E., *Great Power Competition for Overseas Bases. The Geopolitics of Access Diplomacy* (New York: Pergamon Press, 1982).
Harris, K., *Attlee* (London: Weidenfeld & Nicolson, 1982).
Harrison, R. E., Stefanson, V. and Weigert, H. W. (eds), *New Compass of the World* (New York: Macmillan, 1959).
Hathaway, R. M., *Ambiguous Partnership* (New York: Columbia University Press, 1981).
Herken, G., *The Winning Weapon. The Atomic Bomb and the Cold War 1945–50* (New York: Vintage Books, 1981).
Hewlett, R. and Duncan F., *History of the United States Atomic Energy Commission, vol. 2 – Atomic Shield 1947–52* (London: Pennsylvania State University Press, 1969).
Hoeber, F. P. and Schneider, W., Jnr, *Arms, Men and Military Budgets* (New York: Crane, Russack & Co., 1978).
Hughes, E., *Polaris and the Arms Race* (London: 1961).
Huntington, S. P., *The Common Defense. Strategic Programs in National*

Politics (New York: Columbia University Press, 1961).

James, Sgt. E., *Historical Highlights, USAFE 1945–80* (Office of History, Headquarters USAFE, Ramstein: May 1980).

Jane's Weapon Systems, 1982–3, 1984–5.

Johnson, P., *Neutrality. A Policy for Britain* (London: Temple Smith, 1985).

Johnstone, D., *The Politics of Euromissiles* (London: Verso, 1984).

Keeler, J. W., Lt Col, *Third Air Force Historical Brief*, vol. 2, 16 July 1948–31 December 1967 (Historical Division: Office of Information, Third Air Force USAFE).

Kennan, G. F., *Memoirs 1950–63* (Boston: Little, Brown, 1972).

Kissinger, H. A., *Nuclear Weapons and Foreign Policy* (New York: For Council on Foreign Relations, Harper & Bros., 1957).

Kissinger, H. A., *The White House Years* (London: Weidenfeld & Nicolson, 1979).

Kissinger, H. A., *Years of Upheaval* (London: Weidenfeld & Nicolson, 1982).

Knorr, K., *NATO and American Security* (New Jersey: Princeton University Press, 1959).

Kolko, J. and Kolko, G., *The Limits of Power. The World and United States Foreign Policy 1945–54* (New York: Harper Row, 1972).

Lauterpacht, H., *International Law*, vol. 1, 8th edition (London: Longman/ Green, 1955).

Lazareff, S., *Status of Military Forces Under Current International Law* (Leyden: Sijthoff, 1971).

Macdonald, I. S., *Anglo–American Relations since World War II* (Newton Abbot: David & Charles, 1974).

McMahan, J., *British Nuclear Weapons: For and Against* (London: Junction Books, 1981).

McNaughton, F. and Hehmeyer, W., *Harry Truman, President* (New York: McGraw Hill, 1948).

Macmillan, H., *1945–55 – Tides of Fortune*, vol. 2 (London: Macmillan, 1969).

Macmillan, H., *1956–59 – Riding the Storm*, vol. 3 (London: Macmillan, 1971).

Macmillan, H., *1959–61 – Pointing the Way*, vol. 4 (London: Macmillan, 1972).

Macmillan, H., *1961–63 – At the End of the Day*, vol. 5 (London: Macmillan, 1973).

Martin, L., *The Two Edged Sword* (London: Weidenfeld & Nicolson, 1982).

Melnikov, I. A., *The Pentagon. Hotbed of Aggression* (Moscow: Novosti Press Agency, 1972).

Miller, J., *Aerograph 3: Lockheed U-2* (Austin, Texas: Aerofax, 1983).

Millis, W. (ed.), *Forrestal Diaries* (London: Cassel, 1952).

Millis, W., *Armies and Men. A Study in American Military History* (London: Jonathan Cape, 1957).

Montgomery, Field Marshal, *Memoirs* (London: Collins, 1958).

Mosley, L., *Dulles* (New York: The Dial Press, 1978).

Mulley, F. W., *The Politics of Western Defence* (London: Thames & Hudson, 1962).

Neild, R., *How to Make Up Your Mind About the Bomb* (London: Andre Deutsch, 1981).

Newhouse, J., *United States Troops in Europe* (Washington, DC: The Brookings Institute, 1971).

Nicholas, H. G., *The United States and Britain* (London: University of Chicago Press, 1975).

Nixon, R. M., *Memoirs* (New York: Grosset & Dunlop, 1978).

O'Brien, W. V., *The New Nations in International Law and Diplomacy* (London: Stevens and Sons, 1965).

Oppenheimer, J. R., *The Open Mind* (New York: Simon & Schuster, 1955).

Osgood, R. E., *The Entangling Alliance* (Chicago: University of Chicago Press, 1962).

Paul, R. A., *American Military Commitments Abroad* (New Jersey: Rutgers University Press, 1973).

Peacock, L. T., *Strategic Air Command. Warbirds Illustrated*, no. 9 (London: Arms and Armour Press, 1983).

Pierre, A. J., *Nuclear Politics. The British Experience with an Independent Strategic Force 1939–70* (London: Oxford University Press, 1972).

Polmar, N. (ed.), *Strategic Air Command: People, Aircraft and Missiles* (Cambridge: Patrick Stephens, 1980).

Poole, W. S., *History of the Joint Chiefs of Staff. JCS and National Policy*, vol. 4, 1950–2 (Washington, DC: JCS History Division).

Pringle, P. and Spigelman, J., *The Nuclear Barons* (New York: Holt, Rinehart and Winston, 1981).

Record, J., *United States Nuclear Weapons in Europe. Issues and Alternatives* (Washington, DC: Brookings Institution, 1974).

Roberts, H. L. and Wilson, P. A., *Britain and the United States. Problems in Co-operation* (London: Royal Institute of International Affairs, 1953).

Rosecrance, R. N., *The Dispersion of Nuclear Weapons* (New York: Columbia University Press, 1968).

Rosecrance, R. N., *Defence of the Realm. British Strategy in the Nuclear Epoch* (London: Columbia University Press, 1968).

Sams, K., *Nuclear Disarmament Demonstrations in the United Kingdom, 1961* (Office of Information, Headquarters Third Air Force: Historical Division).

Schnabel, J. F., *The History of the Joint Chiefs of Staff. The JCS and National Policy*, vol. 1, 1945–47 (Washington, DC: Historical Divsion, Joint Secretariat, JCS, 1979).

Sella, A., *Soviet Political and Military Conduct in the Middle East* (London: Macmillan, 1981).

Sherry, M. S., *Preparing for the Next War. America's Plans for Postwar Defense 1941–5* (New Haven: Yale University Press, 1977).

Shlaim, A., *The United States and the Berlin Blockade 1948–9. A Study in Crisis Decision Making* (London: University of California Press, 1983).

Simpson, J., *The Independent Nuclear State* (London: Macmillan, 1983).

Skinner, M., *USAFE: A Primer of Modern Air Combat in Europe* (California: Presidio Press, 1983).

Smith, D., *Defence of the Realm in the 1980s* (London: Croom Helm, 1980).

Smith, P. McC., *The Air Force Plans for Peace 1943–5* (Baltimore: Johns Hopkins Press, 1970).

Snyder, W. P., *The Politics of British Defence Policy* (Columbus: Ohio State University Press, 1964).

Spaven, M., *Fortress Scotland. A Guide to the Military Presence* (London: Pluto Press, 1983).

Stambuk, G., *American Military Forces Abroad* (Ohio: Ohio State University Press, 1963).

SIPRI (Stockholm International Peace Research Institute), *Yearbooks* (London: Taylor & Francis).

SIPRI, *Yearbook(s) of World Armaments and Disarmament* (Stockholm: MIT Press and Almquist & Wiksell).

Talbott, S. (ed.), *Khruschev Remembers* (Introduction & Notes by Edward Crankshaw) (London: Book Club Associates, 1971).

Truman, H. S., *Memoirs vol. 2. Years of Trial and Hope* (New York: Garden City, 1956).

Turner, A. C., *The Unique Partnership* (New York: Pegasus, 1971).

United States Air Force Academy, Proceedings of the Eighth Military History Symposium. Air Power and Warfare (Colorado: USAF Academy, 1978).

Urwin, D. W., *Western Europe Since 1945* (London: Longmans, 1968).

Vandenberg, A. H., Jnr, *The Private Papers of Senator Vandenberg* (Boston: Houghton Mifflin, 1952).

Weller, G. A., *Bases Overseas. An American Trusteeship in Power* (New York: Harcourt, Brace & Co., 1944).

White, A., *Symbols of War. Pershing II and Cruise Missiles in Europe* (London: Merlin Press, 1983).

White, R. K., *Fearful Warriors* (London: The Free Press, 1984).

Willard, R. H., Sgt., *Third Air Force Historical Brief 1942–5* (Historical Division, Office of Information, Third Air Force, USAFE).

Williams, F., *A Prime Minister Remembers* (London: Thompson Allied Newspapers Ltd., 1961).

Williams, P. (ed.), *The Nuclear Debate* (London: Routledge & Kegan Paul, 1984).

Wilson, H., *The Labour Government 1964–70* (London: Penguin, 1974).

Windsor, P., *City on Leave. A History of Berlin 1945–52* (London: Chatto & Windus, 1963).

Wohlstetter, A. J., Hoffman, F. S., Lutz, R. J. and Rowen, H. S., *Selection and The Use of Strategic Air Bases* (Rand Corporation, 1 April 1954).

Wohlstetter, A. J., Hoffman, F. S., Lutz, R. J. and Rowen, H. S., *On the Value of Overseas Bases* (Rand Corporation, 5 January 1960).

Yergin, D., *Shattered Peace. The Origins of the Cold War and the National Security State* (Boston: Houghton Mifflin, 1977).

Articles

Alberts, D. J., Lt Col, 'Detterence in the 1980's, Part II: The Role of Conventional Air Power', *Adelphi Paper*, no. 193, International Institute of Strategic Studies (1985).

Aviation Week and Space Technology, 'Looking Glass' and 'U-2 and SR-71', 10 May 1976.

Ball, D., 'Can Nuclear War be Controlled', *Adelphi Paper*, no. 169, International Institute of Strategic Studies (1981).

Barclay, C. N., 'What Happens to Europe if the Americans Leave?', *Army*, no. 11, November 1973.

Barton, G. P., 'The Status of Forces Agreement', *British Yearbook of International Law*, 27 (1959).

Blechman, B. and Hart, D., 'The Political Utility of Nuclear Weapons: The 1973 Middle East Crisis', *International Security*, vol. 7 no. 1, Summer 1982.

Blom-Cooper, L. J., 'NATO's Status of Forces Agreement', *The Solicitor*, November 1957.

Bond, S. J., 'United States Third Air Force – A Short History', *Air Britain Digest*, January–February 1975.

Brenner, M. J., 'Tactical Nuclear Strategy and European Defence: a critical reappraisal', *International Affairs*, vol. 51 no. 1, January 1975.

Brodie, B., 'Nuclear Weapons: strategic or tactical', *Foreign Affairs*, vol. 32 no. 2, January 1954.

Brown, D. A., 'Britain Proposes Defence Plans to USAF', *Aviation Week and Space Technology*, 24 November 1980.

Brown, G., 'Why the United States Maintains Forces in Europe', *Commanders Digest*, 6 March 1975.

Brown, N., 'British Arms and the switch towards Europe', *International Affairs*, vol. 43 no. 3.

Buchan, A., 'Europe, America and NATO', *Survival*, vol. 4 no. 1 (1962).

Buchan, A., 'Europe and the Atlantic Alliance: Two Strategies or one?', *Journal of Common Market Studies*, vol. 1 no. 3 (Spring 1963).

Buchan, A., 'NATO, Partners and Allies', *Survival*, vol. 5 no. 5 (1963).

Burt, R., 'The SS-20 and the Eurostrategic Balance', *World Today*, February 1977.

Campbell, D., 'Target Britain', *New Statesman*, 31 October 1980.

Campbell, D., 'Spy in the Sky', *New Statesman*, 9 September 1983.

Campbell, D., 'Bases build-up', *New Statesman*, 21 October 1983.

Campbell, D., 'Outside the Law', *New Statesman*, 18 November 1983.

Campbell, D., 'Whose Sovereignty?', *New Statesman*, 27 April 1984.

Challenor-Chadwick, L., 'The United States Cruise Missile Programme', *Bradford Schol of Peace Studies, Peace Research no. 2* (1983).

Church, F., 'Reappraising American Policy', *Survival*, vol. 5 no. 5 (1963).

Cordesman, A. H., 'Deterrence in the 1980s. Part I: American Strategic Forces and Extended Deterrence', *Adelphi Paper*, no. 175 (IISS, 1982).

Defence Journal, 'Forward three per cent', vol. 10 no. 3 (March 1979).

Dodd, N. L., Col, 'The Defence of Great Britain', *Asian Defence Journal*, no. 5/78.

Drew, E., 'A Political Journal', *The New Yorker*, 9 May 1983.

Enthoven, A. C., 'US Forces in Europe: How Many? Doing What?', *Foreign Affairs*, vol. 53 no. 3 (April 1975).

Erhardt, C. A., 'Disenchantment between Europe and America', *Aussenpolitik* (4th quarter, 1973).

Facer, R., 'The Future of European Defence', *Adelphi Paper*, no. 108 (IISS, 1975).

Gallois, P., 'US Strategy and the Defense of Europe', *Orbis*, vol. 7 no. 2 (Summer 1963).

Gelber, L., 'A Marriage of Inconvenience', *Survival*, vol. 5 no. 2 (1963).

Gleditsch, N. P. and Wilkes, O., 'Intelligence Installations in Norway: their number, location, function and legality', *Peace Research Institute*, Oslo (PRIO), S-4/79.

Greenwood, D., 'Politics, Economics and European Defence', *RUSI and Brasseys Defence Yearbook* 1975–6 (London: Brassey's, 1975).

Hagerty, H. G., 'Forward Deployment in the '70s and '80s', *National Security Affairs Monograph*, no. 77, National Defense University, Washington, DC (February 1977).

Harris, K., 'Dean Acheson talks to Kenneth Harris', *Listener*, 8 April 1971.

Harrison, S. L., 'NATO Troop Reduction Conflict', *Military Review*, vol. 21 no. 9 (September 1971).

Healey, D., 'The Sputnik and Western Defence', *International Affairs*, vol. 34 no. 2 (April 1958).

Heisenberg, W., 'The Alliance and Europe: Part I. Crisis Stability in Europe and TNW', *Adelphi Paper*, no. 96 (IISS, 1973).

Henshaw, D., 'Whose Finger on the Button?', *The Listener*, 2 June 1983.

Heseltine, M., 'The Atlantic Alliance: an agenda for 1984', *NATO Review*, 1/32 (1984).

Heseltine, M., 'Stengthening Europe's Contribution to the Common Defence: the Role of the Eurogroup', *NATO Review*, 6/32 (1984).

Hunt, K., 'The Alliance and Europe: Part II – Defence with Fewer Men', *Adelphi Paper*, no. 98 (IISS, 1973).

Hunt, K., 'The Alliance and Europe', *Military Balance* (IISS, 1978).

Kissinger, H., 'NATO, the Next Thirty Years', *Survival* (November–December 1979).

McNamara, R. S., 'The Military Role of Nuclear Weapons: Perceptions and Misperceptions', *Foreign Affairs* (Fall 1983).

Martin, L. W., 'British Defence Policy: The Long Recessional', *Adelphi Paper*, no. 61 (IISS, 1969).

Military Enthusiast, 'New Weapons: Europe', vol. 5 no. 32.

Nerlich, U., 'The Alliance and Europe: Part V – Nuclear Weapons and East–West negotiations', *Adelphi Paper*, no. 120 (IISS, 1975–6).

New Statesman, 'Britain's Suicide Pact', 4 January 1958.

New Statesman, 'Buying Brooklyn Bridge', 1 March 1958.

Pfaltzgraff, R. L., 'European–American Defence Burden Sharing', *Atlantic Community Quarterly*, vol. 12 no. 2 (Summer 1974).

Pierre, A. J., 'Nuclear Diplomacy: Britain, France and America', *Foreign Affairs*, vol. 49 no. 2 (January 1971).

Pierre, A. J., 'The Future of America's commitment and Alliances', *Orbis*, no. 3 (Fall 1972).

Rathjens, G., 'NATO Strategy: Total War', in Klaus Knorr (ed.), *NATO and American Security* (Princeton: Princeton University Press, 1959).

Robertson, J., 'Looking back at SAC–UK', *Air Britain Digest* (July, 1968).

Rosenberg, D. A., 'American atomic strategy and the H-bomb decision', *Journal of American History*, vol. 66 (1979).

Schmidt, H., 'The 1977 Alastair Buchan Memorial Lecture', *Survival*, vol. 20 no. 1 (January–February 1978).

Schoenthal, K., 'Bonn-Washington: The Maturing Alliance', *Aussenpolitik*, no. 1 (1970).

Slessor, J., 'The Place of the Bomber in British strategy', *International Affairs*, vol. 39 no. 3 (July, 1953).

Sloan, S. R., 'Crisis in NATO: A Problem of Leadership', *NATO Review*, vol. 30 no. 3 (1982).

Spaatz, C., 'If we should have to fight again', *Life Magazine* (5 July 1948).

Sprout, A. and Sprout, M., 'Retreat from World Power: Processes and Consequences of Readjustment', *World Politics*, vol. 15 no. 4 (July, 1963).

Sviridov, G., 'American Military Bases in Britain', *New Times*, no. 19 (1952).

Szulc, T., 'The National Security Agency', *Penthouse*, vol. 20 no. 8.

Tornetta, V., 'The Nuclear Strategy of the Atlantic Alliance and the "No-First-Use" Debate', *NATO Review*, vol. 5 no. 30 (1982).

Treverton, G., 'Nuclear Weapons and the Gray area', *Foreign Affairs*, vol. 57 no. 3 (Summer 1979).

Treverton, G., 'Nuclear Weapons in Europe', *Adelphi Paper*, no. 168 (IISS, 1981).

Ulstein, E., 'Nordic Security', *Adelphi Paper*, no. 81 (IISS, 1971).

United States News and World Report, 'Britain: Base for an Air Showdown', 30 July 1948.

Van Eekelen, W. F., 'Development of NATO's Nuclear Consultation', *NATO Letter* (July/August 1970).

Walker, P. G., 'The Labour Party's Defence and Foreign Policy', *Foreign Affairs*, vol. 42 no. 3 (April 1964).

Weigart, H. W., 'US Strategic Bases and Collective Security', *Foreign Affairs*, vol. 25 (January 1947).

Wiegele, T. C., 'Nuclear Consultation Processes in NATO', *Orbis*, vol. 16 no. 21 (Summer 1972).

Williams, A. L., 'Is a European Nuclear Force Desirable?', *Atlantic Community Quarterly*, vol. 10 no. 2 (Summer 1972).

Wohlstetter, A., 'The Delicate Balance of Terror', *Foreign Affairs* vol. 37 no. 2 (January 1959).

Wohlstetter, A., 'On the value of Overseas bases', *Rand Corporation* (5 January 1960).

Wohlstetter, A., 'Threats and promises of peace: Europe and America in the new era', *Orbis*, vol. 17 no. 4 (Winter, 1974).

World Today, 'Notes of the Month', vol. 16 no. 3 (August 1960).

Yeremenko, A., 'Critique of United States Bases', *Survival*, vol. 3 no. 2 (1961).

Additional Journals Consulted

Current Digest of Soviet News
Daily Express
Daily Telegraph
The Guardian
Heyford Observer
The International Herald Tribune
Keesing's Contemporary Archives (previously known as 'Facts on File')
New Times
New York Times

Sanity
Soviet News
SIPRI Yearbooks
Strategic Survey (ISS)
The Sunday Times
The Times
Wall Street Journal
Washington Post

Microfilm

Carrollton Press (recently declassified documents on microfilm at Library of
   Congress, Washington, DC – see text).
Records of the JCS, Part 2 (1946–53), *Europe and NATO* (Reel II, Frame
   1391–9).

Unpublished Sources

Converse, E., 'US Plans for Postwar Overseas Military bases', PhD.,
   Princeton University, February 1984.
Kirby, D. J., Maj., 'The Role of Britain as an Advanced Air Base in the Event
   of Future War', Research paper submitted to the Faculty of the Air
   Command and Staff School of the Air University, Maxwell AFB, Alabama.
St Antony's, 'Anglo–American strategic Relations'. Colloquium held in St
   Antony's College, Oxford, 14–17 April 1970.
Viñas, A., 'The Experience of the Spanish–American Bilateral Defence
   Arrangement', prepared for a seminar on Spanish Security Options,
   Instituto de Cuestiones Internacionales, S'Argo, 24–27 April 1980.

Index